LIGHTHEARTED

Breaking free from Heaviness

UTE DEVIKA

BALBOA
PRESS
A DIVISION OF HAY HOUSE

CONTENTS

Acknowledgements ix
Introduction xiii

Chapter 1   Light as a Feather 1
Chapter 2   It's a time of Sea Change 14
Chapter 3   Yes but How? 31
Chapter 4   Encounters with the Miraculous 50
Chapter 5   The Breakthrough of Energy Medicine 68
Chapter 6   Evolving into a Happiness Coach 91
Chapter 7   Coaching Inspires Thinking and Change 118
Chapter 8   Falling in Love with Laughter Yoga 138
Chapter 9   The Magic of Laughter 155
Chapter 10 Enchanted with HeartMath 170
Chapter 11 The Power of Positive Emotions 182
Chapter 12 What I Love About Meditation 206
Chapter 13 Meeting your Self in Meditation 234

Conclusion 251
Exercises 263
Bibliography 281

ACKNOWLEDGEMENTS

This book is dedicated to my mother, Ilse Meinel. She detected my love for reading early on and has bought me many wonderful books since I was little. It was my mother, a courageous English teacher, who sympathized most with my desire to write. And it was she who kept encouraging me to write the book I had dreamt of writing since I was around 10 years old.

Without my mother, I would obviously not be on this planet in this form in the first place. Without her, and the example she gives me as an artist who keeps painting in spite of it all, I wouldn't have been able to create this book. My Mum was my first reader. She enjoyed it deeply when I read the first chapters to her, listening attentively, often with a smile on her face, or tears in her eyes. So Mum, this is for you.

I am also very grateful to the support of my dear friends, Heba Abu Musaed, and Tony Fernandes. Heba's enthusiasm, compassion as well as her exuberant creative energy made me feel it was totally fine when I couldn't write in the years before I finally got down to it, which is actually a big part of the birthing process. And once the writing unleashed itself, she and Tony kept checking in and cheering me to go full steam ahead.

My heartfelt gratitude goes out to Georgine Alicia Kalil who thoroughly edited the book and made countless improvements. I feel delighted about the artistic cover created by Soha Elsirgany. When Soha enrolled in coaching sessions with me as one of my first clients, her dream was to design book covers. Thrilled, I said lightheartedly: Wow, one day you could design a cover for my book.

It amazed us both that this actually happened. When this graceful artist and this editor with her unique sweetness appeared by my side, I felt I got the team in place that I needed to support a good production.

I feel eternally grateful to all the energy healing practitioners who gave

ACKNOWLEDGEMENTS

This book is dedicated to my mother, Ilse Meinel. She detected my love for reading early on and has bought me many wonderful books since I was little. It was my mother, a courageous English teacher, who sympathized most with my desire to write. And it was she who kept encouraging me to write the book I had dreamt of writing since I was around 10 years old.

Without my mother, I would obviously not be on this planet in this form in the first place. Without her, and the example she gives me as an artist who keeps painting in spite of it all, I wouldn't have been able to create this book. My Mum was my first reader. She enjoyed it deeply when I read the first chapters to her, listening attentively, often with a smile on her face, or tears in her eyes. So Mum, this is for you.

I am also very grateful to the support of my dear friends, Heba Abu Musaed, and Tony Fernandes. Heba's enthusiasm, compassion as well as her exuberant creative energy made me feel it was totally fine when I couldn't write in the years before I finally got down to it, which is actually a big part of the birthing process. And once the writing unleashed itself, she and Tony kept checking in and cheering me to go full steam ahead.

My heartfelt gratitude goes out to Georgine Alicia Kalil who thoroughly edited the book and made countless improvements. I feel delighted about the artistic cover created by Soha Elsirgany. When Soha enrolled in coaching sessions with me as one of my first clients, her dream was to design book covers. Thrilled, I said lightheartedly: Wow, one day you could design a cover for my book.

It amazed us both that this actually happened. When this graceful artist and this editor with her unique sweetness appeared by my side, I felt I got the team in place that I needed to support a good production.

I feel eternally grateful to all the energy healing practitioners who gave me sessions over the years and assisted with shedding burdens and bringing more light to my systems.

I also feel deeply blessed for the encounters with my teachers, who inspired me to learn about all those fantastic modalities that have changed my life and are presented in this book. Among them are Leslie Zehr, Sharon Blauer, Anthony Gorman, Ric Weinman, Rollin McCrathy, Jeff Goerlitz, Madan Kataria, as well as Parthasarathi Rajagopalachari. I am also most grateful to my students because it's only thanks to them popping up in my life that I could start teaching.

Last but not least, I am super grateful to the many brilliant authors and writers who keep touching my heart and inspiring my mind through their wonderful books. Listing them would simply take up too much space. However, some of the pearls of wisdom written by some of my favorite authors feel so precious to me that I was drawn to share and discuss them throughout this book.

"We work from within ourselves towards higher consciousness, greater freedom and more complex order to effect a change in the world, first and foremost through our personal evolution."

Barbara Marx Hubbard

INTRODUCTION

Life can be seen in way more colorful ways, lived with way more awareness and so much more joy. As human beings we are all bestowed with huge potential – much bigger than what we actually make use of. Only a fraction of our brain's capacity is normally activated and we're still mostly oblivious of the power of the emotions we feel, and the intelligence residing in our hearts.

We have come to this planet with the potential for happiness. We all share this most important potential of all. This inner spirit of joyfulness is yet to be discovered on a large scale. Most of us are still largely unaware of our innate capability to feel lighthearted. This book offers insights into a variety of modalities that help with getting there.

The majority of people have a wealth of inner gifts they are largely unaware of and incapable to verbally express. These gifts come in the form of a unique combination of wonderful character traits, lovely talents and great capabilities that far too often remain hidden and therefore totally untapped. It's therefore not surprising that so many of us feel that there is so much more we could be and do.

There is a widespread sense that we could show up in life in more vibrant and delightful expressions of ourselves than we usually do. This vague and persistently nagging feeling that we could somehow be playing a bigger game is very common these days. This is one thing we also seem to share as people across nations: the inner urge to grow, to evolve, to make a contribution, to become more aware, and more consistently conscious. This desire has been called 'the evolutionary impulse'.

It's like an unseen force nudging us forward to break free from limitations, unfold and thrive. We have this impulse, nearly like an instinct, to develop our potentials and make good use of them. This is one more indicator that, like everything else in nature, we are programmed to grow and flourish. If we ignore this desire to spread our wings and to fly high, we are bound to turn sour and feel terribly frustrated – even depressed.

There is an incredible wealth of skills and capabilities we carry in our genes that has been passed down to us by a long line of ancestors. These strengths are there for us to make the most of in order to live in ways that are enchanting, caring and thus feel fulfilling. However, our fast-paced materialistic, competitive culture instills more fears than wellbeing. The hectic lifestyle prevents people from finding that space in their hearts where joy and serenity reside at all times.

According to ancient mystical teachings, we are actually meant to live joyfully. While too many of us seem to have forgotten this, we luckily have science now to validate what wisdom traditions have been emphasizing for ages.

There is a growing amount of people all over the world who realize that living in ways that don't express our capability to feel fully present, intensely enthusiastic, or profoundly peaceful limits us in ways that have serious consequences. It's detrimental to our wellbeing and health. The cloud of negative emotions we produce collectively as humanity feels absolutely suffocating at this point in time.

It's very destructive for us, as well as for the environment, when we are out of synch with those tunes of emotions that just by themselves have the power to create harmony and balance in our hearts, and positively impact all those around us. This book presents a variety of approaches and methods from the East and West that effectively address the issue of perpetuated stress and unhappiness and is aimed to assist you to develop the skills that matter most for navigating this intensely insane era with more ease. These capabilities create more lightheartedness.

It comes to us naturally when we feel enchanted. It unfolds when we appreciate and celebrate what's beautiful and beneficial around us. It comes when we find ways to reduce the constant churning of thoughts and feelings about what seems so outrageously wrong with the upside-down world in which we live. Lightheartedness is right there when we decide to giggle a bit, or laugh out loud – even if we fake the laughter for the sake of cultivating happiness. We can easily tune our emotions to its frequency.

Shifting our awareness to our hearts and laughing more often is what creates shifts and breakthroughs that make all the difference. Allowing ourselves to consciously bring on more heartfelt emotions, such as appreciation, wonder, or gratitude is how we can shift our inner state and our focus, again and again. That's it. Nothing else is really needed. In my eyes, nothing is as empowering, as effective and as much fun as practicing the skill of tuning our own inner emotional landscape to the mode of lightheartedness.

Feeling uplifting emotions doesn't only make us feel good. It's soooo freakin good it even triggers rejuvenation on a cellular level. I mean, how good is that? The implications of this scientifically proven fact are remarkable. It's a game changer. The essential role of the emotions we feel as we go about our days cannot be overstated. Transforming the emotions is the crucial factor if we want to excel at anything, or just simply want to live a more satisfying and healthy life.

Emotions create our perceptions, dominate our decisions, and determine the level of coherence and balance throughout our system. Either our feelings sap our energy, get us down to our knees, and lead to shrinking on all levels; or they lift us up, soften us and allow us to expand. As simple as that.

The quality of our lives depends on the emotions we feel. The quality of our relationships depends on what's going on in our hearts. Even though this sounds perfectly logical, most people are not yet aware that we have the ability to shift into light and lovely emotions within minutes.

It's essential to remember that we are not the victims of our accumulated emotional suffering or our bad moods. We can easily change how we feel. The ability to shift into a peaceful and positive feeling state is so precious that it's priceless.

The interest in and understanding of emotions is growing. Countless researchers have discovered important insights into the functioning of the human body, mind and emotions over the past decades. And yet, perhaps due to the nature of funding procedures and highly specialized research in separate disciplines and isolated departments, much of this research has not yet become sufficiently known to a larger public, in spite of the accessibility of free information on the internet.

Most books in the so called self-help genre I have come across usually cover a single modality, often with an underlying attitude of portraying this particular method as being the only effective one to ever consider. Many of the books on happiness, consciousness, emotional intelligence, or various modalities of energy medicine, which are now available in bookstores all over the world, demonstrate this compartmentalized approach. Those authors with an interdisciplinary approach are rare.

Not much has been published from a more general perspective on the important question of how to evolve both, emotions and consciousness – which is what really makes us essentially human. At a time where everything seems to shift, this is a pertinent issue.

These developments have contributed to the fact that there is a whole lot of attention given to the role and importance of our thoughts. Correcting or improving the cognitive processes of the mind is the focus that is dominating the discourse - as well as the market that offers a huge (or uncountable) number of workshops, training events, festivals, conferences, etc. While these mind-centered approaches might be beneficial to some people, I doubt applicability on a larger scale. We definitely need simple solutions that are effective and can easily be practiced on a large scale at this tipping point in time. This is one of the many reasons that kept compelling me to write and publish this book.

The mind is always judging, always off balance. That's the way it works. Great beauty and wonder can only be recognized and experienced by the heart. The ultimate strength that is within each one of us resides in the heart, not in the brain or the muscles. A good example for that is the feeling of wonder, which is something children feel very often, while the rational adult mind prevents us from enjoying this exquisite emotion.

Allowing ourselves to experience childlike playfulness returns us to the largely forgotten realm of wonder. Becoming like children again, happens when we connect to the awe and joy that naturally reside in our hearts.

The much emphasized attempt to replace negative thoughts with positive ones is important, because it is crucial for our survival that we sharpen and focus our minds. However, used on its own, this approach can easily lead us off into an endless battle with the way the ordinary mind works. Fighting our own thinking process can lead to resistance and therefore ultimately more feelings of frustration.

You cannot effectively rationalize, affirm or turn emotions around only by using the mind. It's not possible to clear trauma or deeply ingrained feelings haunting you from the past by thinking positive thoughts. The good news is that there are more effective ways.

The aim of this book is to present various methods to shift out of heaviness and unhappiness that are simple and fun and at the same time deliver fantastic results. Ways to develop more lightheartedness include Laughter Yoga; Coaching; HeartMath; Energy Medicine; Meditation; as well as Deep Relaxation and Ease, which are covered throughout this book.

What is special about it is that a variety of disciplines are introduced and their beneficial effects discussed, but also that two distinctly different styles are used. Each modality is presented in a double way: an autobiographic narrative focusing on my own experiences and development in this field; as well as an analytical description explaining what this method is about and what makes it so important for becoming more lighthearted.

It is my hope that this parallelism of styles, the personal stories I relate together with the description of some research findings and profound thoughts of remarkable authors connects dots between a few essential disciplines. I have always loved to read personal accounts of transformational events and circumstances, which triggered change in people. At the same time I love text books on a wide range of self-discovery modalities. Combining both styles might provide inspiration and a richer understanding of what these methods are and what they can trigger on the personal and collective path of conscious evolution.

At the end some simple exercise are offered to give you keys to stop the mechanism of being driven mainly by toxic emotions and start feeling lighter. The awareness generated through reading, together with a deeper level of integrated knowing and a higher level of energetic frequencies that result from practicing the suggested exercises is a practical approach to accelerate personal growth by becoming more lighthearted.

Outlining the Chapters

The first three chapters have an introductory character. *Light as a Feather* explores the origin of the value given to lightheartedness, which points to ancient Egypt. It depicts the role of the Goddess Ma'at and the importance of the heart in ancient Egyptian culture and mythology for creating balance to fend off chaos. This wisdom is of relevance today as science finally confirms that balance in our heart rhythms is crucial for our wellbeing and that of those around us.

Chapter two outlines characteristics of the messy and yet so special period of time we live in, which is not only change, but epochal Sea Change. A deeper understanding of the serious shifts we are currently going through, can lead to more clarity about the importance of breaking free from the impact of ages of heaviness. This chapter offers a context for the importance of lightheartedness seen through the lens of the very special era we experience. Its aim is to describe the impressive opportunities that come along when we decide to assist with ushering in a new era of cultural and spiritual evolution.

In the third chapter, *Yes, But How?*, I describe my aspiration to become happier since I was a teenager who was brought up in the Middle East and suffered from feelings of awkwardness and heaviness. My intense longing to develop lead to the how-question popping up, and haunting me for a long time. This chapter concludes with a brief outlook on what I learnt in the meantime, creating the context to the modalities then described throughout this book.

Encounters with the Miraculous recalls personal experiences with healing that deserve to be called miracles. These were decisive turning points that instilled awe and set me on a path of learning about energy healing arts. In Chapter Five some modalities of *Energy Medicine* are described and some practitioners quoted to honor their attempts of trying to define the mystery of it all. Various forms of energy healing have become very popular all over the world, which is an indicator for the truth contained in the claim that this is the medicine of the future.

In Chapter Six, I narrate the circumstances that helped me break free from well-paid jobs and led me on a path of *Evolving into a Happiness Coach*. The amount of self-reflection required in this process was challenging, as well as profoundly enriching. In Chapter Seven, I attempt to answer the question what coaching is and how it works. A strong point is made for the importance of fully attentive listening that a coach offers, which leads to a much higher quality of thinking for the client. Developing the ability to think well for ourselves is a crucial part of character building. And it's one important prerequisite to build motivation for taking steps towards personal growth and change.

The next chapter is about the easiest way to go beyond the thinking mind and have some fun at the same time. It describes how I discovered Laughter Yoga and how it changed my life as I turned into a teacher and advocate of this amazing post-modern form of exercise. In *the Magic of Laughter,* I describe what makes Laughter Yoga so special, who created it, and what the many benefits of this practice are.

Enchanted with HeartMath, describes my fascination with rock solid research about the importance of a balanced heart rate for our physical and emotional state, and for the global magnetic field we exist in. The training I took at the HeartMath Institute in California taught me something essential nobody else has ever told me: we have the power to shift our emotions. This is an insight with enormous implications, which are touched upon throughout this book.

The next chapter on *The Power of Positive Emotions* sets out to describe in more detail some findings of research undertaken by the institute, which I find so revealing and relevant, that I quote a whole lot from their publications. The ability of emotional self-regulation, an option of co-creating more smoothness and inner harmony, is a core skill to becoming more lighthearted. This discovery was another game changer in my life that inspired the urge to shout this news from roof tops.

The book would not have felt complete without offering glimpses about the practice of meditation. In Chapter Twelve, I describe what I love about it and how I started to meditate early in life. I also narrate encounters with my guru as well as experiences and insights I was blessed to have during the two years I spent in a little known ashram in southern India. I finally experienced a state sometimes referred to as No-Mind, where nothingness and a sense of freedom prevail. *Meeting your Self in Meditation* attempts to demystify meditation. It is an attempt to define what it is about and what it should rather not be.

The Conclusion sums it all up by promoting the vital importance of ease and enchantment. In order for joy to emerge, relaxation is necessary. By allowing ourselves to shed tension by melting into a relaxed state, we not only become lighter but happier as well. When we reach this state, evolution and healing can form from the inside out. The easiest and most effective way for both to appear effortlessly is to remember intensely that we are indeed allowed to enjoy life.

At this point in time, a large number of people have found meaning through leaving the corporate world behind and turning into coaches, yoga teachers or energy healing practitioners, and many more have similar aspirations. Many of us have learned about different modalities to assist clients in truly holistic ways. Each one represents a unique bouquet of talents. This in itself is very enriching. It's a unique development, something that has never happened before in human history.

This is an excellent time to make the decision to break free from the emotional heaviness that has confined us to inner misery over too many centuries. But of course, this takes courage. Fortunately, there is so much help available to guide us in the right direction. Once we decide to take the first steps moving towards cultivating lightheartedness, a path miraculously opens right in front of us. Osho puts it nicely: "Now the time has come to divorce it. That I call the great courage – to divorce misery, to lose the oldest habit of the human mind, the longest companion."[1]

Luckily, we, as human beings, have lots of wonderful potential. Among many other things, we can develop our capacity to change our feelings, to think about our issues deliberately, to shake off gloominess, and to open our hearts. Each time we feel a pleasant emotion, we divorce its miserable companion. When we shift into lightheartedness, we automatically shift the electromagnetic field that is generated by our hearts. When we shift our own field the global field shifts too. There's a lot to shift. So let's get started.

---

[1] Osho, Courage, New York, 1999, p.62

"The more harmony and balance in one's consciousness and in one's life,

the more it will become a life of beauty, grace, dignity, and efficiency."

A.H. Almaas

ONE

Light as a Feather

Being light as a feather has become a common expression in the English language. It instills a beautiful image of a feather floating blissfully in the air seemingly unaffected by the gravitational pull of the earth. At the same time, the word points not only to the ease and joy that come with lightness but also light as the only antidote to darkness. The state of feeling burdened, bogged down, heavy and dark have become the more common emotional experience for many people in the times we live in.

The mythology and the ideals behind the wonderful state of feeling as light as a feather originate from ancient Egypt. One of the many fascinating aspects of ancient Egyptian culture is the importance that was given to the human heart, which was believed to play a central role in creating and maintaining harmony among people.

In fact, it was the heart, rather than the brain, that was considered to be the source of human wisdom, as well as the center of emotions and memory, the essence of personality itself, and the seat of the soul. It was deeply understood by the ancient Egyptians that human beings are required to cultivate and sustain compassion, balance and lightness in their hearts for the sake of justice and order to prevail in society. Otherwise, chaos and disasters would strike and the annihilation of human life could be the consequence.

In ancient Egyptian times, it was deeply understood that from the physical heart a network of channels (*metu*) emanated that linked all parts of the body together. These channels delivered not only blood, but also air, tears, saliva, mucus, sperm, nutriment and even bodily waste. It is inspiring to note that thousands of years ago in Egypt, people were considered to be in good health if these channels that were regulated by the heart were clear and without blockage.

It was thought that diseases were caused when a channel became blocked – just like an irrigation canal of the river Nile that cannot transport water if it is contaminated by waste. The heart was, therefore, considered the most important organ in the human body and was the only organ that was not removed during the process of mummification. According to some sources, the only real function attributed to the brain was to pass mucus to the nose and it was seen as so obsolete that it was removed in the intricate process of mummifying a deceased person.

It was widely believed that after a person died, their heart, which stands symbolically for the soul, was weighed on a large scale against a feather in the presence of the Goddess of Justice. The degree of lightheartedness determined the fate of the soul of the deceased individual. Only if their heart – or rather the soul - was lighter than an ostrich feather, which symbolized sacred harmony, access to eternal life among the gods would be granted. Otherwise, the soul was devoured by another female goddess in the form of a terrifying demon, and was thought to be extinguished, erased, once and for all.

When we find a story scary, we resist it and miss the point

I found that story very scary as a child. *"How can my heart ever become lighter than a feather?"*, I asked myself when I first heard this explanation of images of the rite of passage of death that is depicted in many tombs. I visited Luxor with my family when I was around 10 years old. At that time, we lived in Cairo, as my father was offered a job there.

That story seemed nonsensical to me back then. Like many others, I took that ancient belief or mythology too literally. I believed that the heart of the deceased was removed, which was obviously not the case. Therefore, I couldn't see the profound meaning that one part of it conveys.

Even many years later, I was quite shocked when I was told about the many conditions that needed to be fulfilled in order to reach eternal life or be devoured by the demon. This sense of fear, which stories like these can bring up, especially in children, made me turn away from them.

Belief systems or approaches that scare people with senarios of punishments aimed at whipping them into compliance with strict rules of what should and shouldn't be done had no appeal to me since I was young. That never changed. Fear-based teachings simply haven't resonated with me. Today, I know for sure that fear of any kind makes us shrink and makes us sick.

Fear keeps old pain that is stored in the cells of the body in place. As has been emphasized again and again by Louise Hay, one of the most eminent pioneers of positive thinking and self-healing in the US who passed away in 2017, as well as by many other remarkable contemporary personalities in the self-discovery arena, fear is the root cause of diseases. It logically follows that identifying and overcoming the fears that were instilled in us through conditioning, as well as painful experiences, is an essential thing to do if we want to heal, expand and lighten up.

Following teachings that contain demons who were devouring souls that weren't light enough or teachings that tell us of souls of 'sinners' who are banished to burn eternally in hell, don't really bring us closer to the ideals of creating more harmony in our hearts and societies. Otherwise, this planet would not be inhabited by a humanity unconsciously driven to self-destruct.

Evolving in more conscious ways cannot be about going back to the past and trying to re-create it. It also doesn't make sense to replace one belief system that operates on fears with another teaching that ultimately instills fears again.

This seems to be an excellent time to extract the essence of the many profoundly beautiful wisdom traditions that have emerged at different times on this planet and leave behind those parts that illicit fear. Instead of focusing on the differences of these teachings, it is more useful to unearth the essence they all have in common. Each of them emphasizes the importance of cultivating feelings of care, compassion and love. The question how to do that can be answered today in more simple and practical ways than ever before.

What is so awe-inspiring about this era of extreme change is that many ancient spiritual teachings are resurfacing in various places on this planet.

A lot of these developments are based on more discoveries of artefacts. They are also carried forward significantly by many intuitive individuals who receive inner messages, or suddenly remember knowledge they had in other existences, or in so-called past lives. While main-stream culture is prone to scoff at the latter, a lot of what is surfacing now is highly interesting and could be very helpful in moving us forward.

It cannot be put into question that ancient Egyptians knew many precious things about astronomy, astrology, sacred geometry, alchemy, harmony and healing that we are only beginning to slowly unearth and understand. Greed for power and corruption led to the downfall of this splendid civilization, like so many others. While more and more people from all over the world are being drawn to Egypt and many books are being published that recover glimpses of life in ancient times in *Kemet*, as many Africans still commonly refer to Egypt, cutting edge scientific research in different disciplines have been presenting findings that actually back up all what was held sacred back then.

The Goddess Ma'at

One of the basic beliefs in ancient Egypt was that order and harmony were maintained by a powerful female spiritual force or goddess called Ma'at who saw to it that principles she stood for were followed by people and upheld by the rulers of the country, namely the Pharaohs. At the same time, it was a central belief that the universe emerged from chaos, which could strike again when the divine principles that guaranteed harmony among people were disregarded. Ancient Egyptians perceived and order and balance as sacred. This harmony was required to be upheld and sustained by individual effort. This is the remarkable part.

This very emphasis on the required individual effort to create and sustain harmony inside us and around us is very much in line what with what scientists and researchers of prestigious institutes as well as effective and therefore successful self-development modalities of today, such as coaching or holistic energy medicine, are essentially about. Basically, they all aim at inspiring individuals to make sustained efforts with the aim to experience more fulfillment and harmony. These individual emotional states ripple out from our hearts and ultimately make an important contribution to the emergence of a more peaceful era.

Sacred balance in society through individual lightheartedness

Ancient Egyptians regarded the ordering principle that the Goddess Ma'at represented to be of such vital importance that the entire code of moral and ethical conduct and law was based on it.

The Declaration of Innocence or Purity that the deceased were judged against in the ceremony mentioned above are described in the *Book of the Death*. In the Papyrus of Ani, 42 declarations of one person are outlined that negate a large number of things the deceased soul had not done in life, beginning with the affirmation, *"I have not learnt the things which are not."* This meant that the person or soul strove in life to devote itself to matters of lasting reality or importance rather than trivial or illusionary matters.

Some authors argue that these 42 negations can be considered the rules of Ma'at, which is debatable. There is no clear evidence for a formalized code of conduct or unified rules that should be followed. More research is needed to decipher the various sources so that a clearer understanding of the essential ethics in ancient Egypt can finally emerge.

Besides, different translations exist of the 42 deeds that were proclaimed as not having been done by Ani during his life and can be found on the internet. Some of the points mentioned below might not have been translated in the ideal way, however, in my eyes, they are most significant to ponder. Apart from the points that rule out murder, betrayal or stealing - which can be found in religions and wisdom traditions all over the world - some of these proclamations even go way beyond religious teachings that emerged much later in human history.

Particularly noteworthy in this time of ecological destruction and violence are the following parts:

- *I have never fouled the water, nor have I polluted the land.*
- *I have not polluted myself.*
- *I have not caused terror.*
- *I have done no hurt to man, nor have I wrought harm to beasts.*
- *I have made none to weep.*

- *I have never uttered fiery words, nor have I stirred up strife.*
- *I have not judged hastily, nor have I judged harshly.*
- *I have not been angry without cause.*
- *I have not acted with undue haste.*
- *I have never raised my voice.*
- *I have done neither harm nor ill, nor have I caused misery.*
- *Each day have I labored more than was required of me.*[2]

The list is impressive. Neither me, nor anyone I know, could honestly say these things about themselves. How many times have we raised our voices or make others cry in only one year? How many times have we judged harshly or become angry for nothing during one month? And how many times per day have we polluted our bodies with toxic foods and the rivers, seas and deserts with their plastic packaging? Unfortunately, we have become used to do all these things too often, and it is about time to examine the ways we think and act consistently, without condemning ourselves for it either – rather, just noting what is going on and how it is affecting us and our planet.

The evolution of human emotionality and consciousness is crucial for human survival

Human behaviors are damaging the planet we live on. As will be shown in the next chapter we are witnessing times of intense chaos. It has been said and written by many spiritual teachers and a variety of authors that this is the time for humanity to either evolve or be wiped out from this planet.

"If we continue with our current practices, we are likely to destroy ourselves. Many of us have seen looming catastrophe, but few of us have realized that this crisis is driving us toward positive change, toward a quantum transformation," says the spiritual visionary Barbara Marx Hubbard.[3] The American writer, public speaker and political activist,

---

[2] For a quick reference of the complete list you can check this: https://en.wikipedia.org/wiki/Maat

[3] Barbara Marx Hubbard, Conscious Evolution, 1998, p.10

Marianne Williamson, has beautifully expressed her indignation over our inability to verbally express feelings about a possible destruction of this planet. "The fact that we go about our lives as though the survival of our world is not at stake is not the sign of a stiff upper lip. It is the sign, rather, of a society not yet able or willing to hold a conversation about its deepest pain"[4]

Williamson has succinctly argued in all her books that facing our pain, including our childhood wounds, is crucial for our transformation. In order to retrieve the joy and the peace that reside underneath all of this pain in our hearts, it seems that nothing less than what has been termed a descent into the underworld is needed. The underworld is an ancient term pointing to the murky areas of the subconscious where a lot of our pain is stored. Facing our pain is necessary if we want to become more lighthearted. More about this issue is explored in the chapter on the power of emotions.

The late Barbara Marx Hubbard, the most eminent pioneer of the concept of evolving consciously into higher levels of awareness and passion, beautifully compares our situation with the metamorphosis of a caterpillar into a butterfly, which symbolizes the ascent from density and cocooning into lightness, astounding beauty and graceful flying: "The breakdown of the caterpillar's old system is essential for the breakthrough of the new butterfly. Yet, in reality the caterpillar neither dies nor disintegrates, for from the beginning its hidden purpose was to transform and be reborn as the butterfly."[5]

The intention and decision to evolve to a higher vibrational level of emotionality and consciousness as represented in the symbol of the butterfly is a choice that each individual is now called to make. This decision to change is the most important one to make. The ongoing and unfolding disasters and multiple crisis occurring around us seem to be pushing us into making that crucial decision to change before it might be too late.

"Only decision will give you action, and only action will become transformation," says the Indian mystic and guru Osho[6]. An essential part

---

[4] Marianne Williamson, The Gift of Change, 2004, p.3
[5] Hubbard, Ibid
[6] Osho, The Book of Secrets, 2010, p.946

of this very needed quantum transformation, according to many spiritual teachers, is learning to live not so much in our heads but going beyond the mind, and living in accordance with the intelligence inherent in our hearts. The HeartMath Institute refers to it as Heart Intelligence.

Osho, who for me remains one of the most radical and fascinating spiritual teachers puts it beautifully: "The greatest problem that modern man is facing is that the mind is trained too much and the heart is completely neglected – not only neglected, but condemned too."[7]

What we know for sure today

As scientific research undertaken by the Institute of HeartMath has shown, emotions such as anger, harshness, aggression, negative judgments etc. lead to an incoherent and erratic heart rate rhythm and a corresponding toxic chemistry in the body that depletes vital energy and shuts down the proper functioning of major systems, such as the immune system, the digestive system, or even the prefrontal cortex, which allows us to think logically. When this part of the brain is not behaving correctly, we can only guess what some of the outcomes could be.

This kind of emotional heaviness, in fact, creates incoherence, or to be more explicit, chaos, inside the body. As we also know now thanks to their research results, the electromagnetic field of an individual heart extends around us and affects the magnetic fields of everyone in the vicinity. Science has confirmed that chaos from the inside-out is the result of heavy emotions, just as the ancient Egyptians taught.

It is interesting that lightheartedness is still a value held very highly in Egypt today. One big compliment among Egyptians is telling somebody that their blood is light.[8] In fact, a remarkable lightheartedness and sense of humor has prevailed in Egypt over the centuries regardless of the circumstances. The ability to crack jokes about authoritarian rulers and some of their actions is one of the many things Egyptians have become famous for. Laughing together has been one great way of resistance for Egyptians. It has become an art form in the age of social media, very much

---

[7] Osho, Emotional Wellness, 2007, p.12
[8] Freely transliterated, it sounds like this: *dammak khafif*

to the dismay of authorities. In spite of the remarkable creative wittiness and loving kindness of Egyptians, it can be easily observed that nowadays a majority of people in Egypt, and indeed elsewhere, are bogged down by the collective post-modern epidemic of anxiety and depression.

Let's face it. Modern humanity is indeed very far away from living a life that is aligned with those ideals that in ancient times were known to induce lightheartedness and were held sacred in various places on this planet. Once we face this fact and truly understand its devastating consequences on the individual and collective levels, we are in a better position to start using tools that shift us out of heaviness.

Living up to these ancient ethical standards that were thought to determine the heaviness or lightness of a human heart and soul requires sustained practices leading to inner balance. Nothing less than self-regulation of emotions and thoughts of a very high degree was necessary if one was interested in an eternal life of the soul after the death of the body. This must have obviously required a level of heart-centered living that points to a very well cultivated intelligence of the heart. It takes effort. Back then, the sacred practices seem to have been reserved mainly for initiates in the temples, and the caste and hierarchy of priests and priestesses, as well as some high ranking dignitaries.

The great contribution of our times which I feel is the most significant ever made is that today knowledge as well as effective practices are available to almost everybody everywhere. Spiritual knowledge has finally become accessible on a wide scale. One could say it has been democratized. And in fact, we can observe a renaissance, a movement made up of many individuals all across the world feeling delighted or even dedicated to contribute to efforts that usher in a new stage of human development.

Looking at it from the perspective of the time we live in, this level of individual transformation has become easier. It can be accelerated through cultivating awareness of one's thoughts and emotions. "Our very cells respond to the thoughts we think – with every word, silent or spoken, we participate in the body's functioning. We participate in the functioning of the universe itself. If our consciousness grows lighter, then so does everything within and around us," says Williamson.[9] In other words, the first step always consists of increasing self-awareness, just realizing and

---

[9] Marianne Williamson, The Age of Miracles, 2008, p.18

accepting what happens in the mind and the body. Checking in for a moment to sense what we are feeling in different parts of our bodies, and how that affects us is the way to go. Based on that awareness we can then choose a feel an emotion that feels better and helps our body to function at its best.

Scientists from the Institute of HeartMath have demonstrated beyond doubt that the key to transforming ourselves and our lives lies in our capacity to lighten up our emotions simply by using our power to change the way in which our hearts beat. Research gathered and undertaken by the University of Laughter Yoga in Bangalore points in the same direction: A few minutes of laughter significantly reduce stress hormones. The biochemistry in the body changes as it is flooded with happiness inducing hormones. Laughter lightens us up. Allowing ourselves to become more childlike and playful makes us feel bubbly and light. Another way is engaging in practices that increase the amount of universal life force energy in our bodies and souls, which is what Energy Medicine is about. Shifting out of heaviness or darkness is indeed simple and natural. These findings are fascinating as they point to a practical and yet joyful way forward.

Summary

This introductory chapter traces the meaning that was given to lightheartedness to its origins in ancient Egypt, where it was considered the most valuable asset.

The extent of lightness of the human heart was the one and only criteria that determined whether a deceased person could be lifted up to the realm of Gods after their death and rejoice in heaven for eternity. When the weight of the heart that stood symbolically for the soul was heavier than an ostrich feather it was extinguished once and for all.

This ancient belief, or mythology, of weighing the heart contains profound wisdom, which is pertinent for us now.

It was widely believed that individual efforts are required to be made by individuals to create harmony inside themselves as well as within their society in order to prevent chaos from spreading and ultimately destroying Egypt, which was considered to be the mother of the world.

Mythologies and spiritual practices from ancient Egypt are surfacing as interest is rising especially at this point in time. Numerous people have traveled to Egypt and wrote about mystical experiences containing memories from past lives in places that were once held sacred.

In spite of a growing variety of individuals promoting certain paths or exercises apparently originating in Egypt, not much is known yet by a broader public about ways to become more lighthearted that must have been practiced back then.

Post-modern science confirms the insights into the importance of the human heart, on which much of the ancient Egyptian spirituality and culture was built.

The HeartMath Institute has proven beyond doubt that the lighter frequency range of heartfelt emotions, among them appreciation, compassion, or gratitude create a harmonious rhythm in the human heart and lead to optimum human functioning. In contrast, the heavy range of emotions most of us feel a lot of create stress responses that deplete our energy levels and lead to chaos in the system.

The era of the splendid Egyptian civilization is long gone. We live in an era that is characterized by accelerating change and a large number of intertwined crises that could easily lead to global chaos.

The next chapter, which also has an introductory character, sheds light on the nature of the very special time we live in. Its aim is to inspire deeper understanding of the many reasons why practicing exercises that effectively build inner balance and pave the way towards lightheartedness are so crucial for all of us now.

"Whenever you withhold love from yourself, you are withholding love from the world...period.

We really need you to stop doing that."

Elisabeth Gilbert

TWO

It's a time of Sea Change

Lightheartedness is not easy to come by nowadays. The opposite is true. Humanity seems to be bogged down to the point of being hell-bent. We live in a challenging era. For most people I know or see around me these are difficult times. That's mainly because it's a period characterized by massive change. That's actually great news. It's just a matter of perspective.

"The best minds of our time are in agreement that you and I are living a radical shift in the world and our lives that's unlike any other in recorded history," says the brilliant geologist and bestselling author Gregg Braden.[10] Many refer to what's going on as 'the shift'. The astrologist and author Dan Furst puts it very matter of factly: "As billions of people on our planet know by now, we are about to enter, or may already be in, something called the Age of Aquarius."[11]

It is an extraordinary time, but it's not exactly easy to grasp how exciting it is to be on this planet in such a special era. Just consider this: what we are witnessing is "one of the very rare periods of a potential evolutionary quantum leap," says the author and leader in the global movement of intercultural understanding Jim Kenney.[12] That sounds pretty enormous to me. "It may be precisely because the implications of our time of extremes

---

[10] Gregg Braden, The Turning Point. Creating Resilience in a Time of Extremes, 2014, p.7
[11] Dan Furst, The Age of Aquarius. How to Ace the Wave of Change, 2011, p.1
[12] Jim Kenney, Thriving in the Crosscurrent, 2010, p.231

are so vast that there's been a reluctance to even acknowledge that we're in the midst of something so big," Braden points out.[13]

He states that "every 5,000 years or so the cycle of the sun and the position of the Earth in space conspire to bring about massive changes in our world."[14] In view of the evidence put forth by many acknowledged researchers from various disciplines it cannot be denied any more that this is a time of transition from one historic and cultural era to another, which carries the potential to be very different in every imaginable way.

There is a lot of energetic pushing and pulling going on as the waves of the cosmic cycle that is ending are ebbing out and the waves of the new age are crashing in on us – at times quite ferociously creating turbulent to whirlpools with violent spins and powerful suctions that seem to drown us. It's a time full of tidal disturbances. These are the beautiful expressions used by Kenney. "Sea change" is the image and fitting metaphor he offers.

I love this explanation because it provides the visual image that really fits the feeling of living in a turbulent time of crosscurrents, which, as he points out so brilliantly, eventually leads to a culturally evolutionary transformation. What can be predicted, according to Kenney's analysis of previous sea changes, is the emergence of progressive new values in every key sector.

Among them are "the likely emergence of evolved human attitudes toward war and peace, injustice and justice and ecological degradation and stewardship."[15] Every sea change advances humankind along the cultural evolutionary spiral, Kenney argues. According to him, only four have occurred since human prehistory.

"Imagine an ocean moment: two waves converging in the same time and space. One is powerful but subsiding, the other just gathering momentum and presence but not yet cresting. At the moment of their meeting they are nearly equal in amplitude and influence. As they cross, who can say which is rising, which is descending? In that moment only the chaos of wave interference exists," writes Kenney. He points out that these transitions and evolutionary shifts in values are never easy and yet, they produce profound inspiration and originality. At the same time cultural

---

[13] Braden, Ibid, p.28
[14] Ibid, p.33
[15] Kenney, Ibid, p.213

confusion and identify crisis occur. The widespread emergence of new values and new ways of thinking always threatens established structures of power, "thus adding a dangerous intensity to an already volatile cultural mix."[16]

The interference of two culture waves unleashes both: "apparent chaos and emerging order." I find Kenney's analysis very inspiring. It brings to memory the harmony and order that the Egyptian Goddess Ma'at represents, as outlined in chapter one. The values and principles that she stands for point to a path that fends off chaos by cultivating compassion, integrity, beauty and devotion for each other, for the earth and for the cosmos.

Braden calls what we are going through now "the time of extremes". And it is exactly these extremes of life that are "forcing us to think differently about ourselves and reconsider how we can sustain our jobs, careers, health and relationships".[17] He points out that in order to make sense of the hardships affecting every facet of society, we are being pushed to look beyond the wisdom handed down to us by our parents, and grandparents. "This is where the message at the core of our most cherished spiritual traditions – our unity with the world and nature's cycles – is now taking on new meaning, and new relevance, in our everyday lives."[18]

The water bearer

The emerging order carries the qualities of the zodiac sign of Aquarius, the Water Bearer. Aquarius is the sign of the genius, the futuristic thinker. It stands for the ability to think outside the box in many ways that are new to us and new to the world. The Aquarius energy is about taking risks, doing or saying something that goes against the "norm." It is the sign of the rebel with a cause. It asks us to take quantum leaps in all areas, as we view the big picture in front of us, and as we trust our genius to see the paths leading to a better future. Aquarius is about breaking up stagnant old patterns so we can reach for our freedom, and march to the beat of our

---

[16] Ibid, p.11
[17] Braden, p.213
[18] Ibid, p.33

own drum. Freedom and liberation are indeed a central part of the values inherent in the sign of Aquarius.[19]

As Furst underlines the ancient image of the Water Bearer that we see especially in Egyptian zodiac images like in the temple of *Hathor* at *Dendera* in Egypt, "most likely evolved in Middle Eastern cultures that saw the waters of the Nile, the Tigris, and the Euphrates, and the wadi rain freshets of Petra as crucial to their very survival."[20] According to him, the truest Aquarian values are: community, cooperation and abundance, while the Piscean age that we are set to leave behind was dominated by beliefs in hierarchy, competition and scarcity. This description clarifies how fundamental the shift of paradigm is that we are currently witnessing.

Coping with intense amounts of chaos and fear

On an emotional level, this shift from one era into another leads to an unprecedented amount of fear that seems to be gripping the hearts of millions of people. Looking at human history, it is quite obvious that the majority of leaders always ruled mainly by instilling fears, while wisdom traditions and religions across the globe through the ages have promoted harmony, love, faith and devotion as the antidote. In the times we are going through now, fear is being instilled in gigantic proportions.

In all possible forms – from worry over losing a job or a partner, to anxiety about uncertainty of the future, to outright panic attacks before leaving the house – fear has become a rampant phenomenon among people of our times. And this is not yet something that many of us like to admit or talk about. "We are coping with intense amounts of chaos and fear, both personally and together," Williamson points out.[21]

We have never been this many people on this planet before. In terms of number of people feeling anxious or afraid, this level is unprecedented. On top of that, media and social media have made it far easier to spread fear in more subtle and chilling ways than ever before. The global economic crisis

---

[19] Find a beautiful article on this issue here: http://soundofheart.org/galacticfreepress/content/aquarius-new-moon-february-8th-love-air
[20] Furst, p.40
[21] Williamson, The Gift of Change, 2004, p.1

hit people everywhere, and the media reported about it all the time, even years after it first hit. At the same time, we are facing an ecological crisis which has become visible. So we can't pretend anymore that everything is just fine.

The widespread fear-mongering is one thing, however, existential fears experienced on an individual level can be helpful trail blazers. Since I was a teenager, my motto has always been: where the fear is, lies the path. Years later, I found a book written by Susan Jeffers with the wonderful title: *Feel the fear and Do it Anyway*. That's exactly what it takes to deal with it: courage to feel it consciously, face it by identifying the worst possible scenario, and then work our way thinking, feeling and acting through it.

It seems that we have arrived at a point where there is a widespread feeling of being fed up of all this crippling fear. One indicator for this development is the amount of books appearing on the issue of courage. Brenè Brown puts it very nicely: "I'd say that the one thing we have in common is that we are sick of feeling afraid. We want to dare greatly."[22] The title of her groundbreaking book, *Daring Greatly*, has inspired me deeply in so many ways that it has turned into something like a slogan, which I am repeatedly referring to throughout this book.

Daring Greatly we must in times like these, when multiple crises converge. "Considering the extreme conditions of our climate, the extreme demands for energy, and the extreme pressure being placed on our economies – all of which are amplified by extreme population levels – it's fair to say that we are living in a time of tremendous volatility," underlines Braden.[23]

The world seems to be already spinning at a different angle on its axis; it's magnetic poles are probably about to shift; the icecaps are melting; the rhythmic beat at the core of the universe seems to be speeding up; huge amounts of storms are occurring on the sun leading to explosions known as solar flares; rivers are drying out; the weather is changing everywhere whatever governments say about climate change; species are dying out at an alarming rate; desertification of formerly green areas is devastating; we have hundreds of thousands of people who have become climate refugees, while unrest and wars are flaring up. The list could fill books.

---

[22] Brenè Brown, Daring Greatly, 2012, p.18
[23] Braden, p.23

Suffice is to say that awareness of these serious problems creates an acute pain as well as an existential fear of being alive on this planet. These emotions are commonly repressed because it's not amusing to feel them, especially with a programming that drives us to avoid pain and increase pleasure. The subconscious pain is as virulent as the fear. It feels like a collective outburst of suffering that seems to be reaching more humongous proportions by the day. Let's own up to the fact that life per se, without anything tragic happening on a personal level, can feel awfully scary.

Many are expecting the end of the world to occur soon. The expectations of Armageddon are widespread, especially among religious people. Intellectuals worry whether the human race will survive on this planet because its destructive behavior is not sustainable anymore and could easily get us wiped out. Braden puts it this way: "Earth cannot sustain our habits. Over 1,000 scientists from various disciplines have honed this idea in a report released by the World Economic Forum, aptly titled *Global Risks 2013*. The bottom line is that the conditions of climate change and the teetering global economy pose the possibility of a 'perfect storm' of crises that will impact the world for a long time to come."[24]

How can we prepare for the unthinkable?

There is a widespread feeling that we should urgently stop playing small and better get started with preparing for whatever could possibly happen in this wild new world. It's just that most of us have no clue how to prepare for that big wave of crap that we gloomily expect to hit the fan at some point. How does one prepare for that? How do you prepare for the unthinkable state of crisis other than by buying weapons, learning how to handle a bow instead of a violin, or hoarding food?

Many people propose to create communities and become self-sustainable. However, going off the grid is not an easy thing to do, and on top of that, many incidents have occurred which show clearly that local authorities in a large number of countries are inclined to make these kinds of attempts even more difficult.

The uneasy feeling of what may still be in store for us in the stormy

---

[24] Ibid, p.27

times of transition has led to a "collective depression among us, not so much dealt with as glossed over and suppressed."[25] The glossing over part is something that people in Western countries seem to be particularly good at. In contrast, the most urgent problems are much more visible in countries that are part of the so-called developing world, including in Egypt.

While the elites are indulging in accelerating consumption patterns, growing deprivation among the majority is difficult to overlook. When more than half the inhabitants of any given country lives in utter poverty, however, we want to define the term poverty, there is ultimately not that much to gloss over. When students in public schools hardly learn how to read and write or patients in public hospitals can't find the medication they need to survive, these issues are plainly visible.

Things have become so difficult in most countries which used to be referred to as "third world" that most people living in them are keenly aware of their multitude of problems. It seems that the majority of people in developing countries know what is not working, and many blame their governments for it. The mismanagement of systems, undermined by corruption is among those things that could remain hidden in the past – but not any more in the times we live in.

When the streets of several areas in Egypt were flooded with foul water due to repairs of the sewage system, many people commented that the crap, which had remained hidden was boiling up so everybody could see it, and smell it too. I found this image to be as drastic as useful since it captures well what we are dealing with. It seems that we are now being mercilessly confronted with the mess we have created collectively, as well as individually, and which we have tried to sweep under the rugs for far too long. It's like we are being forced to clearly see and feel the depth of our collective pain.

The only way, it seems, to get us to face this pain is by intensifying the heavy and dark issues that were kept hidden secrets so that they come up for everybody to see the misery we somehow unwillingly and unconsciously contributed to create. Apparently, as humanity, we need to suffer through a lot of deep emotional pain in this process of breaking our hearts open.

---

[25] Marianne Williamson, The Gift of Change, 2004, p.1

A massive source of emotional pain comes from the absence of caring and loving relationships that so many of us are suffering from. The dysfunctional way we generally relate, or rather not relate to each other as people on this planet, has become very obvious. Inability or unwillingness to communicate openly, which leads to emotional disengagement, is a root cause. An unprecedented number of marriages break down. Even friendships and business partnerships seem difficult to keep intact and harmonious. And as our relationships break down, our hearts break again and again.

As painful as that is, it is ultimately a good thing. Things have to sometimes take a turn for the worse in order for us to move on to the next evolutionary stage. What is breaking down here is nothing less than the old paradigm of the supremacy of patriarchy. The new wave is already ushering in feminine empowerment. It has been said and written many times: *Only what we can feel, we can heal*. And a lot of this earth, and its rivers, seas, and forests are in need of healing, as much as we are. The so-called outer, such as the earth, is a reflection of the inner planes. Healing, just like happiness, is an inside job.

The evolutionary impulse is becoming more demanding on us as the whole planet is shaking and spinning in new and unknown ways, and the ground we stand on seems more unstable and uninviting than ever. On a personal level, it often feels like we relentlessly get kicked in the butt. These kicks can come in the form of unexpected experiences, which either force us to move out of our uncomfortable comfort zones or to hit rock bottom.

The vulnerability that comes with more awareness

What becoming aware of the sheer extent of feeling hurt and wounded in so many parts of our bodies and psyches does with us is not easy to bear. One of the emotions that are difficult to get used to in this process of becoming more conscious of what is going on inside us is vulnerability. The most important thing I learned from the brilliant researcher, activist and bestselling author Brenè Brown is that vulnerability is the core of all emotions and feelings. "To feel is to be vulnerable," she says.[26]

---

[26] Brown, p.33

The definition of the Latin word *vulnerare* includes the meaning of being capable of being wounded or open to attack or damage. In a world driven by masculine values and ways of thinking, most of us fear vulnerability because it makes us feel so out of control and helpless, so exposed - to the point of feeling naked. It's highly uncomfortable. Also, because we have been taught to look suspiciously at emotions and feelings and brand them as a form of weakness, there is an underlying fear of all the dark emotions lurking in the basement.

However, it is worth understanding that "vulnerability is the core, the heart, the center of meaningful human experiences," as Brown poignantly points out.[27] "If we want to reclaim the essential emotional part of our lives and reignite our passion and purpose, we have to learn how to own and engage with our vulnerability and how to feel the emotions that come with it," she argues.[28] "If we want to be fully engaged, to be connected, we have to be vulnerable. If we want greater clarity in our purpose or deeper and more meaningful spiritual lives, vulnerability is the path."[29]

In contrast to commonly held beliefs about vulnerability being a weakness, Brown points out that weaknesses often stem from a lack of vulnerability: "when we don't acknowledge how and where we are tender, we're more at risk of being hurt." She offers a brilliant and innovative definition of vulnerability based on her research on the heavy emotions, foremost shame: "I define vulnerability as uncertainty, risk and emotional exposure."[30]

So when we ask the question, "what do we do with all this pain?" the answer is: we take the courageous way to face it, feel it, bear it, accept it and shift it. There is no other way. If we don't face our wounds and heal them, the thriving adult we intend to become stands no chance. The juicy things we dream to experience simply can't happen if we are bogged down by many layers of unhealed pain and repressed emotions. Hardheartedness prevents us from developing our potential for sinking into the joyful moments and basking in them.

In the effort to deal with pain, we might not even know if we are

---

[27] Ibid, p.22
[28] Ibid, p.35
[29] Ibid, p.61 and p.34
[30] Ibid, p. 39 and 34

processing, or just suffering through it without any major release occurring. And yet, the main recipe remains: to face it. Because otherwise, suppressed pain is bound to show up in other forms: among them unhealthy and unloving behaviors and attitudes, aches and pains, diseases, or a hell of a lot of fatigue. The problem for many of us is the habitually conditioned resistance towards taking action to improve the way we feel. *Daring Greatly* is in fact needed to show up, feel good, and flourish. Only then can we live lighthearted.

"The entire world is completely upside down. But the good news is, how many people know this," says Williamson.[31] It is precisely the discomfort of this knowing that propels us forward in the search for a way forward. This is what gets many of us to start the search for relief and recovery. The booming wellness and coaching industries attest to this development.

The rest of this book is about modalities that offer brilliant solutions to reduce and eventually heal our pain. In fact, the Aquarius Age offers us a very different view on pertinent issues, such as our health. "The current sea change is very good news indeed," emphasizes Kenney.[32]

Boiling it down to one issue that can be remedied

The other day somebody said to me: "You have a problem." I laughed, and then I was surprised as well about the sharpness of the sarcastic answer that shot out of my mouth before I could think: "Only one?" I retorted and started laughing. *Layers and layers of seemingly endless problems*, I thought. As numerous healers point out, our system is imprinted by the memories and energies related to all the problems we face individually, as well as collectively as humanity that seems to be on the brink of being hit by several intertwined disasters. *Oh how I wish it were only one problem*, I observed myself thinking. However, maybe it can all be traced back to one single core problem? That would be kind of nice. It would give us more motivation to focus on the remedies.

Pondering on this issue, I believe that we can sum up the multitude of

---

[31] Williamson, The Gift of Change, p.23
[32] Kenney, p.12

problems in one issue that can be remedied: we have been forgetting and turning away from the cosmic principles that Ma'at symbolically stands for. These are also themes of other prominent figures revered by ancient wisdom traditions. I am not referring to the persona of the Egyptian Goddess of Justice and her comeback to prominence, or how she might be worshipped again in her role of a goddess.

The point I am driving home is that the knowledge about the cosmic forces of harmony and chaos that ancient Egyptians held sacred is very relevant today. Lightheartedness is a way to fend off chaos. It's that important. Retrieving, becoming conscious of and honoring these principles is an essential step to evolve and move forward into a more harmonious and serene future. And this is what can be done on the individual level. Even while we are at home, simply through taking time to remember, reflect, re-align and readjust our internal navigation system.

Kenney puts it this way: "The ancient human-Earth relationship must be recovered in a new context, in its mystical as well as in its physical functioning. There is a need for awareness that the mountains and rivers and all living things, the sky and its sun and moon and clouds all constitute a healing, sustaining sacred presence for humans which they need as much for their psychic integrity as for their physical nourishment."[33]

Braden stresses that, "we have been led to believe that we are separate from one another. We've been taught that we are essentially powerless when it comes to the healing of our own bodies or our ability to influence peace in our communities and beyond."[34] The new paradigm, which emphasizes our inter-connection, is popping up all over the internet. It's definitely spreading. Oneness is a key word, and a hashtag that's buzzing.

Kenney poignantly points out that "the quality of life in a time of sea change depends to some degree on whether we feel as though we're riding the old wave down and out or riding the new one in."[35] It's helpful to remind ourselves again and again that the profound misunderstanding about being separate from another and from nature as well as the outrageous

---

[33] Thomas Berry, Evening Thoughts: Reflecting on Earth as Sacred Community, 2009, quoted by Kenney, p.203
[34] Braden, p.55
[35] Kenney, p.221

mistreatment of planet earth that are coming with that package are part of the outgoing wave. So let's wave goodbye to them.

Being part of worldwide efforts to ride the new wave in is the most exciting thing to do nowadays. It is about aligning our thinking, feeling and actions with the values of the Aquarian Age and dropping more and more of those thoughts, limiting beliefs, and self-destructive habits that are remnants of the old era we are moving away from. The clear understanding that long-term generational life on Earth is impossible without a harmonious relationship with the planet itself and with all forms of life is what the new waves are bringing in.

A deepening ecological awareness and commitment to do something about it are among the signs characterizing successful navigators of the new ear. Kenney argues that converting our desires for a balanced relationship to nature into action will determine whether the present sea change succeeds or fails.[36]

Honoring the incoming age

Creating a conscious relationship to water is one way to honor the incoming Aquarian Age and at the same time replenish our vital energy and feel more nourished at an essential level. The Japanese scientist Masaru Emoto has demonstrated in his amazing research that the tiny particles forming water are imprinted and affected by human thoughts and words.

Emoto deserves to be called "one of the most important water researchers the world has known." He offered evidence for the emerging understanding of the new paradigm that our thoughts and intentions impact the physical realm. For over 20 years, until he passed away in 2014, Emoto studied the evidence of how the molecular structure in water transforms when it is exposed to human words, thoughts, sounds and intentions.

His extraordinary life work is documented in the New York Times Bestseller, *The Hidden Messages in Water*. In this book, Emoto "demonstrates how water exposed to loving, benevolent, and compassionate human intention results in aesthetically pleasing physical molecular formations in

---

[36] Ibid, p.226

the water while water exposed to fearful and discordant human intentions results in disconnected, disfigured, and 'unpleasant' physical molecular formations. He did this through Magnetic Resonance Analysis technology and high speed photographs."[37]

Something as simple as writing the word "love" on a jug of water, totally changes what we take in. We can also channel high frequency vibrations into a bottle of water before drinking from it. This is especially advisable in case of dealing with a plastic bottle that has been transported over long distances and was exposed to damaging influences and loads of low frequency energies on the way. This is a simple little exercise that makes a huge difference. It's in line with traditional and often forgotten rituals of saying a prayer before eating and blessing our food. It's the attention and intention that matter. There is a lot we can do purely on an energy level to nourish ourselves in more profound ways at a time when many of the elements we ingest have become toxic to our bodies and souls.

As Furst stresses so aptly, "the link between Aquarius and water is inescapable now at this time of planetary water crisis, as great stretches of Earth's surface become desert and corporations who call water 'blue gold' aim to buy it up." He goes on to say that the challenge of Aquarius and the question of water "both invite us to decide whether water is an *It* – a colorless, odorless tasteless thing to be controlled and traded – or a *She*: a single conscious being who is sacred and the same in every cup of water we share, every drop of rain that falls on us, every lake and river we cross, every ocean that is the eternal source of birth and wisdom."[38]

This example, so well expressed, shows how crucial our perceptions and our ways of thinking are – especially in times of sea change. We cannot afford to keep defending the outworn beliefs about hierarchy, competition and scarcity that have brought us to the brink of collapse. What we need most is a revolution of consciousness, as the Indian sage and guru, Osho, pointed out repeatedly. It's time to wholeheartedly embrace the big new wave that promotes more joyful and abundant ways of living for all people on this planet.

A perpetuated focus on scarcity and lack will only bring us more

---

[37] For a well written article on Emoto's research, see (https://thewellnessenterprise.com/emoto/

[38] Furst, p.41

of it. According to a much repeated saying, *energy flows where attention goes.* Hopefully, this will become common knowledge one day. Brown succinctly calls scarcity "the never enough problem." I like this term very much because it points to the fact that the world, even in view of the splendid abundance and beauty of nature, cannot quench our thirst for the spirit of life that gives rise to the Self. Nothing material, and not even the most wonderful human love relationship, can ever be enough to satisfy the longing of our souls for the source of infinite bliss. On some level we know that, and yet we keep straying like hungry souls, desperately trying to fill ourselves up with all kinds of substitutes, which is ultimately perpetuating the painful sense of scarcity that impoverishes us more and more.

Brown argues that the term abundance, which is widely used nowadays not only in New Age circles, is not the counter approach to scarcity. Interestingly she defines the opposite of scarcity as enough, or wholeheartedness:[39] "Wholehearted living is about engaging in our lives from a place of worthiness."[40] The shortest way to develop an inner sense of worthiness is to unleash our inherent potential for joy. When we feel happy, we automatically feel worthy.

It's intriguing to remember that we can now much more easily arrive at a stage when we finally allow ourselves to feel worthy. The reason for that is that the worthiness of our Being is out of question. It simply cannot be disputed any longer, not after quantum physics proved that we are all made of and connected by the same tiny energy particles and space. In the miraculous dance of micro particles and space from which all life emerges, everything and everybody is interrelated. Therefore, we are all infinitely worthy. Period.

---

[39] Brown, p.29
[40] Brown, p.10

Summary

The volatility that is created by the rare kind of shift we experience now contains many dangers as well as tremendous opportunities for a major change in the ways we do things on this planet.

Numerous people, especially the young, feel a tremendous sense of urgency to do something useful that leads to transformation and make a positive contribution to this world. A part of that collective urge is due to the evolutionary impulse that is driving us, as well as the idealism that characterizes many of the themes that the new era we are about to enter brings with it. However, another part is fear-based, which can create major set-backs.

There is a pushing and pulling of two gigantic forces going on that is tossing us around in opposing directions. One wave is pulling us into the old paradigm build on convictions of scarcity, survival instinct, ruthless competition, and merciless authoritarian ways of ruling. The incoming wave pushes us forward to feel a strong urge for freedom, social justice, cooperation, creativity, abundance, as well as spiritual connection and awakened human consciousness to gain ground.

The period of transition from one historic age to another creates a large array of raw and mostly negative emotions that can easily bring us down without anything dramatic having happened in our own lives. Fears are as rampant among people, as is depression that is spreading like a virus all over the world. These heavy emotions hang over us like black clouds. When pressure and tension become too much, we tend to shut down and easily get sucked into a downward spiral.

On the other hand, an unprecedented amount of higher electromagnetic frequencies are pouring into our world and can lift us up to magnificent heights. A constantly growing number of people are making wonderful contributions to the many endeavors of evolving into a species that feels more compassionate and lighthearted. We are supported in many miraculous ways as we stand at the brink of either self-destructing as humanity or making a quantum leap.

Making excellent use of this crucial time boils down to cultivating the art of navigating the chaos with more ease and joy. It takes artistry to amplify the vital life force because we need a lot of fuel for the journey towards fulfilling our deepest aspirations. A central part of this transformation is about finally arriving at the point of recognizing and feeling our own worthiness.

You have to be an artist to successfully surf the huge waves of sea change, which are characteristics of our time. Flow, intuition, inspiration as well as emotional and spiritual intelligence are crucial assets. The rest of the book is about those paths that offer major support in developing this much required artistry.

The next chapter is an introduction to my personal story that depicts an early urge for transformation. It sets the stage for the narration of my own experiences with the modalities described in the following chapters of the book. There is no logical timeline in those as significant turning points are described in the context of each modality and are therefore not ordered in a chronological manner.

*"To whatever extent I find the miraculous key
to the transformation of my own life,
to that extent I will help change the world."*

Marianne Williamson

THREE

Yes but How?

How to become more lighthearted, more loving, and wiser has been a question I have asked myself since I was a teenager. It took me many years and a whole lot of unpleasant emotions before I could come up with good answers to this important question. In fact, the "how" question freaked me out at times.

Being German, I tend to overthink. So, I felt particularly inspired by the possibility to go beyond the realm of the thinking mind, to transcend the thinking process and with it, the suffering it commonly instills. I imagined that when I reach that state of possible human development, which I saw as the ultimate pinnacle, I would be calm, compassionate, warm, balanced and full of love.

In a way, it was a wonderful thing that I had had these high aspirations already as a teenager. However, the yearning they brought up also contributed to perpetuate a sense of inadequacy, frustration with what is, as well as attachments to how I felt things should be. That was topped off by impatience to reach a destination that sometimes seemed so far away that it looked like it was totally out of reach.

"How do I get there?". This question kept popping up. Over the years, it had become nearly too painful to keep asking. Whenever I had a discussion about essential values, or Asian wisdom traditions with people dear to me, who would remind me of the ideal of becoming unconditionally loving, or fully awake, my response was, "yes, great, would love to be like that, but how?".

Looking back, I realize that for many years I felt that I hadn't progress enough spiritually and hadn't become calm and loving enough. I had done most of the exciting things in life that I had wanted to do, such as becoming a journalist and living and reporting in the Middle East, or moving to India and meditating for two years in an ashram, writing a first book, and discovering love. I had had a wonderful life. And, yet, I kept looking mainly at what was not yet good enough about me to qualify as being that liberated and enlightened person I had been longing to be.

Apart from the slow pace of self-development that annoyed me, another of the challenges was that there is such an incredible amount of readily available teachings, systems, techniques, tools and spiritual teachers out there. This in itself seems to create a lot of confusion. We try out one way and when it doesn't seem to work, we check out another modality. As Osho has pointed out, "every seeking is a seeking for a technique."[41] I can say now that my search has led me to fantastic places where I found answers.

There simply comes a point when something changes, seemingly by itself. First, in a subtle way, nearly unrecognizable. It might take time to realize that, yes, there has been a certain shift. Something has changed. A time arrived when I realized that I definitely felt a lot better about who and where I was and what I was doing. I did in fact, finally fall in love with my life. And from this love, I was able to turn into a much happier person.

I remember reading a book by Osho around seven years ago. I came across a part where he strongly emphasized that if you are not even in love with yourself and your life, you are dangerous to others because you create misery for those around you. The two little words 'not even' had the strongest effect on me. *Oh my, oh my, not even in love with myself*, I kept thinking. It shocked me a little that after all those years I hadn't even seem to have reached the first rung of the ladder leading to spiritual awakening.

---

[41] Osho, The book of Secrets, p.943

It takes everyone this long

This is why I found it very comforting to read the following sentences of Marianne Williamson: "Don't worry that it took you so long to get to this point. It takes everyone this long. We know nothing until we know all the ways that we're not the way we should be."[42]

Williamson's following description of the process describes well what I experienced. Discovering succinct explanations of what we went through is a huge part of the joy of reading. It makes us feel understood, less alone in our experience. So here it is: "What is it about spiritual knowledge that takes so long to digest?" she asks.

"The trendy nature of much contemporary seeking would lead you to think that you spend a year or two at the ashram and *voila!* you are at the mountaintop. But my experience argues otherwise. It takes a decade to understand the basic nature of spiritual principles, another decade while the ego tries to eat you alive, another decade while you try to wrestle it to the ground, and finally you walk more or less in the light. Anyone who thinks a spiritual path is easy probably hasn't been walking one."[43]

My experience has been like that too. Many things needed to happen that eventually lead me to the breakthrough I was yearning and praying for. Nasty bosses, dramatic break-ups, menopause, a whole revolution breaking out around me, the passing of my father, the loss of a well-paid job and way of work, and many other small or big things that triggered feelings of pain and sadness.

A sea of sadness

I realized that all that sadness held me back from evolving towards more lightheartedness. It seemed I was moving some steps forward but then many steps backwards. I feel that for most people development happens like that. It's never a straight line you walk on consistently, but contains many detours and loops.

Also it dawned on me that thinking about the reasons for the sadness

---

[42] Marianne Williamson, The Age of Miracles, p.29
[43] Ibid, p.28

was not really helpful at all. As Daniel Goleman says in his bestseller *Emotional Intelligence*: "Worrying about what's depressing us, it seems makes the depression all the more intense and prolonged. In depression, worry takes several forms, all focusing on one aspect of the depression itself – how tired we feel, how little energy or motivation we have, for instance, or how little work we are getting done."[44] I don't think that I was ever depressed in the clinical sense, but haunted by melancholy and a sea of sadness.

Now I know that a lot of the emotions I have felt since my childhood were modes that simply felt familiar and therefore comfortable. One of those emotional modes in my case was sadness, which I had been carrying with me like a heavy suitcase since I was a little girl without really knowing what I felt so sad about. Early on, I realized that I was more serious than others; that unlike most people around me, I would actually really like to be alone and spend time reading and thinking.

I also understood that this tendency didn't seem to make me particularly endearing to most people. And being likable is about the most important thing at that age – perhaps at every age. It just seems to be more urgent and dramatic when we are teens. Like many teenagers, I often felt lost and forlorn and somehow burdened by what I observed around me.

One of my few childhood friends would tease me when I would enter the gloomy mode and tell her I couldn't join her to go to the beach during our summer vacations because I needed to read and think. "Oh come on, wrap a rope with an anchor on it around your neck and throw yourself into the sea," she would respond laughingly. I didn't find that funny at all. All it did was to increase the feeling of being complicated and different from others. I didn't know how I could or would ever fit in.

Along with the notion of not fitting in, which made me feel unlovable, I also carried around the belief for a long time that I was stupid and at the same time too serious. I didn't particularly like the other children in kindergarten or school and yet I felt sad that they didn't seem to like me either. It's not that I was bullied or treated badly in any way, as it happens to so many other children. I just simply felt alone, awkward and bogged down.

These feelings persisted for a long time. Like a background color in a

---

[44] Daniel Goleman, Emotional Intelligence, 1996, p.71

painting, they remained there, fading a bit sometimes and then again, at other times, becoming very prevalent and painful. Like a familiar baseline that my system reverted back to again and again, whatever I did.

Many times I found myself wondering what the reasons were for this persistent gloominess that would hold its grip on my heart. In contrast to many people I knew or saw around me, I had a very good life. No childhood abuse, no trauma, no poverty, no real hardships or difficulties, no parental divorce, no war, no rape, no violence of any kind, not even one serious illness. None of these unfortunately very wide spread things happened. And so I felt that in view of the grave miseries around me, I had no right to feel that sad.

Ancestors in our emotional landscape

Miseries do not have to occur directly to us to feel bogged down by them. It took me nearly 50 years to understand that a whole lot of that sadness wasn't really mine in a strictly personalized sense. That is what we do as children – we see our parents suffer and instinctively want to lift that weight from their shoulders. We take on their suffering, such as, for instance, the sadness that descended on my mother when her mother died of cancer, or the trauma of my father who was forced to serve as a child soldier during World War II. As some spiritual teachers have pointed out, we are actually here to teach our parents and help them to lighten up – contrary to what parents usually feel they are doing.

When I first read Goleman's book, I understood that I belonged to these people who suffer from what he termed *chronic anxiety*. That was quite an awakening for me. After all, I had already mediated for years, however, the description he offered was clearly fitting, just as it fitted both of my parents. In addition to their difficult childhoods in Nazi Germany, moving every three years to a different country and with my father changing careers in between, they became irritable and worried.

Now I understand that. As a child, I soaked it up and thought it was normal to feel like that. A lot of that anxiety, irritability as well as that melancholy actually belonged to my parents, as well as their parents and their ancestors. A lot of this Germanic heaviness seems to have been stored in our DNA.

The collective nature of things

Another component was the collective human sadness and anxiety that I seemed to have been empathically picking up quite strongly. The psychologist C.G. Jung has coined the term and concept of a "collective sub-consciousness," which has become widely debated and was applauded by many who connect the prior seemingly separated realms of psychology and spirituality in their thinking and writing.

As I learned through reading, I belonged to those people that are now commonly called *empaths*. I am very susceptible to the moods and feelings of others, and am affected also very much by natural phenomena, such as full moons, eclipses, solar flares, earth quakes, tsunamis, etc.

It is also worth adding that there seems to be a very collective nature of emotional modes, which seems more prevalent to me in Egypt than in other places. Perhaps because it is a very family oriented society, or because it's so densely populated, or because of the emotional nature of many Egyptians who share their feelings quite openly. Whatever the numerous reasons could be, we seem to move through a whole lot of emotions together around here in ways that are more noticeable than in Western societies where people tend to live more isolated lives, live further apart from each other, and are less expressive about their feelings.

All these are possible explanations for emotional states that have no apparent root causes in a personal story. Apart from that there is also the explanation of past lives, which has always made sense to me. Perhaps because I was born in India, it seemed naturally plausible to me since I was a teenager. It simply seemed impossible to learn everything there is to learn on this planet in only one life. I also couldn't understand why we should wait for the afterlife to find ourselves either in paradise or in hell. This I clearly felt were the states we would need to deal with, or rather co-create, while here on earth.

I had this feeling, more like an inner knowing, that I have been around many times before. It's not usually something I like to debate, because my experience is that discussions about personal beliefs don't bring us anywhere. I have never felt drawn to past-life regression therapy either. I sensed that I had enough to figure out about this life first that I might get lost in gathering endless glimpses about past lives drawn out of context, which would add confusion and not lead me to enlightenment. And yet, my relationship with Egypt seemed to be mysteriously linked to the past.

Egypt is my home

But it is the present that is of most concern to me. The here and now has a lot to do with where I live and what I do. At this point of my life, I am living in one of the special Megacities. I live on an island on the river Nile, pretty much in the middle of Cairo, *Al Kahera*, the victorious city. It has a majestic air to it. It is bursting with aliveness. It is one of the most densely populated areas in the world and one of the most polluted cities on this planet. Life in Cairo is intense. It's taxing and tiring. It also often feels exhilarating.

This city is full of various layers of visual reminders of different bygone eras of architectural and aesthetic splendor. A lot of it is peeling off, hidden under many layers of dust and neglect. It gives you the impression of crumbling and decay. It generally has become rather shabby. And yet for me, this is part of its unique charm.

At its fringes, nearly conquered and swallowed up by the city that keeps relentlessly stretching out further and further into the desert areas surrounding it in all directions, stand the pyramids, the most majestic of all sights to me. I have no words to describe their glory.

Each time I see them popping up from afar, a sense of childlike happiness descends on me. *There they are! I have seen them! Yeeaaahhh!* That's my immediate emotional response. And I think that conveys more than trying to classify the emotion or to describe the view, not to speak of the mysteriously strong spiritual force or energy the pyramids continue to emit in their mind boggling miraculous ways.

These energies that emit from all the places that were held sacred in ancient Egypt, can feel very strong at times, especially during eclipses or solstices. There is an amazingly intense spiritual energy in Egypt, way more than in other places I have visited. In fact many people from around the world are drawn to Egypt because of its splendid ancient civilization.

Many books have been written about it. Many of the well-known spiritual teachers from the West have been leading groups to visit temples and tombs constructed by ancient Egyptian queens and kings and, of course, the pyramids. The government is not fond abut foreigners meditating in the pyramids, and misses out on the opportunity of promoting Egypt as a prime destination for spiritual tours. However, some of the big teachers still ended up getting special permissions for their groups to spend a night or early morning to meditate in one of the great pyramids. Rumors have it that large sums were paid in exchange.

Some of the less known teachers travel here regularly, or have settled in Egypt for a while to bask in the energies. Many of them have received glimpses of the healing rituals that were held in temples. Many have re-established a connection to some of the gods or goddesses that were once worshiped in ancient Egypt and say that they feel guided by them. Some of them went on to teach ancient healing modalities, such as Sekhmet Healing, Egyptian Reiki, Egyptian Aromatherapy, Kemetic Yoga etc.

Childhood in Egypt

For me, Egypt is not a touristic experience, not a fleeting encounter with the exotic, not a search for the past. It's my life lived among Egyptians that has formed me and shaped me. It's my home, and I love it dearly. The first time I came to this splendid country I was around three years old. My family stayed with friends in a gorgeous Mediterranean little beach house in *Agami,* and we spent the whole summer on a very long white sandy beach right by the turquoise sea. This set the standard for me. This was how a proper sea should look like.

When my parents took me to the North Sea in Germany for the first time, I was around six years old and felt terribly disappointed by the view of many kilometers of grayish color, slick, extending out all around us where people, for reasons unknown to me, were enjoying walking in the mud. The equally murky and sad looking sea far out there *ran away,* as I put it. It puzzled me, and I asked my parents how come the sea ran away from us. I just wouldn't have it. *This is not a nice sea,* I concluded very seriously. That was my verdict back then. I was never able to change it.

Until now, I simply have felt that Egypt has some of the best beaches in the world, in spite of all of the efforts to damage the beauty of its coastlines by building plenty of resorts made of grey or beige colored cement houses that ultimately have the look of shoe boxes, stapled up close to each other, remaining empty through most of the year. And yet, there are still simple camps with bamboo huts right by the sea, or eco-lodges in some of the most pristine natural environments in various areas of the country. The vastness and raw beauty of the desert is stunning, and efforts of conservation are increasing.

Whatever is built or done around me in the name of progress doesn't change my basic feeling: Each time I cross one of the bridges in Cairo and look at the Nile and the splendid row of five star hotels and boats seaming its shores in the core of the city, my heart beats quicker. I love Cairo. Many Egyptians can't really seem to wrap their heads around it. They wonder how a German citizen, who could leave any time and live happily ever after in Germany would choose to live in Egypt. The dream of finding a way to reach Germany and start a new life there is very wide-spread.

When you love something or someone, you don't have logical reasons for it. The mind would like to find them and churn up some rationalization. However, it's the heart from where the sense of loving and belonging originates. And the mind will never understand it, nor even tolerate this strange illogical state for long. It rather creates confusion and disturbances.

Cairo simply feels more familiar, more like home to me than any other place in the world. I arrived to live there with my family when I was nine years old. We came from Beirut, where we had lived for three years before that. I was born in India and lived in Turkey during the preschool period. I loved to go horse riding next to the pyramids. I loved the palm trees. I loved the smell of the river, and I loved trips to Upper Egypt or to some of the long white beaches by the Mediterranean Sea. And I loved the extraordinary lightheartedness of Egyptians – even though, I wasn't able to describe it back then. There is a special spirit in the air in Egypt that I found nowhere else.

When I was not yet 13, my parents felt that we should move to Germany. It was the most traumatic culture shock I ever experienced. I did not want to live there or have anything to do with it, and since that time my main wish was always to return home to Egypt. My mother reminded me recently that whenever she would ask me what I wanted as a birthday or Christmas present, my standard answer was: *I want a flight ticket to Cairo.*

Early on, I informed my parents that when I was grown up, I would move back to Egypt. When we announce something or ask for something persistently, we eventually get it. I have been based in Egypt now since nearly 20 years, and I can't really see myself leaving. That's just simply how my life unfolded.

When you are a second generation expat, it is often very difficult to feel happy in your country of origin, because you didn't grow up there. The nature and the people there don't talk to you and touch your heart in the same way you feel in those places that are more deeply familiar. Your soul simply can't soar.

What is also different as a second generation expat is that you dive into the culture way deeper than an adult who settles abroad. As a child, you soak up the atmosphere and it becomes a part of you because you experience the emotions of people more intensely than an adult can because grown-ups are more confined to the realm of the mind and all the judgments it brings up. And it is the emotionality of Egyptians and the amount of beautiful feelings that they can generally so easily generate from their hearts that I have come to love on a deep level.

The gloominess after the Egyptian Revolution

Things changed a lot after the January 25 revolution in Egypt. The years after 2011 that first brought up so much hope, enthusiasm, idealism and aspirations have been a profoundly challenging time for everybody I have come across or heard of, as these feelings were crushed and turned into their opposites.

One might be tempted to argue that because it was hard for me in many ways, I only perceived the hardships of others more sensitively. Or that I attracted only people to show up in my life who resonated with the wavelength of the kind of feelings that I kept feeling. However, the fact remains that many others told me that they also see this phenomena happening all around them. It was like the whole possible range of heavy emotions boiled up and flooded over.

There seemed to have been a collective soup of feelings that descended upon us like a black cloud containing a lot of these ingredients: fed-up, frustrated, frazzled, uneasy, stuck, hopeless, resigned, apathetic, resistant to taking any action, helpless, bored, overwhelmed, fragile, fatigued, fearful, restless or even outright struck down in any kind of dramatic way. In a nutshell: sucked dry and lifeless.

Becoming aware of all these kinds of depleting and often plainly annoying emotions is not exactly a fun thing to do, which is why so many people seem to prefer living in denial, or take all kinds of drugs to numb the pain. And yet, facing our worst emotions is fundamental for our evolution, individually and collectively as a species.

As Williamson says so nicely: "If you avoid the pain, you miss the gain."[45] I have come to feel beyond mere intellectual understanding that it's ultimately through facing our emotions that we evolve. This is valid for the individual as well as for the collective level.

It's the emotions that move us forward

Like for many others a lot of ups and downs occurred in my life. The ride was not a smooth one. As we have seen in the last chapter, this is part of the dynamic of the crosscurrents and whirling energies that are typical for times of sea change. I would often set goals and set out to do something differently only to be thrown straight back to square one. I often felt frustrated because of the sheer amount of resistance that would pop up, making it look impossible to ever achieve any of them.

Menopause hit me unexpectedly early when I was not even in my mid-forties. I suffered from heat flashes and would often wake up in the middle of the night bathed in sweat and feeling terrified. Tons of doubts, questions and worries visited me in loads of sleepless nights. Going through a divorce was another experience that left me feeling as if my heart was being torn apart. These two issues together left me feeling sapped of vital energy and haunted by irrational fears that my life as a woman had come to an end and I would never feel sensual or attractive again.

These dark nights of the soul feel so terrifying because they break us open at our core and all the stuff that we have tried so hard to hide from ourselves, the painful memories, the secrets, the shame, the injuries, the nasty words we heard from lovers, or we said to others, all of that jucky stuff is exposed leaving us feeling naked, and utterly unlovable. The many

---

[45] Williamson, The Age of Miracles, p.57

ways we felt rejected jump into our memory and make us realize the many ways we rejected ourselves, by not honoring our bodies, our intelligence, our hearts, not recognizing our unique and ultimately sacred beauty. The rawness of feelings leads to honesty, and we are delivered to a new level of clarity. In this painful process of recognizing ourselves, layers of social conditioning are being peeled off and we are being cleansed.

And then suddenly a breeze of fresh air comes in from nowhere, a new perspective appears, a wave of blissful feelings caresses us and we realize that there is a new softness where we felt bitter and hard before. These kinds of awakenings occur so that our hearts can be purified.

Awakenings don't happen to everybody, because not everyone is ready to wake up. However, we all get many chances to experience dark nights and difficult periods when the ugly stuff comes up. While we go through them, these experiences are messy and painful and don't feel graceful at all. And yet, they are very precious because they ultimately deliver us to a place from where we can see our truth, accept it and stand in it. Awakenings deliver us to our hearts. They help us to feel more compassion for ourselves and for others.

I didn't know that coming out on the other side of these experiences would make such a difference. I was very skeptical when I read that midlife could be a great time of empowerment for women. Like many others, the fear of aging was stronger than the ability of allowing the thought that life in my 50s or 60s could be anything close to fantastic. Now I see the same skepticism in the eyes of those clients in their 40s who are afraid of turning 50 when I tell them this.

Truth be told, I have never felt as inspired, free, empowered and content as in my 50s. And there's this knowing that this development is just another beginning. While some of my classmates are thinking about their retirement plans, my feeling is that I am just starting to come out of the closet and have many exciting years ahead to roll.

What made a big change, apart from the awakening moments, was that I started taking many different courses and that made me feel incredibly excited and inspired. It was like a whole new world opened up for me. Earlier than I had planned, circumstances unfolded that led to an end of my existence as a long-term expert, working for international cooperation agencies. I felt I wasn't ready and hadn't saved enough money to make it on my own, and tried to hang on. And yet God, or the divine, or the universe, or life, or whatever you might be comfortable with calling the unnamable, obviously had other plans for me that I just couldn't see. The unknown is always a scary place to step into. So yes, I went through and faced a whole lot of fears that kept popping up again and again during one messy decade.

The good thing is that over time I managed to navigate the opposing forces in increasingly better ways. An important part of this was learning the lesson of accepting those duller days when I felt unable to accomplish anything of what I would have liked to see happening. I kept going for energy healing sessions when I felt I was getting caught in one of those downward dynamics. And slowly I started listening more often to my intuition and moved forward just upon a hunch.

Life has a mysterious way of unfolding on its own. During my first trip to London to take a class in energy healing, I got a magazine in one of the spiritual bookstores that were a fascinating discovery on its own. I loved diving into them and would lose any sense of time there. The last 20 pages of this magazine were filled with advertisements for retreats and workshops on an incredible variety of topics. I had no clue that this kind of world even existed before reading that magazine. None of this was available in Egypt at that time.

I remember vividly how I sat in a coffee shop, looking at this last section in that magazine, my eyes opening as wide as my heart. I felt a strong desire to be a part of this movement to the point of feeling a pain aching deep in my heart. I realized that I really wanted to be able to spread useful knowledge and assist others to evolve through offering these kinds of workshops. Somehow I have arrived at that place. This is a part of what I do now. I love it. And I love how it all unfolded and fell into place in spite of all the fears and tears and ups and downs and the messiness of it all.

Only at hindsight some of the significant developments and turning points that got me to where I am now make sense. I started taking courses in energy healing arts because I experienced a healing miracle that I describe in the next chapter. This lead to the discovery of the existence of something called coaching. Enrolling in *The Coaching Academy* in London, from where I eventually obtained three diplomas in distinctively different areas of coaching, lead me to a lady who offered me another important clue on my very first day there. This turned around my life. I strongly feel that I was led to the University of Laughter Yoga in Bangalore. And the enthusiasm I started to develop for Laughter Yoga very much to my own surprise led me on a path that brought me to the door steps of the HeartMath Institute. One thing always leads to many others.

None of these beautiful paths would have created the changes I have experienced on their own. As blissful as meditation can be, or as wonderful giving or receiving energy healing sessions can be, on their own, they didn't create the transformation I finally experienced. When flanked by the deep level of self-reflection and determination to achieve my goals that came with developing into a Life Coach, as well as big doses of extended laughter and emotional self-regulation techniques, things changed in way more tangible ways. This is the reason I feel so passionate about mixing approaches and studying way more than just only one modality.

Many practitioners mix modalities because the combination of a variety of self-development tools creates remarkable breakthroughs. Many of us are drawn to study many things as the era when there was only one brand of spiritual or religious practice in town is luckily over. It is one of the grand opportunities of this very exciting era of Sea Change we live in that gives us the opportunities to keep expanding our knowledge and experiences in ways that have never been possible before. And each one of us who is ready and keen to change is led to those paths that work for them. What we seem to have in common is that the longing for transformation is usually created by deep emotional suffering.

Only now I can see the range of heavy emotions I suffered from for so many years as the blessing they turned out to be. As Goleman points out: "The single mood people generally put most effort into shacking is sadness."[46] This was exactly the case for me. It was this feeling of being fed up of the suffocating sadness, which had become so intense that it seemed to suck the life force out of me. This was what motivated me to find ways that would lead me out of it. Moving away from it was the logic behind the motion. These emotions were the reason for my quest to feel happier.

Without this persistent sadness or chronic anxiety, I would have never made all the beautiful discoveries that have become so precious to me. Thanks especially to the sadness I discovered the beauty of Laughter Yoga. Without it, I might have dipped my toes into this strange laughter delivery

---

[46] Goleman, ibid, p.69

system and simply left it at that. I would not have dived so deeply into it. I would not have come to see it as one of the most wonderful forms of exercise. To miss out on the joy it gives me to make others laugh would have been a real pity.

If I would have already been a perfectly happy person to begin with, it is also very improbable that I would have been drawn to fly to California, crossing thousands of miles over the ocean, which was quite terrifying for me, to attend a training of the remarkable HeartMath Institute. It is precisely the discomfort or even agony of inner suffering that gets us moving. This trip turned out to be an eye-opener. I had no clue before that it was possible to change my emotions at the drop of a hat.

If I hadn't felt so fragile, fatigued or weak so often while doctors would usually find no medical reasons for these states, I would not have been drawn so strongly to seek alternative treatments that work for me. Energy healing brought in higher frequency energies that shifted me out of states in which blockages were so dense that I was stuck in a state suffering. Many times it has helped me tremendously to get out of a health or emotional crisis. It has enriched my life and provided a growing sense of security that people who either don't know about it yet, or choose to take a skeptical stance, are missing out.

The how-question was finally answered. I started experiencing more states of inner joy without doing strenuous practices or living in the bliss field of an Indian ashram. I could catch myself more often when I felt gloomy and shift out of it. Suddenly I could better accept situations that would annoy me before, or keep up a sense of gratitude for my life. I would laugh more often, or find myself sitting somewhere with a big smile on my face.

I started consciously enjoying staring into the space around me. Becoming aware of that emptiness around things, the space in between them, which flows through everything and connects everything to everything, made me feel delighted and enchanted. Now, it happens often that I become aware of a sense of contentment.

One of the main reasons for this development is that the mental bugging that went on and on over the past decades, the nagging inner voice that was trying to convince me that things should be different, has finally begun to subside. That in itself was an enormous relief.

The realization sank in that I am living exactly the life I always wanted to live. I didn't fall into the trap of massive self-exploitation, like many entrepreneurs or passion-preneurs seem to be doing. I am not constantly on the phone. There is no multitasking, no crazy pressure, and no ugly office. I make a lot of time for my own enjoyment of life, such as playing with my dogs and dancing. I love what I do now, and it gives me a tremendous sense of satisfaction that I never felt while working in any of the well-paid jobs I had before. While I have come to appreciate many aspects of my life over the past years, and have gradually felt more and more grateful for it, I could not have expressed it in this explicit manner before.

Somehow, I was able to allow myself to slow down and live a laid back life and enjoy it with less of those moments where the inner critic raises its ugly head to tell me that I should be more active, should get up earlier, should earn more money, should be more out there, should be more disciplined, should develop greatness, or should be doing anything else than what I was just doing. Instead, I could feel more often how blessed I was to be able to live exactly the way I did. In a strange way, it was as if the many days and periods I spent on my sofa feeling too much physical pain or fatigue to do anything, and becoming aware of the need to accept the non-doing, giving in to a state of just being, have started to bring in a beautiful harvest.

The connection to another level of consciousness is made simply by remembering to connect to pure awareness, and boom, a different feeling state, a different biochemical state appears. These feelings were so pleasant that I remembered more often to connect. It became easier and more fun. Just as Williamson points out: "If in fact the highest, most creative work is the work of consciousness, then in slowing down we are not doing less; we're doing more."[47]

Not that much in my outer world had changed. It's the quality of the inner world that eventually shifted and created all the difference. What Osho describes so well in the following quote just happened by itself: "A saturation point comes when you have asked again and again "How? How? How? – and ultimately the "how" falls. Then you can surrender."[48]

---

[47] Williamson, The Age of Miracles, p.33
[48] Osho, The Book of Secrets, p.943

Summary

The desire to evolve spirituality and feel lighthearted has inspired me since I was a teenager. While this aspiration triggered a spiritual quest and ongoing personal development path, it also perpetuated a sense of feeling not there yet and 'not good enough'.

Over many decades, again and again I felt as if I was gripped by a persistent heaviness that bogged me down. Like anything else, the reasons for this sadness were multi-causal. A part of the sadness we carry is not ours in a personal sense. We carry the issues of our parents and ancestors and that can feel like a very heavy burden.

The desire to shake it off and turn into a happy person kept growing. It was the main motivation to move forward and keep going.

Living in Egypt as a second generation expat makes me visibly different from most people around me, which often made me feel very uncomfortable when I was young and wanted to blend in. At some point, the issue of a well-defined national identity lost its importance.

Living in the exciting cosmopolitan city Cairo, I keep meeting people with intercultural backgrounds and a profound interest in self-development and spirituality. By taking many courses in different places, I realized that there are people on this planet who resonate with me. Finally, I have found my tribe.

Digesting spiritual knowledge can take a while. Self-Development is not one straight line forward. It's messy and often painful, usually characterized by many ups and downs, with progress and set-backs alternating, sometimes at a crazy speed, while at other times feeling stuck can prevail for what feels like an eternity. Awakenings are not graceful moments but they deliver a lot of grace.

Many people try something and if it doesn't seem to produce any results, they wouldn't feel motivated to try again. One of the most important aspects that I like to convey through narrating my story is that I simply kept moving forward. Whatever the inner or outer obstacles were, I continued taking energy healing sessions, attended classes, tried new things and kept re-inventing myself over and over again.

A multitude of events and miraculous occurrences were needed so that I could come to experience a phase where I eventually enjoy more conscious feeling states of contentment, fulfillment and gratitude. Life has a miraculous way of unfolding on its own, which only makes sense at hindsight.

In the next chapter, I narrate my first encounters with energy healing practitioners. These encounters made deep impressions on my psyche and constituted turning points because I was healed from a variety of afflictions that could have developed into quite debilitating states. The miracles I experienced raised a keen interest in learning more about energy healing arts.

"You have the power to heal your life, and you need to know that."

Louise Hay

FOUR

Encounters with the Miraculous

Releasing the energetic imprints of trauma and pain to heal our souls and our bodies is an essential path to lightheartedness. Taking or giving energy healing sessions is among the activities I enjoy most. It's usually deeply relaxing. Something always gets released. Afterwards, there is a sense of relief and revival. There's more lightness in the system, more ease. Something flows better, feels better.

Additionally, there is a sense of having been nourished at a profound level, from deep down inside. This in itself provides for a deeply felt sense of being comforted, taken care of. It restores the sense of feeling safe that comes from the realm of the soul. On a soul level, most of us do not feel threatened at all. That's where we soar and fly high in feelings sates of bliss and joy.

Most of us have lost this soul feeling that all is well early in life. Living without a conscious connection to our souls has become the habitual mode for far too many of us. We take that as normal. That's simply how it is. Many don't seem to really know anything else, at least not with the rational mind that has become so powerful at this point in time.

This delicious sense of being held and cared for, provided for and loved prevails in the realm of consciousness, or divine essence and seems to have a tendency to get watered down or, even at times, evaporate in the three dimensional world we became so used to living in. What remains is a vague sense of longing for it, which comes through the soul. However, most of us are too hurt, too distracted, too brainwashed to take the time for getting in touch with our souls. Many people would even doubt that we have one – especially in many Western societies.

Energy medicine brings me back into realms that the mind has no access to. For me, energy healing is a necessary part of maintenance of the system. The set-up of body, mind and soul requires showers of vital energy to keep functioning well. It's not a luxury. It's actually a must.

I am writing this while being aware that must-dos, shoulds and have-tos don't really get us to move. If anything, the attitude of "I have to" only creates more resistance. What works well, is allowing oneself more flow, allowing relaxation, allowing pampering, allowing release of pains and tensions, allowing softening….

What I am trying to bring across here is that simply by living on this planet we have accumulated many, many dense layers that are carrying tension, anxiety, worry, fear, pain, emotional wounding, trauma, distress, sadness, anguish, guilt and shame, etc. You name it, we are all haunted by it in one way or another. Activities in which we can drop or peel off some of these heavy layers are very much needed by our system, which is already struggling to keep going in the toxic environments we are exposed to every day.

I consider it a huge blessing that I have come across energy medicine and have had several experiences that truly deserve to be called miracles. Whenever I was feeling really miserable and was in need of emotional or physical healing, a healer would show up unexpectedly and tangible transformation happened. This kind of miraculous support started to happen when I was in my thirties. I guess before that, I just didn't really need it or wasn't ready to receive this kind of gift. Looking back, I realize how important these encounters were for me and my personal as well as professional development.

Back then, I had no clue that my fascination for energy medicine would increase and eventually lead me along to a path that consisted of discovering the thrill of taking many courses in various energy healing arts. At the time, it just felt like the most natural and obvious thing to do. In fact, there seemed to be no other alternative.

Ute Devika

How I was cured from arthritis

Once upon a time, when I was in my early thirties I worked as a Gulf Correspondent for the German Press Agency (dpa) in Bahrain, which seems like a different era to me now. Bahrain is a tiny island state in the Arabian Gulf, which has witnessed periodic waves of unrest. Reporting on it got me repeatedly into trouble. This job was way more stressful than I thought it would be. After nearly three years of working in Manama, I was expelled. I was given 24 hours to pack and get out of the country. The panic I was in during those days while outwardly maintaining my cool defies any description.

When I arrived at my parent's home in northern Germany feeling like a refugee, I was not only under shock, but traumatized. Only that back then neither me nor my parents knew what a trauma is – much less how to deal with it. The only thing I felt I knew and had been trained for then was how to write. Since I was a student, I had used my typewriter to integrate and digest problems. When psychotherapy became popular among university students in Berlin, where I studied philosophy, mass communication and political science, I actually joked sometimes that I didn't need therapy as long as I had a typewriter or computer.

So the first thing I did just for myself was to write down the sequence of events that led to my departure from Bahrain. What I had never experienced before was that my whole body started trembling while writing. My legs were shaking, and the process was so painful that it drained me to the point that I felt fears creeping in. Yet my need to write down some of the things I went through was unshakable. After some months, I left to Italy to retreat into seclusion in the country side to read and write. This undertaking created such a huge strain on my psyche, my body actually developed arthritis.

I suffered mainly from strong pains in the joints of my hands. It reached a point where I couldn't really use them anymore - at least not for carrying heavy bags from the supermarket, or cleaning the house. I bandaged my wrists and gave them as much rest as I could. Eventually, it got so bad that I couldn't type anymore. Writing was what I had been most yearning for and what I was also most afraid to do.

A doctor I finally consulted told me that there was no cure for arthritis and that I would end up in a wheelchair in less than 20 years. I was shocked, as if somebody had hit me on my head. Like many doctors who took years of studying conventional medicine and built their identity and pride on this accomplishment, he was oblivious of to any alternative therapies. Probably this *stranger*, all puffed up by the superiority of his book knowledge, would have scoffed at the idea that I could possibly be cured. This diagnosis that was delivered in such an ice cold way got me moving.

It's exactly when this kind of drastic verdict is passed down to me, or somebody threatens me with terrible consequences if I would do a particular thing, that a rebelliousness kicks in, which seems to be rather deeply ingrained in my character. Now I realize that rebelliousness is not an easy trait to let go of, especially since it seems like it served me well many times in my life. The good thing was that the determination that I simply would not have any sort of this kind of scenario happening to me became very strong. And that, it seems, was what was most needed for me to be healed.

A neighbor told me about an energy healer she frequented for her aching knees. I felt intrigued and immediately called the lady to arrange for an appointment. We both felt a lot of love for each other from the very beginning of our first meeting. Oliva was the name of this special woman, who some people called a witch. My heart is filled with gratitude for her. She was a very warm Italian woman in her mid-fifties who had no children and bestowed a whole lot of motherly love on those who came to see her for support and healing.

Oliva asked me to sit in front of her and started to ask me some questions while she took notes and looked up things in a huge book. From time to time she would peek over her little reading classes into my eyes and beam a smile at me. I felt that she looked right through me. Her intuitive way of understanding me and the condition I was in fascinated me. I had never witnessed anything like that before.

She simply knew that I wanted to write a book but was literally scared to death about actually doing it. She stated that as a plain fact. I was stunned. Hardly anybody knew what I was planning to do. In view of the waves of paranoia that would get hold of me, I had been very secretive about my plan. Strangely enough Oliva had been working in a big publishing house in Milan for many years before she moved to the countryside and turned into a healer. Perhaps she had seen many authors suffering from writer's block to the point that their wrists got frozen. I never asked her.

Oliva searched for a homeopathic remedy in her big book. When she found a few, she used a pendulum to figure out which one would work best for me. I had never seen a pendulum before. However, her dowsing felt natural because in Oliva's presence I felt entirely accepted and loved. Her prescription was simple and logic: Apart from the homeopathic drops, I was supposed to take regularly, she suggested a lymph drainage massage every week to get the toxins moving out of my arms. On top of that, Oliva recommended that I eat well, sleep a lot and take long walks in nature every day. She made it a point that I should attend her yoga class twice a week.

Lying down on her massage bed was the best part of the cure. I had had regular massages for years before I met Oliva. I had always loved to be massaged, but lymph drainage was a new experience that I came to enjoy tremendously. It was a tender stroking, no oils, no pressure - just gentle movements from the fingertips up to the shoulders using just a little bit of powder. She tenderly called me 'Stellina', meaning little star in Italian, and beamed her loving smile. I felt I was in heaven.

I am quite sure now that this extraordinary lady, who looked like quite an ordinary, slightly chubby Italian housewife - except for her big brown eyes that revealed so much depth and love – Oliva, also channeled energy. I didn't ask her though what exactly she did. I simply surrendered. That was possible because of the strong bonding from the heart that miraculously happened when we met. I simply adored and trusted her.

At that time, I didn't know anything about energy healing. I was fascinated that Oliva was a member of a spiritual group and had a teacher who was a self-proclaimed Italian master that had written a few books and offered classes and retreats. My plan at the time was to travel to India, stay in an ashram, enjoy group meditations and gain the inner peace and strength to be able to write about what I had experienced in that little island state. I eventually did that, and much to my own surprise I stayed in a raja yoga ashram little known outside India for two years where I experienced incredible states of inner bliss. But that's another story. You can read more about it in Chapter Twelve.

The whole point of this story is that within three to four months the pain in my wrists was gone and the arthritis was completely healed – never to return. I felt emotionally more balanced and stronger. In fact, I felt strong enough to move on with my life and travel to India for another superb adventure. Only that this time it wasn't about my career. In that area, I felt I had done enough for the time being. Now it was time to dive into the realm of the heart in order to discover the soul.

This is what energy medicine can do. It can heal conditions that some doctors define as incurable. How that happens is ultimately mysterious. Focused intent of the healer who brings in a big dose of high frequency energy to boost the self-healing mechanism of the body and release blockages is a major component. Willingness of the patient to heal is another. That implies readiness to let go of the emotions and the trauma that are root causes of the symptoms showing up in the body.

In my eyes, healers who deserve that term are spiritually evolved enough to go into a meditative state, empty their mind of thoughts and dive into pure consciousness or nothingness. This is how they hold the space for healing to occur. The self-healing mechanism of the body gets a massive boost while high-frequency energy moves around in the body and smoothens out the edges – much like a defragmentation program helps a laptop to function better as files are defragmented. As much as we try to find logical explanations, ultimately energy healing happens in the realm of the miraculous.

There are many definitions of energy healing. Some of them sound very complicated. They give you the impression that energy medicine is difficult to practice when the opposite is true. At the end of the day, for me, it's all about feeling better. That's what really counts. And that has been the case after most energy healing sessions that I have taken over the years with different healers I have been lucky to meet.

Recovering from an accident and learning about Reiki

Around five years later, when I was working as a consultant for an international organization in Alexandria, I was involved in a car accident. I had been sleeping on the back seat of the car while traveling from Cairo to Alexandria during the night when the driver smashed into a small car, which was, as a result, totally wrecked. My head and knees banged into the seats in front of me and I suffered a shock. Luckily, nothing grave happened to anyone involved. What I carried away from this accident were aching knees and a strong headache. Doctors could not find any reasons, no fractures, no concussion either. Yet, the pain prevailed, and became nearly unbearable after long hours of sitting at the computer.

I started searching for a practitioner of energy healing and was led to a young man who was a Reiki Master. He gave me quite a few sessions, during which I felt very relaxed and comforted. I felt I was being bathed in warmth and nourishing energies. My condition improved a lot. He said that my body was soaking up the universal life force energy like a sponge and was in need of large quantities of it.

His suggestion was to teach me Reiki so that I would not become dependent on him or on taking sessions and spending a lot of money for it. I very much liked the fact that he wanted to empower me to heal myself. That is how I took the first course in a gentle and effective energy healing art originating in Japan, which unknowingly to me back then came to play an important part in my life.

In the following months, I placed my hands on my head and knees a lot, invoking the energy to flow and enjoying the heat my hands would suddenly generate. Especially when I got into any car, or felt a bit tired, stressed or shaky, I would lean back, breathe deeply, put my hands on my knees and bring on the Reiki energy. Around four months later, these efforts proved to be fruitful: there was no more pain in my knees and my head.

Another healing miracle

Around ten years after I was cured from arthritis, my body developed another potentially dangerous health condition and I unexpectedly experienced another miracle. A cyst grew on my uterus, and as it was not in it but on top of it, doctors called it a non-malignant tumor. It had the size of a golf ball and stayed under observation for a few years without need for intervention by the doctors I consulted.

At that time, I lived in Cairo and went for regular check-ups to a competent female gynecologist. At some point, this tumor started bleeding and moving. I got a high fever and a very strong pain kicked in. As is often the case when we are feeling very weak, I didn't have the inner strength to recharge my system with Reiki by myself. I was going down.

The doctor said that now the time had come to remove this tumor through an operation because the spouts of fever and pain would be recurring. I felt terrified. This irrational and deep seated fear was created by the thoughts that I would die if someone would open up my solar plexus area with a knife and remove a part of my uterus.

Maybe I had been influenced by watching some Samurai films, where these people committed suicide when they failed at something by slitting open that exact part of their bodies. The Japanese consider the *hara*, as it is called, to be the center of vital power and the seat of the soul. I don't really know where this fear came from, but I was so scared of having to undergo an operation that I was ready to do anything to avoid having to do that. I frantically called an energy healer I had met during a party a few years before. Her name was Linda. She was originally from the Netherlands.

"How can I help you?" was the first thing she said on the phone. "Please help me," was all I could answer. I was surprised and moved by my own request, because at the time I was certainly not the kind of girl that would ask anybody for help. I started crying. Her voice was very calm, reassuring and warm, when she asked what was wrong. When I outlined the problem, she briefly described that she practiced a new form of hands-on energy medicine called VortexHealing® and asked me to set a date and pass by soon. "I am sure that I can help you," she said. That was definitely what I most needed to hear.

Linda was one of the pioneers of energy medicine in Egypt, and she was one of the first people who had the courage to open a center dedicated to healing arts. She had worked as a tour guide in Egypt as well as various other African countries, which surely added to her remarkable skills to really see and understand the needs of people. Most of all, she was centered, open-hearted, kind and harbored no doubts about the effectiveness of the brand of energy healing arts she practiced. When I came to the center, she gave me a glance, then she laughed and hugged me. I felt like mother earth herself was embracing me.

Linda said that there could be various causes for this fibroid, and that she knew of many cases in which growths like these had vanished through energy healing. She suggested that we should work on various parts of my system and address several emotional issues. In a down-to-earth way, she said that it would be good to take a package of ten sessions. I agreed, even though the ten sessions amounted to what seemed at first like a big sum. Looking back, I feel she would have deserved 10 times the amount, taking into consideration what an operation would have cost me financially, not to speak of all the risks and side effects of an intervention of this magnitude, not to speak of the possibility of dying.

Most of the sessions were relaxing to the point that I fell asleep sometimes. Other than that I felt nothing. She kept asking me after the sessions what I had felt. I was a bit embarrassed to say that I didn't sense anything going on other than a comforting feeling of warmth in those places where she put her hands on my body. Sometimes I felt restless and had many thoughts moving around in my head. One evening tears started rolling down my cheeks in large quantities without me feeling particularly sad about anything. Neither was I sobbing, nor did I know the reason for that strange flood of tears. Linda said it was a form of release, which made perfect sense to me.

During one of the sessions, she said she would be performing a psychic operation, and there might be some slight pain. That was the only time I had the sensation of needles pricking me deep inside my uterus. However, so strange as those things sounded or felt to me at first, I didn't question Linda. I lay down on her massage bed and gave her the permission to do whatever she felt was necessary to do. I tried to let go of thinking, focused on my breath and my heart, enjoyed to softness of the nature sounds that her little CD player produced. Most of the time, I surrendered.

That summer when we were done with the ten sessions, I planned to spend some time with my parents in Germany. Only then I asked my mother to book an appointment for me with her gynecologist who was specialized on tumors and required bookings many weeks ahead. Given the fact that my mother had breast cancer before, and tended to be overly worried about me, I didn't want to burden her with the knowledge of a tumor sitting on my uterus. Obviously, she immediately knew something was wrong and had sleepless nights until my arrival and the date with the doctor. Both of us felt very tense when we left for that appointment. My father was also feeling very alarmed.

And then it happened: The doctor could not find any tumor whatsoever.

Not a trace of the fibroid could be seen on the screen. I couldn't believe it and kept asking her to check again. She in turn couldn't believe that there had been a growth in the first place and that it apparently had vanished through energy healing. I had not taken along the many results and images that could prove the existence of a growth as big as a golf ball that had been sitting there for many years. She kept repeating: "There is definitely no tumor anywhere in or on top of your uterus."

We left dumb founded. My mother was thrilled, totally changed. She was all bubbly and chatty and kept exclaiming how wonderful that was. I was speechless for quite some time. We had ice cream in an Italian café to celebrate. When we finally returned home, my father sat on his armchair in the entrance staring at us, looking battered and pale. Due to our delay, he had assumed that I had been advised to go straight to the hospital to be operated on the spot. I told him what had happened.

My father, an intellectual of caliber, a man of science, who refused to believe in anything and needed solid proof based on scientific research for everything, looked into my eyes and gravely said the following sentence to me: "These kind of miracles do happen." I couldn't believe he said that. It was one of these unforgettable moments.

For years, we had argued vehemently about the value and importance of meditation or yoga, the possibility of enlightenment and the existence of various energy vibrations, which he felt was all nonsensical. And then he simply stated what was obvious to him at that moment. A miracle had occurred. The utterly astounding thing was that he obviously felt that it was entirely possible.

To my own surprise, I could not wrap my head around it that easily. I had always believed beyond doubt in miracles happening to others. I read about modern ones in various books and articles, and I firmly believed in the healing miracles that were performed by Jesus Christ. However, I just couldn't believe that it had happened to me.

Sure enough I had been hoping and praying for it. However, I suddenly realized clearly that deep down inside I must have doubted all along that this could possibly happen to me. It came like a shock – a most positive shock, but, nevertheless, a profound shock. This is when I became aware of the subconscious belief sitting somewhere in my system that I was not worthy of a miracle. Kind of like "Who am I for this to happen to me?" For weeks on end, I just didn't get it.

This was the turning point. This is when I realized that if VortexHealing® could produce these kinds of results, I absolutely needed to enroll in classes and study it. I also knew that this miracle was just the beginning of a healing journey that I intended to take seriously. I suddenly felt clearly that there were many more issues that needed to be released from my system, not only a fibroid the size of a golf ball. Now I had the proof that it was entirely possible. And as it turned out, this knowing is very precious.

Knowing versus believing

When I started travelling to London and Amsterdam to take classes in VortexHealing®, I felt I was entering the Harry Potter world. This rather new brand of energy healing, which is not yet widely known, is a spiritual path to awakening that aims to assist students to release as many layers of conditioning as possible and discover who they really are at their innermost core. It is also a very powerful method to release blockages, flood the system with a wide range of different transmissions of high frequency energies, release some root causes of diseases, which can reduce symptoms showing up in the body, even working on the most subtle levels and patterns in the DNA.

As we progressed, the things we were taught sounded quite weird at times. Whether it was about angels that came in to assist us with shifting particularly heavy energies, past life experiences that some people started perceiving, the exercise of trying to remember an animal past life, or highly developed extraterrestrials from an unheard of planet who apparently attended the class but remained unseen, the range of issues that would get some people to raise their eyebrows or frown was quite large.

I kept thinking that if this would happen to some people who were already drawn to attend such advanced courses of an energy healing art, how much more would those people frown who reject the idea of energy or spiritual development in the first place? In Harry Potter terminology it boils down to the question: What would the 'muggles' think and say? But then again, who cares? I mean really, those who don't believe in miracles or doubt the existence of realms that can be called magical, will find out in their own time on their own terms. So, whenever somebody started voicing some doubt during the breaks in which we were all suddenly most keen on munching large amounts of delicious cookies, I would simply say: "I don't care about the strangeness of some of these things. All of this is not really important. I know it works. And that's what counts for me."

I came to understand that there is a huge difference between believing in something and knowing it. Belief takes mental effort. You sometimes try hard to get yourself to believe in something. A belief system is a construct of thoughts. Therefore, it breeds doubts. The mind always finds reasons to dissect and undermine any belief, so the nature of a belief is ultimately pretty fragile. It can break down and vanish into thin air any time.

Knowing arises from experience. You know something for sure because you lived it, felt it, experienced it and digested it. Knowing cannot be taken away from you. I am not talking of theoretical knowledge that comes from reading books, or something we picked up from a teacher or a trusted friend. Knowing is not book-knowledge, it's not information borrowed from others; it's not about abstract concepts or dogmas, either. It arises from integrated experience. It's your own truth.

What I know for sure, to paraphrase the inspiring question of the famous American talk show host Oprah, is that energy healing works. It doesn't always produce the outcomes the mind would trick us into desiring. A particular ailment might not be healed, but instead something else gets better. It relaxes and nourishes us, it shifts us out of stuckness, it gets the juices flowing. It restores balance and wholeness, helps us to recover faster and it rejuvenates us on a cellular, genetic and quantum level.

Energy healing is not what some lazy people wish for: you take one session and everything gets miraculously cured. Usually, it takes some willingness and effort. However, in some cases, instant healing also happens. After relating the healing miracles that happened to me, at the end of this chapter, I would like to share a few situations where I became the conduit of astounding transformations when I finally started putting my hands on people.

Miracles happen

One day, I was happily sitting at the back of a plane to London looking forward to taking another course in VortexHealing® when I heard somebody in front of me moaning in pain. I felt the impulse to offer help, but felt too shy because I had hardly had any experience in channeling energy to anybody other than myself. Somehow, it felt like I was asked to prove what I had learnt before taking another round of training. The noises of agony became so loud that flight attendants became aware of it and an announcement was made, asking if there was a doctor on board. In no time, many people appeared and there was a lot of commotion around the suffering young man, who related that he had been in hospital in Egypt and was on his way to a clinic in London due to kidney stones that were moving. When all of them left, I got up, and sat next to what turned out to be a very handsome young man. He was bent forward and had wrapped his arms around his belly. I asked if he would allow me to do some energy healing on him.

He looked up at me with astonishment and then said slowly, "I don't understand what you can do for me but if it helps I would go for anything." I asked him to sit straight and breathe deeply together with me while I placed my hands on his arm and side. I said an internal prayer, asking for divine help as I had no idea how I could possibly help. After a few minutes, his breath calmed and his muscles relaxed. Ten minutes later he smiled and started chatting me up. The plane was delayed, and while we kept circling over London, I kept channeling. An announcement was made that all passengers were requested to remain seated while a crew of first aid responders would carry one passenger out of the plane.

He turned his head to look at me with an amazed expression and said: "I have no idea what you did, but I feel good now." When the medical crew arrived immediately after we landed, they were surprised to see that the young man could walk on his own and was joking with them as if nothing had happened. He sent me an email a few weeks later telling me that the kidney stone came out as soon as he was in hospital and that he had suffered no further pain.

One day a woman in her thirties called me and asked for an appointment for an energy healing session. She had heard about me from a friend who took some sessions with me. The first thing I realized when she came was that there was a strange contrast between the remarkable sweetness of her facial expression and many kilos of overweight that she struggled to carry like a heavy shield. She looked bogged down, and there seemed to be a grey color around her.

She told me she held a good position as an assistant in a big firm, and then came straight to the point. She related that she suffered from persistent pains all over her body since she was young and that she was very much burdened by something that she had never shared with anybody. She chose me as a healer not only because she had heard good things about me, but mainly because she trusted that as a German living in Egypt, I would be able to keep the things she told me strictly confidential. I did promise her that. And so she told me her sad story.

When she was nine years old, she was repeatedly sexually abused and raped by a relative who threatened to kill her if she would ever talk about it to anyone. She was too scared to tell her parents and kept this horrible secret buried inside her. Since then, she had suffered from chronic pain, felt a lot of anxiety, and hardly any friends or social contacts. Obviously, she also took to eating a lot to put on such an amount of weight that would not make her look attractive to men. It helped her to feel safer.

I asked her to lie down on a sofa and got a little stool. Before starting, I prayed for a healing miracle. It took much longer than usual because I had no clue how I could possibly help in such a case. I called on Mother Mary and Jesus Christ to come in and help this lady who was suffering so badly from something horrible that was done to her when she was just a child. When I started to feel calmer, I put my hands on different parts of her body —wherever they were drawn to.

So much energy was flowing through me, I started to sweat profusely and sometimes my body made sudden movements, like shuddering. At the same time, there was an incredible sweetness coming in that felt so very graceful. Since I am not a very visual person, it surprised me that this lady conveyed to me after the session that she had seen many images. One of them was that I pulled out black energy out of her body that turned into something like red wool, which I wrapped up into a big ball. Another image she saw was that Mother Mary came in and put her hand on her shoulder, which to her had felt most comforting.

When she came back for the next session, I would not have recognized her if it hadn't been for her weight. She was glowing. Her face had a different color. She kept giggling like a little girl, and had the most angelic smile I had ever seen. She was happy to say that all her pain had vanished. For the first time in her life after the abuse, she was free of pain and didn't feel bogged down. She kept thanking me. I kept saying that it definitely wasn't me who performed this miracle. I had just been allowed to be the vehicle for it. She didn't come again for sessions. The work had been done. We are in contact until today through social media, and sometimes she pops up online to thank me again.

One day a friend of one of my clients called and said he needed my help because he felt extremely depressed. When he arrived, he narrated that he suffered from intense headaches and neck pain every day, that he had no appetite and would even forget to eat, and that he hadn't felt any emotions for a few years. His face looked dark even though he was pale and his eyes looked stern and lifeless. His face had such a grim expression that he said people would tend to be afraid of him.

I gave him a massage and then channeled energy to him for half an hour. It was an intense session and my body started shaking a lot. A few days later he called me to thank me and relate that he enjoyed being free of pain. For the first time in years, he could eat with great joy. He said that he cried after hearing a sad story from a friend and that he felt grateful for feeling emotions again. Somehow, he had just forgiven his father, who he had held grudges against for years. On top of that, he said he found himself smiling a lot.

When he came back for another session, I could see the transformation. He looked like a different person. The layer of blackness that I had sensed around his whole body was gone, and even his skin color looked as if it had been whitened. I felt incredulous. It gave me goose bumps. This is what energy medicine can do. It's mind-bogglingly wonderful. It never stops amazing me. The way it works is mysterious. One thing I know for sure now: Miracles do happen.

Summary

I was healed from rheumatoid arthritis by a very loving homeopath and healer in Italy when I was in my 30s. What got me to see her was a medical doctor telling me without the slightest hint of mercy that I would be sitting in a wheelchair within ten years.

Rheumatoid arthritis is a debilitating disease that could have crippled me. Therefore, I feel that the encounter with Oliva was indeed one of the big blessings I received. This miracle and the love and gratitude I keep feeling for the remarkable woman who was the conduit for it, has changed the course of my life. Just that I didn't know that back then.

One of the results of a minor car accident was that my scull and knees were in a lot of pain, in spite of the fact that doctors could not detect anything that was visibly injured. This triggered my search for a practitioner of energy healing. I discovered a Reiki Master who taught me this nurturing energy healing art from Japan and inspired me to heal myself. Within four months of charging my own system daily with this wonderfully soothing life force energy, the pains were gone.

I was diagnosed with a benign tumor sitting on top of my uterus. At some point a doctor suggested that it needed to be removed. I felt terrified of an operation, irrationally convinced that I would not survive it. This got me on my knees, and I was guided to Linda, a practitioner of VortexHealing® from the Netherlands.

Linda was a super positive pioneer of energy healing in Egypt. I took ten sessions with her, and the tumor disappeared. I had a hard time to grasp that this miracle actually really happened to me. As a result, I understood clearly that I needed to enroll in courses to learn more about this contemporary energy healing art. And so I set the sails to embark on a journey that took me to many fantastic places.

Circumstances unfolded in a way that nudged me forward to lay my hands on people and channel healing energies. In contrast to my experience with coaching, developing into a practitioner of energy healing was not a conscious goal I set out to achieve. It rather happened by itself in spite of my initial resistance. Now it gives me tremendous joy to teach Reiki courses and channel energies to others.

In the next chapter, I attempt to define in more rational terms what energy healing is about even though I know that it's ultimately mysterious. At first sight, this might seem contradictory. It is important to honor our own innate skepticism when it comes to mysterious healings, which is born of the rational mind's desire to understand what's going on. It sure felt very important to me and took a while until I could wrap my head around the fact that miracles happen.

"No matter how it may seem to you, your body is actually a collection of energies, flying in close formation."

Bradely Nelson

FIVE

The Breakthrough of Energy Medicine

Consciously tending to our health and wellbeing is needed if we are to prosper. For me, this means updating our bodies' "energy software" to adapt to the world of extremes we live in and regularly recharging our vital energy to cope with the numerous challenges we are facing. At this point in time, energy medicine is more crucial than ever.

Given how sick we are collectively as humanity living on an ailing planet, healing our many imbalances and dysfunctions is vital. "If you are to thrive, you must participate in the evolution of your body's energy patterns," say Donna Eden and David Feinstein.[49] And according to them, this is exactly what energy medicine does.

The Indian Master Reiki Healer, Maharaj Krishnan Sharma, points out that each one of us represents a vast potential to grow and develop emotionally, psychologically and spiritually. He states plainly how important this personal evolution is: "Our present world demands such growth and development."[50]

In other words, evolving to upgrade our energy system that was designed for living in the wild to higher levels of coherence, resilience and

---

[49] Donna Eden, David Feinstein, Energy Medicine, 1999, p.3
[50] Krishnan Sharma, The Practical Book of Reiki, 2008, p.47

joy needed in order to successfully navigate the chaos of transition into the Age of Aquarius is not just an option if we want to survive. It's a must, especially if we aim at becoming lighthearted.

One of the essential things that we literally have in our hands to recover and feel way better is energy medicine. Energy healing arts in general contribute in many miraculous ways not only to heal all kinds of ailments but to make us feel more peaceful and fulfilled and live lives that are characterized by deeper engagement from the heart and a profound sense of connection from the soul.

"Using the principles of energy medicine, you can optimize your body's natural capacities to heal itself and to stay healthy. You can bring renewed stamina to a tired body, fresh vitality to a wary mind, and new bounce to a sagging spirit," argue Eden and Feinstein.[51] They go on to emphasize that "healing is an inside job," where energy is the medicine and troubled energies requiring repatterning are the patient.[52]

Achieving a state of harmony within is the purpose of balancing and healing the energy centers in the body located along the spine, now quite commonly known as *chakras*, explains the author and teacher of *Polarity Therapy*, Maruti Seidman: "When harmony is achieved, a person's consciousness can then weave the thread of love through her spiritual, mental, emotional, and physical beings. This will harmonize all her energies with the universal life force energy."[53]

Dr. Bradely Nelson, the founder of *Emotion Code* says this: "How healthy you are is directly related to how balanced your energy field is. Energy healing works to restore and maintain the harmony of the energy field, so that the body can remain vitally healthy."[54] The keyword here is harmony, which is ultimately about coherence and balance. Most authors on the subject I have come across emphasize that energy healing is mainly about restoring balance.

"All systems in nature move towards balance. The body always moves towards *homeostasis*," say Stephen Co and Eric Robins.[55] Co is a much

---

[51] Eden & Feinstein, p.1
[52] Ibid., p.11
[53] Maruti Seidman, Balancing the Chakras, 2006, p.6
[54] Bradely Nelson, The Emotion Code, 2007, p.123
[55] Stephen Co, Eric B. Robins, M.D., Your Hands Can Heal You, 2002, p.28

revered Master Healer of a modality known as *Pranic Healing*, which is one of the traditional energy healing arts originating from India that have become popular all over the world, including in Egypt. "Many health problems result from an energetic disturbance that is ultimately caused by the subconscious mind trapping a negative emotion or limiting belief in the body," argue Co and Robins.[56]

According to Nelson, any issue we can possibly have has underlying imbalances. He emphasizes that much of our suffering is due to negative emotional energies that have become 'trapped' within us. Interestingly he detected that the heart has a tendency to create an energetic wall around itself when much pain is stored there. I have tried an *Emotion Code* session during which a heart wall was removed by a certified practitioner. After that session I felt so light that I literally had the sensation of walking on clouds. I could hardly feel the asphalt under my feet and seemed to be floating home. It was an amazing experience. Nelson is the only person I have come across who discovered the walls around our hearts and who lectures on the importance of having them removed. I can definitely attest to the difference it makes. When the aim is to feel lighthearted it makes a lot of sense to free the heart from any constrictions that might have formed around or inside it.

Unprocessed emotions become trapped in the body

The subconscious mind, which is responsible for distributing life force energy through our systems stores traumatic or painful memories all over the body to hide them away from our attention, because it is programmed to protect us from harm, danger and experiencing pain. "In order to prevent these memories from surfacing to your conscious mind, where they would be replayed, your unconscious mind, acting on its prime directive to protect us, frequently 'clamps down' on the memory: it contracts or constricts tightly the smooth muscles or internal organs where the memory is stored. Clamping down is a specific type of resistance to feeling negative emotions," say Co and Robins.[57]

---

[56] Ibid., p.37
[57] Ibid., p.29

These understandings and explanations of reputable healers and teachers point to the emotional nature of imbalances. Emotions that are not dealt with through feeling them, expressing them and eventually processing them in such a natural sequence, can haunt us years later by 'somatising' or sinking into the body and causing symptoms of distress. What we don't deal with on a conscious level, will eventually come back to bite us in the butt. The conclusion is that in order to feel lighter, it's essential to create more equilibrium in our inner emotional landscapes through making a conscious effort to feel more uplifting and nourishing emotions. You can read more on this issue in chapters ten and eleven.

The point I am making here is that a growing number of medical doctors are aware that widespread functional disorders, such as asthma, urinary infections, migraines, high blood pressure or irritable bowel syndrome, have so called "psychosomatic" or emotional and, therefore, ultimately energetic underlying causes rather than anatomic ones. The cell biologist Bruce Lipton points out that an increasing body of research suggests that our hyper-vigilant lifestyles, where we are besieged by multitudes of unresolvable worries and, therefore, chronically elevated stress hormones, is severely impacting the health of our bodies. "Almost every major illness that people acquire has been linked to chronic stress."[58]

It is not surprising then that at the same time more and more people seem to lose trust in conventional medicine and the astounding power of the pharmaceutical industry and its lobby which backs it up and fights alternative treatment modalities that would, once chosen widely as the preferred path to take, lessen their considerable profit generation. "Indeed, one reason why so many now distance themselves from allopathic medicine is the drug vampires, and the white-coated technicians who do their research and speak in their commercials, cannot accept and have no interest in the spiritual basis of true healing," writes Dan Furst.[59] He succinctly adds that "it is a safe bet that those who keep prescribing all the pills and sprays are not yet ready to endorse such remedies as love and intention."

The main ingredients of the various frequencies that are being channeled in diverse forms of energy healing are in fact love and consciousness. Eric Pearl puts it so very nicely: "The love upon healing is based is the love upon

---

[58] Bruce Lipton, The Biology of Belief, 2005, p.121
[59] Dan Furst, Surfing Aquarius, 2011, p.121

which life and the universe are based. It's not hormonal or 'I've got to have you' love, nor is it teary-eyed 'I feel for you' love. It's the all-encompassing love for creation and consciousness. It's the love that allows you to get out of your ego, get out of the way, and be both the observer and the observed, thereby allowing the patient that same gift. It is the love that allows the power that *made* the body to *heal* the body. This is when the transformation takes place. This is when the *light* and *information* flows. This is love."[60]

The internationally renowned psychiatrist, physician, researcher, spiritual teacher and lecturer David Hawkins points out that healing is a consequence of compassion. "In an energy field of 600 or higher, almost anything has a tendency to heal," he said.[61] Hawkins developed a Map of Consciousness, which is like a roadmap whereby one can measure one's internal state. Over 20 years of research and Kinesiology tests, or muscle testing, with thousands of people underlie the development of this numerical scale of the consciousness or energy level that was calibrated from 0 points all the way to the highest end of 1000 points.

Within this scale, Hawkins identified 17 different levels of consciousness marked by different points on the scale. Moving from the 0 to the 1000 mark represents a shift in one's emotions and world view from shame and hate to the highest attainable level of enlightenment at 1000. The level of 500 corresponds to love. The level of 600 mentioned above interestingly corresponds to the level of peace, while the emotion attributed to it is bliss.

Restoring balance, not to speak of love or bliss, at a time where every segment of life feels so topsy-turvy might seem like a nearly impossible endeavor. This can leave us with a sense of dread that is bound to create resistance - especially when we read books on healthy lifestyles that tell us to do a whole lot of difficult things we should do. However, this makes energy medicine even more important, also because it's so easy to do and such a pleasant practice. Let's face it: the ancient tenant that our state of health is tied to our supply of *prana* or *chi* energy makes sense.

"Matter follows energy. That is the fundamental law of energy medicine. When your energies are vibrant, so is your body," say Eden

---

[60] Eric Pearl, The Reconnection, 2001, p.131
[61] David Hawkins, Power vs Force, 2013, p.244

and Feinstein.[62] Co stresses that when the *prana* is plentiful and pure, we are in good physical and mental health. When the opposite is the case, we typically experience some sort of health problem.[63] Sharma points out that this non-physical energy animates all living things and is the primary energy of our emotions, thoughts and spiritual life. When there is a restriction to its flow, we are more vulnerable to sickness.[64]

The logical conclusion is that increasing the flow of high vibrational energies in our systems is the first step to feeling lighter and better enabled to move forward with renewed stamina. Regularly charging ourselves with *ki* or *chi* energy will over time harmonize our energies more and more with the creative universal force, which some authors refer to as pure consciousness or awareness, universal intelligence, divine energy, or spirit. Healing our energy systems, including our souls, looking at it from this bigger perspective can then be understood not only as actively cultivating more wellbeing by reducing symptoms of agony or pain, but as an essential step towards becoming more rounded, whole and lighthearted.

The spiritual nature of energy medicine

The VortexHealing practitioner Bette Hanson also points to the various dimensions that energy medicine commonly deals with. "Energy healing works purely with the energetic level of our being. Energy healing is thus by nature 'holistic,' she writes in a well written article on her website. Hanson stresses the fact that energy healing is increasingly recognized as a quickly growing professional phenomenon: "In general, it describes any form of healing that works on the energy system to rebalance, restore, clear or smooth out the flow of energy in your body. It can address physical illness and emotional or mental disorders, and can also promote high-level wellness, peak performance and spiritual awakening."[65]

'Smoothing out' is a beautiful and precise description of what is happening in an energy healing session. I am not a very visual person. I

---

[62] Eden and Feinstein, Energy Medicine, 1999, p.23
[63] Stephen Co, Eric B. Robins, M.D., Your Hands Can Heal You, 2002, p.37
[64] Krishnan Sharma, The Practical Book of Reiki, 2008, p.113
[65] Bette Hanson's website can be found through this link: www.bettehanson.com

usually don't see the energy bodies around people commonly referred to as auras, neither do I see lights moving during a session, nor do I get images about the life of the client. I found out over time that this is what many of my clients are actually scared of. So no, I don't see through people. I am not endowed with clairvoyant powers as some psychic healers are. However, I have had a few visual insights, or visions that came to me over the years quite unexpectedly.

Once I was in a deep meditative state and my mind started pondering over the question how life force energy moves to heal us. What I was shown was that the tiniest subatomic particles that form our molecules, atoms and cells often move in string formations, and that the dance of these energetically connected strings can be out of synch, with some little edges poking out here and there. When high frequency energies came in, the image changed dramatically. When I saw that image, the advertisements for hair conditioners came to my mind. Dry and brittle hair in those ads look just like that, I thought. And when smoothed out by the advertised product, the hair looks strong and shiny. This smoothing out happens on the most minuscule and subtle level. This is what happens in my experience. Dr. Eric Pearl, the founder of *Reconnective Healing*, describes it very clearly.

Pearl was a successful chiropractor with a well going practice in Los Angeles who suddenly felt drawn to move his hands over certain parts of his patients' bodies, which gave way to more effective results. Some of the clients started to receive messages from spiritual entities during these sessions. The first messages that they kept receiving was that he was "bringing light and information onto this planet."[66] Pearl has appeared on many American TV shows and became famous for the mindboggling amount of healing miracles his patients experienced.

Later, when he was told that he was reconnecting 'strands and strings,' Pearl came to the following conclusion: "It appears that the most fundamental particles of the universe aren't really particles at all. They're best described as loops of 'string' that vibrate at specific frequencies."[67] Reading this quote was what I needed to remember and validate the vision I had. So smoothing out the stands and strings by bringing in love and

---

[66] Eric Pearl, The Reconnection, 2001, p.79
[67] Ibid, p.93

light is what most energy healing practitioners ultimately do. Pearl makes the point that feeling better is not enough and is by far not the only thing that happens in a healing session.

What's going on in this kind of holistic treatment is in fact far bigger than that. "Healing, as we often think of it, may well be about the alleviation of symptoms, diseases, infirmities, and other noticeable hindrances to full functioning. Healing is also the restoration of the person to spiritual wholeness," says Pearl. He defines it like this: "In essence, healing is this: the release or removal of a block or interference that has kept us separate from the perfection of the universe. Yet, healing is about our evolution, and also includes the evolutionary restructuring of our DNA and our reconnection to the universe on a new level."[68]

Like numerous other practitioners of ancient or contemporary healing arts, Pearl strongly emphasizes that healing is guided by the "higher Intelligence of the universe," He points out that there is a transfer of information in a form of spiritual communication. "What we are doing in Reconnective Healing is definitely more along the lines of healing through Spirit or spirituality."[69]

Sharma defines what is happening by describing the deeper meaning of the word Reiki. Reiki is presumed to have originated as a Tibetan Buddhist healing technique, which was thousands of years old and became forgotten, until it was rediscovered and simplified for modern use in the late 18th century by Mikao Usui in Japan. The word *rei*, as used in Reiki, can be interpreted to mean spiritual consciousness or God-consciousness, as well as supernatural knowledge, referring to the wisdom that comes from God or the higher self. *Ki* is the life force, or universal energy, animating everything. It has also been called bio-plasma, orgone or odic force. In the practice of healing, divine consciousness or intelligence guides the flow of life force energy.

A definition seems needed to take a closer look at what that means, as terminology is a tricky thing, especially when it comes to such subtle matters, all the more if they could interfere with our belief systems in the existence or non-existence of God, or the divine, or whatever you wish to call the unnamable. Spirit seems the word best suited for all. It is often

---

[68] Ibid, p.110
[69] Ibid, p.96

defined as the all-pervasive, intelligent energy of creation. The soul is often described as its subtle manifestation on the individual level.

At the end of the day, poetic words best seem to point to the realm of mystery: "To work with a person's energy is to touch a person's soul as well as a body," Eden and Feinstein point out. When all our energies are brought into harmony, our bodies flourish, they underline. "And when your body flourishes, your soul has a soil in which it can blossom in the world. These are the ultimate reasons for energy medicine – to prepare the soil and nurture the blossom."[70]

Bringing our energies into a greater harmony and consciously reconnecting to spirit that is all around and inside us is essentially at the core of healing. "Healing comes about through unity and oneness," Pearl so succinctly says.[71] In ancient times, healing came about through practices aimed at assisting a person to discover themselves and grow spiritually in order to consciously immerse themselves into the divine realm, such as in temples in ancient Egypt, or sacred places where yoga masters taught students in India.

Nelson underlines that the existence of the "Human Energy Field" has been a basic tenet of the healing arts for a very long time: The Hindus understood the vital, life-giving force which permeates and gives life to all things to be *prana*, an understanding going back 5,000 years. The Chinese taught that this energy is called *chi*, and understood that if it is imbalanced within an individual, the result is poor health. And the list could go on to point to many diverse cultures all over the world.

The revival of ancient wisdom

Undeniably, there is a huge new interest in the old knowledge that was held sacred in highly evolved, as well as in so-called primitive cultures. Ancient and indigenous cultures knew how to heal people through the use of sound, color, movement, flower essences, oils, herbs and touch – which basically boils down to light, frequency, vibration, resonance, and energetic informational exchange.

---

[70] Eden and Feinstein, Energy Medicine, 1999, p.26
[71] Pearl, Ibid, p.173

The ancient traditions of the Egyptians, the philosophies and practices of the Hindus, most religions of the East, as well as indigenous cultures, such as the native American culture, promoted energy medicine, which was successfully practiced. In fact, "for most of humanity's history, natural healing was the only game in town."[72] The emergence of numerous energy healing modalities that are in one way or another based on such ancient understandings is one of the most valuable things I see happening now. It gives us the possibility to explore different types of healing and figure out what resonates with us at different times. It also gives us the possibility to actively and consciously participate in our own healing process, which is affecting the energy field around us. Eden and Feinstein see the revival of energy medicine as "one of the most significant cultural developments of the day for the return of energy medicine is a return to personal authority for health care, a return to the legacy of our ancestors in harmonizing with the forces of nature and a return to practices that are natural, friendly and familiar to body, mind and soul."[73]

One of my teachers, the founder of *VortexHealing*®, Ric Weinman, emphasized repeatedly in class that energy healing is going to spread widely in the near future, and that our services as energy healing practitioners would be very much sought after. Norm Shealy, the Founding President of the American Holistic Medical Association goes a step further: "Energy medicine is the future of all medicine," he was quoted as saying publicly.[74]

Reiki, and other traditional types of energy healing, such as Pranic Healing, as well as many of the contemporary types, including Tetha Healing, Emotional Freedom Technique (EFT) or Quantum Healing and Emotion Code, have already become popular in many countries around the world. The emerging new paradigm and practice is both: ancient and contemporary, moving side by side and enriching each other. Ancient insights are rediscovered and revived, while new forms are perceived and downloaded.

There seem to be large numbers of people somewhere out there who feel called to channel information and go on to promote new healing modalities. A good example is, for instance, *Divine Empowerment*, which

---

[72] Eden and Feinstein, Ibid, p.30
[73] Ibid, p.4
[74] Ibid, p.3

was founded by a courageous and gifted young woman in Britain. As you read this another type of energy healing is probably being born somewhere. The internet is full of buzz in this realm. And this, I feel, is just the beginning. At the same time, the essential part of the new paradigm – unity consciousness – is also being experienced as well as researched by a growing amount of people.

The vast quantum web of connection

The remarkable author Lynne McTaggert, who writes about results of cutting-edge scientific research, documents evidence in her book *The Field* that everything is connected to everything else by one big sea of energy. Her research reconciles mind with matter, classic science with quantum physics, and science with religion. Unlike most other authors I have come across, she is dedicated to raise awareness of scientific proof that "all matter exists in a vast quantum web of connection."[75]

"The closer scientists look, the more they discover how dependent on, and finally indivisible from, everything is with everything else," writes McTaggert. "When particle physicists get down to the bottom layer of matter, there isn't really anything there." She goes on to point out that, therefore, even the word 'particle' with its suggestion of a separate and corporeal reality is a misnomer. "Although we classify everything in the universe as separate and individual, individuality at the most rudimentary level, does not exist."[76] In the most basic sense, she says, "there is no such thing as a thing."[77]

I love the way this outstanding author attempts to describe what is emerging as a new picture in plenty of research undertaken in the past decade: "Subatomic particles more closely resemble a tiny coalescence of energy, a smeared out, uncongealed puff of vibratory nothingness," she says. Our rational mind is usually focused on seemingly solid objects, however, let's not forget that what surrounds them and what they are essentially made of is space, or nothingness. Pearl points out that "if you

---

[75] Lynne McTaggert, The Bond, 2011, p.xxiv, (Ibd.,p.xxiii).
[76] Ibid, p.8
[77] Ibid, p.xxvi

extracted all the empty space from a human body, the resulting chunk of matter would be proportionate to a golf ball sitting in an empty football field."[78]

During one of the intense meditations we had when I was initiated to the Reiki master level, I felt more than I saw that the density of my body was illusionary, a trick of the mind and the senses. First, it felt like my body was somehow melting or dissolving. However, I soon became aware that I was shown an image for what seems to be more accurate. I saw that I was made of a whole lot of luminous tiny little particles floating around together. They were jetting through the air with enormous speed, some of them firing up more light, and they seemed to be happily dancing with each other. I was stunned and felt inexplicably exhilarated and uplifted. *Ahhh, that's how it looks like and feels like*, I thought. This experience, I already felt back then, was offering me a very significant insight.

In fact, the rather mindboggling attempt to describe what energy medicine is all about cannot possibly be undertaken without trying to gain an understanding of what practitioners ultimately deal with. In contrast to the concern of medical doctors, energy healing practitioners are not so much focused on the specific affected organs, tissues, cells, molecules, atoms or sub-atomic particles, neither on root causes for disturbances, but deal more with what McTaggart and others have termed *"the space between things"*, which animates all life forms and miraculously holds them all together. Energy Medicine works through allowing insubstantial energies to move around differently and dance more happily.

The German scientist Max Planck, who can safely be called one of the greatest minds of the 20th century, and is considered the father of Quantum Theory, made the following statement when he was awarded the Nobel prize for physics in 1919: "As a man who has devoted his whole life to the most clearheaded science, to the study of matter, I can tell you as a result of my research about the atoms this much: There is no matter as such! All matter originates and exists only by virtue of a force which brings the particles of an atom to vibration and holds this most minute solar system

---

[78] Pearl, ibid, p.185

of the atom together... We must assume behind this force the existence of a conscious and intelligent Spirit. This Spirit is the matrix of all matter."[79]

This insight points to the fact that research results from the frontiers of science, which McTaggart gathers and analyses so brilliantly, are ultimately not that new after all. It's just that many of us needed over a hundred years to be able to take that information in, build on it and get ready to swing with a larger paradigm shift that is not confined to physics.

The new story or paradigm that is emerging around the globe is based on the recognition that nothing is separate from anything else. It is exactly this connection, this bond, in which life happens, in which information is constantly exchanged. It is this interconnectivity, this intrinsic bonding that defines us at our core. This is very different from the saga of separation that was hammered into us during the old age, which is luckily on its way out.

Bradely describes well what we all deep down know to be true because we can feel it: "The reality is that the entire human family is connected energetically. When people are suffering and dying on the other side of the earth, we feel their distant cries and anguish on a subconscious level and we are darkened by it. When something tragic happens in the world, the whole world feels it subconsciously, and is affected by it. On the other hand, when wonderful things happen in the world, we all are brightened together."[80]

The old story that has shaped our mindsets for the past 300 years that we are "isolated beings competing for survival on a lonely planet in an indifferent universe," needs to be cast out urgently argues McTaggart.[81] It has brought us too many catastrophic developments already. It is a truly remarkable achievement that more and more scientists are now assisting us to discover and form a more accurate understanding, which is basically a holistic view of ourselves as inextricably linked to everything.

This is the time to accept and integrate these fundamental insights, which radically turn around everything we have been taught so far.

---

[79] Here quoted from Bradely Nelson, The Emotion Code, 2007, p.102. See also https://en.wikiquote.org/wiki/Max_Planck

[80] Ibid, p.46
[81] Lynne McTaggert, Ibid, p.xxiii

"Nature's most basic impulse is not a struggle for domination but a constant and irrepressible drive for wholeness."[82] Indeed, this finding alone, which casts out the world view dominated by Charles Darwin's theory of evolution through natural selection and necessary struggle for existence, has the potential to revolutionize and truly evolve the way we live, work and love.

Once we hold this understanding in our awareness, the inherent drive for cooperation and partnership can come to the forefront of our awareness so that we can start to live in harmony with our essential nature that is more in alignment to the new age. McTaggart offers an important contribution to the emerging new paradigm of the Aquarius Age that is fundamentally shaped by the insight into the importance of living in deep connection. It replaces the old story of ruthless competition and battle that continues to destroy us and the planet we live on.

"Applying these new discoveries to every aspect of our lives requires nothing less than making ourselves anew," she poignantly puts it. This, she says, involves training ourselves to see 'I' only in relationship to others - as many Eastern cultures have taught and are still postulating today. It demands shifting our focus "from the smallness of the self to the expansiveness of the space in between."[83]

It seems to me that the urge to shift and recreate ourselves anew that I feel in many people around me is accelerated by the sheer amount of stress our systems are exposed to every day. As hard as that is to cope with on a daily level, it appears that it might be the necessary evil that finally motivates more and more of us to make some of the changes, which at first might seem uncomfortable.

"With tens of thousands of artificial chemicals in our food, high concentration of pollutants in our air and technology-induced electromagnetic radiation everywhere, the immune system is on constant alert, a 'code orange' emergency response that drains your energy and depletes your life force." This is what Eden and Feinstein say at the outset of their much acclaimed classic *Energy Medicine*. And this is exactly what so many people around the world are becoming more conscious of.

It is perhaps even more the case in so-called developing countries than

---

[82] Ibid, p.xxv
[83] Ibid, p.xxvi and p.163

in the West where the levels of our daily doses of toxic intake through all kind of pollution constitute such an outrageous assault on our bodies that we can really feel it - even if we are habitually numbed out. When things are becoming extreme in their proportions, you can't really miss out on them any longer, even if you would prefer to continue living in denial. Things have become so bad for so many people that we are collectively shaken up to realize some uncomfortable truths about the way we live and burn up energy on this planet. The desire to evolve to a new level is growing.

Even if we don't feel it in these brutal ways as we do in the megacities in emerging markets, it has become more obvious to more people that we mostly live in environments that are biologically unfamiliar and unhealthy to us and that the body's energy intelligence is operating very much outside its familiar scope of competence. We are now called to go beyond our biological programming of survival instinct that has shaped such a big part of our collective history and determines much of our predatory behavior until today.

This is the time to give in to the yearning of the soul, which is to dance with life. In the deepest essence, our true nature is stillness and vastness, infinite expansion. The awareness of it is accompanied by feelings of bliss, peace, joy and love. To consciously choose again and again to expand and to thrive in the face of a worldwide system built on fear and exploitation is the most revolutionary and, yet, at the same time the most loving choice we can possibly make.

Making this choice is imperative. How fantastic would life be if this would become the priority for most people on the planet? Think about it: Thriving is simply the best thing we can do for ourselves, for those we love and for the human collective as a whole. It's the most important contribution we can possibly make to our collective evolution.

It's not as difficult as you might think

In contrast to what some traditional spiritual masters have taught, becoming aware of nothingness is not difficult at all. As the famous spiritual teacher and bestselling author Eckhart Tolle has repeatedly pointed out, we can train ourselves quite easily to focus less on the objects we see around us and more on the awareness of the empty space in the background. Looking for the space between thoughts, and things means focusing on no-thing, or no-form. That's nothingness. It really is easy to recognize once you get the hang of how good that actually feels.

Starting to practice energy medicine on yourself or others is also very easy. This insight is based on my own experiences as the eternal student I see myself, as well as in the role of a teacher that I have naturally grown into a few years ago. When I came across the following quote of Eden and Feinstein, my heart made a little jump: "You need only knock on the door to arouse the two-million-year-old healer dwelling within you." It rings a bell to me that "our healing abilities still reside in our ancestral bones, our healing hands, our compassionate hearts, and our intuitive brains," as they so beautifully put it.[84] Pearl also emphasizes that "at this time of our transition, healing is a capacity shared by all."[85]

Reviving these skills and further building on them through practice, therefore, cannot possibly be a difficult quest to accomplish. One of the reasons why I love to teach workshops about the energy healing art of Reiki is indeed because it is simple, gentle, effective, pleasant and very easy to learn.

Some healing modalities teach a large number of levels stuffed with complicated practices that contain many technicalities that give you the impression of studying a form of human engineering. However, energy healing ultimately is neither about techniques, nor about trying to find and analyze causes for disturbances, which is a mind-driven and ultimately futile attempt in view of the fact that every phenomena is multi-causal and interrelated to everything else.

My experience is that anybody can learn to consciously feel, connect to and channel life force energy. No prior experience with energy healing or spiritual practices is required for starting. After the first two-day course of Reiki, you know the basic hand positions and techniques for sending healing energies to yourself and others. Once the initial doubt whether it's working or not is overcome by students, the inhibition of placing their hands on somebody and of channeling energy usually vanishes into

---

[84] Eden and Feinstein, p.30 and 31
[85] Pearl, Ibid, p.139

thin air. This often happens in class during the practical part of energy exchange.

Many of my students who never had a Reiki treatment before attending class are dumbfounded how comforting and good it feels when a fellow student places their hands on them at specific points and their hands become hot or sometimes cold from the amount of energy they are channeling. What holds us back is doubt. It always does. As much as I am grateful for an upbringing that taught me to doubt belief systems or dogmas, as much I know now that if we want to become excellent at anything, the doubts are better dropped rather sooner than later. This is the reason why I am convinced that it is useful to teach some basic techniques to beginners.

Once the steps to take are clear to them, their doubting minds recede, and then the healing can happen by itself. From level two onwards, I tell my students that it's not about a fixed sequence of steps to take, and that they should get out of their thinking mind and instead allow their hands to move and play freely and allow their intuition to guide them to the spots to place their hands, instead of following protocols.

This is one of the reasons why I enjoyed reading Pearl's book so much. He describes exactly this insight into the necessity to step back, take oneself out of the picture, stop all that trying to send energy, but allow to receive and let a "Higher Power" guide. "Not only did the energy know where to go and what to do without the slightest instruction from me, but the more I got my attention out of the picture, the more powerful the response," he says.[86] It takes trust in what is happening by itself to get to that stage.

One of the remarkably gifted students I had the pleasure to teach and attune to the Reiki master level unknowingly used the very same words as Pearl when she told me how tremendously she enjoys giving sessions. "You're allowing your mind to reach a place where you are not exactly awake and not exactly asleep – where you are somewhere else," she exclaimed. I thought that this is actually the state described as *yoga nidra* in ancient yoga scriptures. This is exactly what they call *yogic sleep*, I said. You are in between, not here, not there. The next day, I read this very quote in his book. She hadn't read the book and yet used exactly the same words, which to me is another indicator for the understanding that

---

[86] Ibid, p.108

thoughts are not our own individual creation but are rather freely floating energy formations in a quantum soup of energy.

What Pearl adds to this sentence might clarify what I am trying to bring across: "This is the place where healing energy comes to Earth," he writes. I couldn't agree more. He also emphasizes that with the ongoing shift, we now exist within a much larger set of parameters, and need no longer to throw salt into the four corners, or shake negative energies into bowls of water, nor spray ourselves with alcohol solutions or wear amulets. We also don't have to stop eating pizza. "We need not use our conscious minds in an attempt to determine what is 'wrong' with a person so that we know how to 'treat' them. We now allow ourselves to simply *be* – be with the person and understand that the uncertainty will be taken care of."[87]

In my eyes the significance of the following insight, which has been taught by numerous meditation teachers and which Pearl puts so well, cannot possibly be overstated: "Our lesson is to learn to *be*. The freedom of *being* will extricate you from the oppression of *doing*. Herein lies the seed of *knowingness* that has the capacity to take you beyond all of this world's knowledge."[88]

So, what seems most essential to practice is a state of relaxed and yet fully present being that is not obstructed by obsessive thinking, not only for those who aspire to become energy healing practitioners, coaches or wellness therapists, but for everyone aspiring to become more aware of who they truly are. Meditation and mindfulness are beautiful practices to cultivate this state of pure beingnes, and you can read more about that in chapter twelve and thirteen. And yet, you don't need to be an experienced meditator, yoga teacher or vegetarian to easily focus on feeling the incoming energy and immerse yourself into the experience of simply enjoying the ride.

Sharma underlines that Reiki is not only a democratization of the ability to heal, it also makes a level of spiritual transformation available to non-meditators that has usually been reserved for those with a meditative path.[89] So, drop the drive to become perfectly peaceful, non-judgemental and compassionate first, which can become a major excuse for not actively

---

[87] Ibid, p.204 and p.116
[88] Ibid, p.116
[89] Sharma, ibid, p.15

practicing any of the energy healing arts. It is a simple state of allowing that gets you into the flow and the groove of it.

Even to a beginner, giving a Reiki session to somebody commonly feels like an infusion of gentleness and inner peace out of nowhere that takes you out of the limits of the mind and transports you into another realm. Just like that. Most people notice after taking Reiki courses that changes simply happen by themselves in their lives. Many unforeseeable or miraculous things are reported in books as well as by my students to have happened. What happens is an attunement of the system to higher frequency energies that causes changes in various ways, one of them can be profound healing.

Healing requires space & stillness

Taking our own recovery and healing seriously and practicing it in gentle ways requires space – often a lot of it. The space to take time for ourselves to do absolutely nothing, the space to experience stillness and go within, the space to ask important questions, and to become more aware of who we are at our core and what we are most longing for to experience in life. The inner aching and longing we encounter in that space brings us into more connection with all that is. It teaches us how to become more fully alive. What happens is nothing less than a journey into the underworld, which can feel very uncomfortable, scary and even painful at times, but which eventually leads us to burst open into feeling way more enchantment than we thought possible before taking the first steps of this journey.

Energy medicine is a wonderful practice that has the inherent potential and power to release not only blocked energies, but also limiting beliefs and issues that are a central part of our conditioning and our emotional suffering. In fact, it is a great way to release more and more layers of this webbing of conditioning that is imprinted all over our bodies. It is this conditioning that comes not only from our childhoods, but from the experiences of our ancestors, as well as collective memories, which keep shaping our perceptions and therefore our reality.

The potent power to release this deep seated programming is perhaps the main reason why energy medicine has the potential to lead to higher levels of spiritual awakening. It allows us to break free, as if an invisible egg around us cracks open and the accumulated pain that is part of the core ego structures gives way like an opening in the clouds revealing bright sunshine, so that pure consciousness can become aware of itself. Becoming aware of awareness is what brings us a feeling of bliss originating right from the source. It is the lightest and most beautiful feeling I know. It's beyond happiness.

Summary

Upgrading our energy system that was designed for living in the wild to higher levels of coherence and resilience is needed to navigate the chaos of transitioning into the Age of Aquarius. It's not just an option if we want to survive, it's a must, especially if we aim at becoming lighthearted.

One of the essential things that we literally have in our hands to recover and feel better is energy medicine. Bringing our energies into a greater harmony and consciously re-connecting to spirit is at the core of healing. Energy Medicine works through motivating insubstantial energies to move around differently and dance more happily.

When these intangible energies are vibrant, so are our bodies. When the opposite is the case, we typically experience some sort of health problem. Energy healing is mainly about restoring balance.

Ancient and indigenous cultures knew how to heal people through the use of sound, color, movement, flower essences, oils, herbs and touch – which basically boils down to light, frequency, vibration, resonance, and energetic informational exchange.

All illness comes from depleted energy that stops flowing properly due to blockages. The greatest drainer of energy is emotional and mental stress that can erode the vital energy in the body to an extent that major systems stop functioning well.

Increasing the flow of high vibrational energies in our systems is a crucial step towards feeling lighter and healthier. Regularly charging ourselves with *ki* or *chi* energy harmonizes our energies with the creative universal force, which some authors refer to as pure consciousness or awareness, universal intelligence, divine energy, or spirit.

Energy healing contributes not only to heal all kinds of ailments but to make us feel more peaceful and fulfilled and live in ways that are characterized by deeper engagement from the heart and a profound sense of connection from the soul. It is a practice with the potential and power to release limiting beliefs, trauma, as well as issues that are part of our conditioning and our emotional suffering.

Healing is a capacity shared by all. It's easy to learn. Anybody can do it, even though there seem to be some people who have a greater talent. Taking our own recovery and healing seriously and practicing it in gentle ways requires space – often a lot of it: The space to take time for ourselves to do absolutely nothing, the space to experience stillness and to go within.

Healing so that we can thrive is the best thing we can do for ourselves, for those we love and for the human collective as a whole. It's the best contribution we can make. The next chapter describes a modality that is also aimed at inspiring and nudging individuals to thrive.

"There is an art to imparting strength and confidence, to inspiring and heartening what is already within us. In many ways, to encourage is to help the heart unfold."

Mark Nepo

SIX

Evolving into a Happiness Coach

Learning to develop into a professional coach has taken many years. It was a gradual process. One part of it was attending courses, watching training CDs and reading a lot about coaching. The other consisted of applying the theory with so-called trial clients, which was an entirely different story.

The third element was documenting these sessions in filling out forms, which required an awful lot of reflection on what went well and what didn't. I also had to identify as well as commit to taking concrete steps towards further improving my own performance. At times, I felt that I hadn't done so well and knew exactly what the reasons were. Sometimes, I simply had no clue what I could do better or what steps I could possibly come up with to become more effective at coaching. Not being able to figure that out, made me feel helpless. It could also lead to procrastination, or avoidance of filling out all those many coach record sheets that I needed to qualify for the diploma.

What I wasn't prepared for and hadn't read in books was that each client confronted me with aspects of my own issues, as if they needed to be brought up for deeper levels of inspection and understanding. Here are just some examples of this strange occurrence to illustrate how difficult it felt sometimes: One of my first trial clients complained about not being adequately recognized at work and suffering from many pent-up feelings of humiliation. Yup, I certainly know how that feels. Another felt she wasn't organized enough. Oh boy, tell me about it. Someone else came along who was struggling with menopausal distress and fears about getting older. Yeah, that's a bummer. Another person felt a lot of disappointment and resentment during a break-up. Outch. And so on and so forth.

Facing my own issues

Whatever it was, I recognized that I had all those issues too and needed to come to terms with them so that my thoughts, judgments and emotions would neither lead me to think thoughts clouded by my own emotions around that issue during the session, nor get me to spontaneously exclaim, *I know exactly what you are talking about.* As 'normal' as these human reactions are in private conversations, according to common coaching standards, such behavior is considered quite inappropriate and unprofessional.

At times, the confrontation with that much rather unresolved stuff freaked me out quite a bit. Sometimes, I felt a need to slow down in order to reflect, set goals of my own in all those areas, and integrate new ways of thinking about them and about me. I consciously took a lot of time for myself, not only for introspection and self-evaluation but also because I started to realize on a deeper level that I needed to be as relaxed and at ease as I possibly could in order to create a suitable environment inspiring clients to think for themselves and map out their own path to lightheartedness. I also made it a point to engage in at least one activity each day that would infuse more emotions of fulfillment and happiness. Looking back, I realize that this was one of the most precious aspects of the process of growing into a coach.

I had always felt that I was pretty aware of the issues bothering me. However, it was only when I started coaching others that I realized that many things had remained a bit hidden and were being brought to my attention. As overwhelming as it could feel at times, it taught me many things about myself and accelerated my own growth like hardly anything else.

While I didn't seem to be able to make much progress with some issues for what felt like a long time, in many other areas, I felt nudged into taking action on the spot. Self-development seems to happen in leaps or in what can seem like a painfully stretched out period. "Growth, both individual and collective, can take place either slowly or suddenly," says the psychiatrist and author David Hawkins. He points out that growth and development are irregular and non-linear.[90]

Some insights were priceless

A good example was one young woman who told me on a fateful evening that she felt reluctant to take responsibility for anybody and had the greatest difficulty to commit to anyone. This, she said, was her biggest problem. I had the gloomy feeling that there was another reflection of what could be said about me as well. *Not again*, I found myself thinking. The resistance against realizing more and more issues, which apparently wanted to be resolved would sometimes become very strong because it could feel like more than I was able, or willing, to handle.

However, on that very evening I sat on my sofa after the session, filling out my form sheet, and reflecting on what I could do to overcome this tendency, which had crept in at some point in my life. I realized that what I really wanted to commit to, other than my own evolution, was neither a task, nor a single calling or profession, nor a relationship to a man, but a dog. I had wanted to live with a dog since many years, and suddenly I just knew that I could be very committed to taking good care of a dog. I also realized that if I didn't act on this insight immediately, I would probably never fulfill my old desire of living with a dog. And so I did.

This is how, through the help of a friend and colleague, I discovered an extremely cute Griffon puppy, who turned out to be the most unconditionally loving companion I have ever had. This step changed my life. Years later, I took in an abandoned and abused *Shitzu*, and these two little furry fellows give me an incredible amount of joy on a daily basis. Some insights won during reflection about how well I was coaching others were indeed priceless.

A similar sense of being overwhelmed happened when I started reading about issues commonly associated with the energy centers called

---

[90] David Hawkins, Power vs Force, 1995, p.249

chakras. I was shocked to find that most of the descriptions of various symptoms indicating imbalances in each and every chakra reflected so-called weaknesses I tended to suffer from. *Oh my God, this one too*, was a thought that kept popping up. This, at first, felt like a terrible discovery, which seemed to confirm the old conditioning that something was wrong with me at a fundamental level.

After a while, however, it dawned on me that there seems to be large number of common themes that human beings are confronted with – especially at this point in time – which are part of the experience of being and evolving in a physical body on our planet. I have realized that experiencing these issues was not an indicator that there was something 'wrong' with me on a personal level. We all have a whole lot of issues to deal with. That's simply how it is. Once I accepted this insight, I could see that the ability to notice and feel numerous issues actually brought with it an increase of empathy for others who are suffering from them and are struggling to overcome their challenges.

A dear friend called me one evening after reading half a book on chakras. "Oh my God, I have all those symptoms described there. It's terrible, I don't know what to do, and I read only about the first three energy centers," she said in a very dramatic tone. I couldn't help laughing. *Welcome to the club*, I replied. *We all have these issues. Nothing to worry about.*

The process of thinking about one's issues without dramatizing them, or going into self-berating, is actually very precious. For the development of higher degrees of awareness, it's essential. Given the fact that the majority of people are living in a state of fear and/or denial, it's a privilege when we become more conscious of those areas in our lives where we feel unsatisfied or frustrated and can recognize the wounding that lies underneath. This is how understanding oneself arises. Even though the issues don't go away, reflection helps us live with them as we learn to accept them.

Awareness together with the coaching approach is curative

In my experience awareness alone is not necessarily always curative, as many authors keep postulating. It's the coaching approach that tackles the crucial question how to deal with an issue and take it forward. Many of us are aware that we have an issue, but that doesn't mean that we are capable or ready to resolve it by ourselves and take constructive actions that bring about solutions. This is where the support of a coach comes in very handy. Coaching not only creates awareness on deeper levels, but also the motivation to start doing something about an issue.

Some so-called issues or problems seem urgent and call out to be remedied by taking immediate actions aimed at creating solutions. Others require first to be accepted, or rather embraced before we can develop the inner strength to do anything useful about them. It sounds simple. However, acceptance is not a state that most of us arrive at easily.

As long as we are in a state of non-acceptance, we resist what is. And as long as we are stuck in resistance, the issue is bound to persist. I have read many books of Neale Donald Welsh and the one sentence that he repeated over and over and that stuck most in my head was: "What you resist persists." Knowing that intellectually is one thing. Arriving at acceptance of an issue we are used to struggling with is quite another.

Many times I would just sit on my sofa, making sure I was comfortable, breathing a bit deeper and thinking about what I would really like to see happening about a particular issue, or in a certain area of my life. I would allow all kinds of thoughts to come up and swirl around in my mind and just watch them. After a while, I would reach for a pen and a notebook and write down my preferred scenario, and some thoughts about it, or memories from the past that popped up and seemed significant at the moment. I would scribble away and then sit back again and feel into the desired outcomes, kind of like an inner film. Then I would take a few deep breaths and decide to let it all go.

I would continue to sit there and breathe and allow myself to relax into the recognition that I wasn't where I desired to be just yet, but I knew where I wanted to go and that therefore everything was ok. "All is well." This beautiful little sentence sometimes turned into something like a mantra to repeat internally in order to remember that there is some kind of mysterious Divine order unfolding, which I might not be aware of most of the time, but nevertheless am an inseparable part of. This was one of the ways how I started to consciously cultivate more acceptance of what is and what shows up in this moment.

Careful questions about what we could possibly learn from a particular issue, or what could be useful for us about it in the future coupled with a whole lot of most attentive listening from a coach leads to a process in which we can arrive at accepting what happened, or how we feel. From here, we can gently move forward through coming up with a vision, formulating a concrete goal, and taking little steps towards it, one at a time. This is exactly what makes the coaching approach so powerful.

Breaking through resistance

One of the many beneficial aspects of the journey towards developing into a competent coach consists of becoming acutely aware of the huge amount of resistance that most of us revert to automatically when it comes to feeling the painful emotions that are hidden away in the basement and thinking about ways to induce changes in how we feel and act. The ego-mind abhors change. And the subconscious mind is keen on protecting us from remembering painful situations and reliving them. Resistance is, therefore, a mighty force to reckon with when we want to make changes.

A big range of largely unconscious and really unhealthy strategies are set in motion with the sole aim to keep us safe through playing small. They can take many forms. It was quite a shock when I read a very long list of behaviors or strategies that are forms of resistance to avoid feelings, which was published for a while on the website of Christian Pankhurst, Life Coach and founder of Heart IQ. The list includes physical, mental, emotional and relational strategies. Among them are:

- digestive issues, increased amount of aches, fatigue, addictions, obsessing, compulsive shopping or overeating, watching television, spending a lot of time on the Internet, creating drama, etc.
- Distracted mind, self-doubt, cynicism, adhering to dogma, sense of entitlement, procrastination, routinely running late, thinking you are superior, wasting time on unimportant things, making excuses, thinking you are always wrong, etc.
- Keeping a high stress level, judging others, lashing out, guilt, worrying compulsively, shame over past choices, anger and judgment aimed at yourself, constantly bitching about your life

and others, frequent lying, being frustrated easily, making fun of others, numbness, denial, boredom, etc.
- Avoiding relationships altogether to avoid internal pain, avoiding asking anybody for help, staying in a relationship that is not fulfilling you, tolerating abuse of any kind, going quickly from one relationship to another to avoid being single, being manipulative or hurtful to a friend or partner, being extremely critical of others; acting dishonestly with a partner, etc.

Even though this is only a fraction of the possible behaviors, this is a very long list to stomach. Most of us display many of these strategies habitually, and they become especially pronounced the moment we decide to set the sail towards creating something new. So yes, there's an awful lot of gooey stuff we do to avoid feeling our feelings and to avoid changing perspectives and thought patterns that would elevate us and, therefore, make us feel better. "It would seem that most people are willing to die rather than alter those belief systems that confine them to lower levels of consciousness," says Hawkins.[91] That is a bizarre and sad occurrence.

Reading such a list can feel very daunting because we recognize all those behaviors that we would actually really like to drop. We might also feel ashamed at some deep level that we are engaging in these kinds of behavior in the first place. Given how many resistance strategies we tend to have in place at the same time, switching out of them seems like a mission impossible.

The function behind resistance is to keep us safe

Understanding the function of the limiting assumption that hides behind a dysfunctional behavior feels liberating. It was very helpful for me to make a list of all behaviors I would engage in and ask myself what the purpose of this behavior was. Reflecting on the real reason behind each behavior, I discovered that they were all aimed at preventing me from becoming too successful, going out there and shining my light, or speaking

---

[91] Ibid, p.247

my truth, and thriving because this was perceived as very dangerous by the subconscious mind.

This thinking exercise confirmed what I had read before: dysfunctional behaviors are ultimately strategies aimed at keeping us safe. They were born out of a collective memory of human history during which being outstanding in any way equaled a death sentence.

It's a gruesome fact after all that women who had knowledge about herbal remedies and became known for their healing talents were sought out, branded as witches, brutally tortured and burnt or hanged during the Inquisition of the Catholic Church. This practice went on for over three centuries all over the Western world. Estimates of the numbers of women killed in the name of God to enforce one particular belief system and pave the way to a male dominated religion and medical profession vary. Some sources say there were more than one million victims, other estimates are much lower. Who can tell? In any case, the witch hunt has rightly been called genocide.

Contemporary witch-hunts have been reported from Sub-Saharan Africa and Papua New Guinea. Even today, there exists official legislation against witchcraft in Saudi Arabia and Cameroon. This is a reminder of the fact that brutal oppression of people who dared to come up with scientific discoveries or a different belief system did not only happen in the Middle Ages. Human history is full of examples.

In communist countries, it was especially dangerous to look different or be outstanding in any way. The same goes for ruthless authoritarian patriarchal regimes that persist all over the place. These practices are not a matter of the past. They continue unabated until today. Writing about issues that are contrary to the officially sanctioned view of things still brings thousands of courageous people into prisons and exposes them to the most horrendous forms of torture in numerous countries all over the world.

Keeping your head down, while looking and acting like everybody else has been a necessary survival strategy over the biggest part of our history and in most countries. And this is exactly what we have been conditioned to do through our genetic programming and our social upbringing. It's deeply engrained. The realistic conclusion of the individual subconscious is that standing out can cost you your head.

And what could possibly make you more outstanding than becoming visibly successful and glamorously shiny? So, breaking free from all those subconscious strategies that are aimed at keeping us safe by playing small seems like a daunting undertaking. It takes a massive amount of courage. There is hardly any bigger challenge than that. It needs us to be *Daring Greatly*.

A coach can make this process simpler, by asking questions that unveil the limiting assumption and replacing it with a freeing one. Sometimes it can be that easy to break free from a thought pattern that keeps us believing that we don't have what it takes to succeed. Coaching also gets us to focus on one issue at a time, which makes things less muddled up. Once we have the goal clear and formulate it in a simple sentence we like, stating what we want in a positive way and in present tense, going about achieving it seems more do-able.

Going through some of my many notebooks, I realized that I wrote down certain goals again and again, for years on end. Some of them I have achieved. However, my experience is that certain goals bring up a lot of resistance, which makes it important to keep them in our awareness by saying them out loud and writing them down many times. Eventually, they sink deep into the subconscious, and some mysterious way towards realization is carved out there.

At the right time, something gives in and we suddenly find ourselves moving forward with ease. When that happens there is a tremendous sense of satisfaction and joy. We don't understand anymore how come we remained stuck for so long, but we understand on an intuitive level that it was all this time of feeling so helplessly stuck that delivered us to this very point where we can appreciate and celebrate the breakthrough all the more.

Asking great questions is essential for growth

Being aware of what really matters to us is precious because it gives us a deep sense of understanding ourselves, even if we are not yet in a state to make as many of the changes we would like to see happening. Having a competent coach walking at our side, helps with the development of self- acceptance and self-compassion. Another major benefit is that having clear goals gives us a sense of direction and purpose. We feel less tortured by confusion and stop drifting through life.

Leaving desired outcomes to the universe to care of or surrendering to God is not the same as drifting. The latter indicates aimlessness and lack of clarity. Drifting like a piece of wood in a river that is tossed around is not to be confused with the spiritually elevated state of floating in which one is well aware of being divinely supported and protected. Surrender is when there is a knowing of my path and my will and yet there is an allowing and inviting of the will of God to prevail. Drifting usually happens out of resignation and frustration. It's a way of giving up. It seems to be very common, especially in the region where I happen to live because there are only small areas or pockets that allow for something that would deserve to be called self-determination.

It seems fair to say that most people in the Middle East don't have the freedom to make many choices on their own, whatever the economic strata they come from. One reason is the tribal nature of conservative and religious societies in which the often extreme forms of individualization more common in Western countries are rare exceptions. It's the extended family that guarantees support and survival in case medical treatments are necessary, not health insurances or the government. It is also the network of the extended family, or tribe that can secure employment opportunities for the young generation through connections. Therefore, decisions about which schools should be chosen and which marriage partners are deemed acceptable are still widely depending on the agreement within the clan. Even the choice what to study, if one is privileged enough to have the chance to enjoy higher education, is determined by something else than the personal preferences or talents of the student. It is solely determined by the level of grades obtained in the final high school exams.

When you can neither decide what you would like to study, not where you would like to work, the choices you can make about life are not exactly huge. It is therefore not surprising that the majority of people seem to be quite unaware of what would make their hearts sing. In spite of that situation, or perhaps because of it, coaching has become popular during the past five years in some of countries of the region, including in Lebanon, the United Arab Emirates and Egypt.

The amount of young coaches who suddenly started offering their services on the internet within a rather short time frame is surprising. And as it is often the case when something becomes a trend, the programs offered to train aspiring coaches are quite dubious. The other day I came across an online program for 25 dollars. The amazing thing was that it included exactly the same headlines for classes and subjects that well-known and reputable institutions offer. So that could be creating a lot of confusion. When newcomers ask me how to become a coach, I always recommend enrolling in a high quality training program in order to get the support and feedback needed in the development process. I don't really think that an online program would do the trick.

Unfortunately, for the reputation of this valuable profession, I have also seen some coaches offering trainings that seem rather incomplete while asking for quite astronomical sums to be paid. So thoroughly checking programs before enrolling is well worth the effort and might save a lot of money spent on little in return. Contrary to what a lot of people seem to think, it is not easy to grow into a competent Life Coach.

One part of a good training program is that students are required to demonstrate their coaching skills in front of assessors. *The Coaching Academy* requests their students to coach some of their trial clients through the entire protocol of the structured coaching conversation during 30 minutes via Skype with an assessor listening. The assessor then gives feedback and discusses with you how to improve your performance. Depending on the diplomas the student has enrolled in, it varies how many of these Skype tests are taking place.

In my case, I flunked in the very first test of this kind. Never had I failed in any exam before. I might have had bad grades, but not passing was new and, therefore, came as a shock. I felt utterly deflated for a while. It took a lot of effort to counterbalance and eventually overcome the voice of the inner critic, which kept screaming at me that I obviously don't have what it takes to ever turn into a good coach.

What did I do 'wrong'? During the otherwise honestly quite brilliant coaching conversation I asked the client one closed question and one leading question. *What? That's it? You got to be kidding me!*

First, I felt that it was outrageously unfair to deny me passing the test for such a tiny transgression. This point of view was obviously shared by my mother as well as the trial client, and close friends sympathizing with the poor-me-drama that I fell into. However, this incident turned out to be of big service to me. At hindsight, we can always see the blessings hidden in difficulties. Since that day, I hardly ever asked anybody again a question that could be answered only with either a yes or a no. Such a question is aptly called a 'closed question,' because it doesn't allow anyone to open up to talking. Yes or no? End of discussion.

A leading question is even worse. I have observed these kinds of question sometimes with inner discomfort in numerous other people over the years. When somebody asks you, "wouldn't you agree that this supermarket is dreadful?", or even worse, for example during a massage, "it feels great, doesn't it?" they are obviously not interested in your own point of view, or truthful response, but only in validating their own opinions. There is no room for any discussion, either. There is no space for you to even start thinking, much less daring to express a different perspective. What happens is actually a form of manipulation. And what I observed, thanks to this experience as one part of the excellent training, is that quite a lot of people do this habitually. Usually, they keep remaining totally unaware of the inner nature of the questions they so regularly keep asking.

Coaches are required to ask questions that start with 'how', 'what' or 'when'. That's when the other person's mind is challenged and set in motion in order to come up with an answer in at least one sentence or more. Then you can start talking.

Even the why-questions are usually strictly avoided, because they more often than not provoke a defensive response. Many why-questions are really awful. Such as, "why did you start smoking again?", or "why did you catch a cold?", or 'why did you gain weight?" How can you possibly reply without feeling judged and cornered?

The result is the end of sharing, maybe even the end of your willingness to talk to the person asking this kind of stupid questions. This would then be another case of breakdown of communication due to lack of awareness. We have got too many of those instances on all levels of society already. Asking sensitive, well-crafted questions just at the right moment is a requirement for non-violent communication, which we as humanity on this planet are so much in need of, especially at this crucial point in time.

I had thought that due to the fact that I worked many years in journalism and was a curious, engaged and also well-trained young reporter who was keen to ask people all kinds of questions, I would be pre-destined to steer coaching conversations with ease. However, this turned out to be an illusion. Asking a coaching client great questions is an art that requires a lot of practice, situational and emotional awareness, as well as a big dose of intuition.

Breaking free from the rules

I feel very grateful for the thorough way in which I was trained, and will never forget how I failed that exam. It certainly took me a long time to be learn, how to stick to a certain sequence of structuring the coaching conversation. During the training period it made perfect sense to me. However, I realized that it also made me feel anxious about forgetting something or not getting it right. Even after I passed my final exams and received my diplomas, I kept the habit of assessing how I had been doing. I could always point to something that didn't go so well that I could improve.

Here are some examples: Either the ratio of listening towards talking had been overstretched, or I had given in to a client insisting on giving them advice, or I had allowed my mind to drift off because I felt tired, or the time management didn't go well for me as many clients felt so comfortable that they were reluctant to leave. I could find lots of things to criticize and had to consciously remind myself over and over again to find way more things to appreciate than criticize, like many authors and organizations recommend as rules for giving feedback and making assessments professionally.

The time came to let go of the common coaching protocol, at least partially. My clients have been most instrumental in teaching me the most about developing my own style. With some clients, the standard structure would simply not work. When they decided what they wanted to talk about, I would have to ask them what they wanted as a result out of the session, to establish a so-called session goal. At that moment, something in their minds would get blocked. They would look at me with an expression of utter confusion and helplessness. I realized that I could not go by the book and insist on identifying a concrete outcome only in order to establish a measure for the success of the session. I had to accept that they really didn't know what they wanted out of it, and that they just wanted to talk about their issue and didn't give a damn about any measurable results.

At other times, I realized that it was something I had related during the conversation from my own life concerning the issue at hand that inspired them and got them to think. It happened a few times that I thought I had been sharing too much of myself instead of just asking questions. But when they came back they said something on the lines of, "what you told me last time about the problem you faced with your boss really inspired me and I realized something important."

Sometimes I felt it was required of me to talk a bit about the collective challenges we go through at this point in time to reassure the client that they were not alone with their issue, and that is was a quite common one affecting many other people. It was in those moments that I could sense the atmosphere changing. There was a noticeable drop in the level of worry or tension they carried with them. They would instantly ease up.

Once I felt awful after a session because I had become quite harsh, telling a client very bluntly that I was unwilling to waste my time any longer with listening an umpteenth time to an ongoing story that emphasized her role as a victim. I had lacked self-management and allowed myself to become upset, and realizing what I branded as a transgression from my side made me even more upset – this time with myself. However, once again I was surprised by the reaction when the client came back. With a beaming smile, she thanked me for the tough love. She said it was exactly what she had needed to hear. Nobody else could have spoken to her like that. And it was exactly this spontaneous outburst that allowed her to realize what she was doing and to eventually shift out of the victim scenarios she had been playing in her mind over and over again. Not that I took this incident as a green card to get angry at clients, but hey, sometimes tough love seems like the only way to go.

Working with a client with an autoimmune disease that she kept secret from her family and friends was another eye-opener. This client hardly ever answered any question in a direct manner. I would get to hear long and vague responses that seemed to come from a position of either habitual denial or equally deeply ingrained defensiveness. It forced me to ask very simple questions and reduce their quantity. This client had a strong need to talk about the state of her health and the many worries she entertained about it. That's the main thing she wanted, to finally share her agony with somebody who would understand, somebody she could trust to keep the secret.

I explained to her that I was not a psychotherapist, but she insisted that it was me that she wanted to talk to and nobody else. What I needed to do was to trust that this would help her. It was a challenge for me to give up the structure altogether and remember that coaching in whatever form is supposed to go along with the agenda of the client. She turned out to be my most loyal client, coming to me for over two years.

The goals that she did identify took her a long time to reach. However, eventually she did. She started to experiment with different kinds of sports. She went to see a holistic physiotherapist and a nutritionist. She even travelled to the US to get a diagnosis from the most prominent doctor specialized in this field. She created her bedroom more beautifully as her safe space. Her blood test indicators improved and gradually she became much more self-confident. That was something incredibly beautiful to witness. We got to know each other very well and we also got to appreciate each other a whole lot.

Creating my way - #devikastyle

It was mainly the not usual clients, those who faced serious challenges, who got me to think about unusual methods. One teenager told me during the first session that he was gay. Homosexuality is not only strongly stigmatized in Egypt but criminalized by the penal code as well. Having lived for nearly ten years in Berlin, homosexuality is surely not one of the things that can shock me. This is why I could remain perfectly natural about this issue, other than most Egyptian coaches known to me could have done.

While extracting a list of his talents, this young man told me that some of his schoolmates thought he was a very good actor. One of his goals was to develop more inner strength and self-esteem. Since he couldn't really put in words how that would feel or look like, I asked him to mimic this for me. "Stand up and walk like a strong guy, then sit down and sit like a self-confident man," I requested. And there he was, right on, with a perfect performance. We both laughed. And he understood why I asked him to keep faking it until he got there.

That moment was his breakthrough. He consciously developed the most confident body language I have ever seen in a teenager. Motion follows emotion and vice versa, so with just a bit of practice he felt more and more authentically self-confident. It was like he turned into a new person right in front of my eyes. He was absolutely brilliant.

Another 17 year old told me in the second session that he was a cutter. Luckily, I could keep a poker face and not fall into the emotional temptation of demonstrating any kind of motherly reaction. My natural curiosity helps me in these kinds of moments. "Hm," I said. "That's interesting. Many young people in the West do that now, but I have never met anyone doing it. How would you feel about showing me how you do this?" He did, and I got to see one arm full of scars.

Then I asked him to roll up the shirt of both arms and have a good look at all the cuts. I spared us both the sight of his legs. "How do you feel when you look at your arms?" I asked. All of a sudden he looked very sad and vulnerable. "I feel that I want to stop doing that," he replied after a long silence in a voice that was so low that I could hardly hear it. I sensed that he was having a hard time holding back tears. "Ok great, then let's get started," I said.

I proceeded to tell him in the most matter of fact way what I was capable of in that moment, which was very emotional for me too, that this issue exceeded by far the competence and scope of a Life Coach, and that I was not a trained psychotherapist. He replied that he had seen some psychotherapists before and didn't trust them, because all they did was to medicate him for depression. I also told him that I would only coach him through stopping the cutting if he promised to call me the moment he was about to do it again. And that I needed to involve one of his relatives in case this would actually happen. We agreed on that with a handshake. He kept this promise.

I decided on the spot that infusing him with the emotion of appreciation was the best way to go and suggested to do HeartMath exercises together. I asked him to commit to doing them regularly. He had a strong scientific interest and took to the HeartMath system like a duckling to the pond. He simply loved it and his intelligent brain got totally involved with it.

He called me when he was on the verge of cutting himself again, and luckily I could talk him out of it. And then, by himself, he informed the relative he trusted most and they talked about it a lot. I also talked to that relative a few times over the phone. He never cut himself with a knife again. He owned up to his repressed feelings of anger and understood where they came from. He simply refused to continue turning this anger against himself. And he finished school with brilliant grades.

The magic effect of appreciation

The more I practiced coaching others, the more I understood that appreciation is the key to personal transformation. Appreciation is a core element of love. We can't love anybody or anything without appreciating. And in contrast to the overused word love, appreciation feels doable. Anybody, even the most depressed person, can like and appreciate something in front of them, even if it's a cup of coffee. This emotion of liking something, or someone, and being liked, satisfies one of our most basic needs: the need for feeling connected and loved.

This need could be easily satisfied if we could make it a habit to notice something good and say it to those around us. "People need this and benefit from it instantly," says Kline. "Showing appreciation, short, accurate, genuine, is vital. I think we should become seed-sowers of confidence and intelligence in the people around us by doing this simple thing," she emphasizes.[92]

This is one of the reasons I have incorporated the approach of Appreciative Inquiry as a tool I regularly use. It has become an integral part of my style of coaching. Appreciative Inquiry (AI) was pioneered in the 1980s by David Cooperrider and Suresh Srivastva, two professors at the Weatherhead School of Management at Case Western Reserve University. It's basically is a change management approach and process that focuses on identifying what's working well, analyzing why it is working well and then doing more of it.

The main tenet of Appreciative Inquiry is that an organization will grow in the direction in which people in the organization focus their

---

[92] Nancy Kline, Time to Think, p.64

all the attention is focused on problems, then identifying dealing with them is what the organization will do best. If all ⸺n is focused on strengths, however, then identifying strengths ⸺ding on those strengths is what the organization will do best."[93] ⸺etty much at the beginning of the coaching process, I ask my clients ⸺ame any talent or character trait that they can possibly appreciate about themselves. In most cases, people name around five items and then give up. "That's it," they tend to say with a shy expression. The conditioning that we should be modest and humble, and not engage in self-flattery or, God forbid, any form of self-glorification, seems to sit very deep – especially in the Middle East and Asia.

However, I just won't have any of that and keep asking. And this is when the 'buts' kick in. Sort of like this: "Yes, I am intelligent but I am also disorganized." Keeping them from focusing on the 'but', as soon as they say something positive about themselves is really hard work. Sometimes, I start wildly guessing about talents I feel must exist, and my intuition leads me increasingly well in this exercise. I won't give up until I have at least 25 to 30 traits. Then I read the list to them. What happens to most female clients at this point is disbelief. Most of them tear up. There is a release of tears coupled with an enormous emotional relief when a predominately negative self-image begins to crack and break down.

It's mindboggling how well we know our shortcomings and how keen we are to talk about them, while we acknowledge all the things that can be appreciated about us so little. I have observed that most people have no idea about talents and gifts they bring with them into this life. According to Tom Rath, one big problem is that most people are unaware of their strengths, or unable to describe them, or those of the people around them. This lack of awareness of strengths comes at a high price. It more often than not leads to a lifetime of feeling unfulfilled, frustrated and out of place.

When we have such a list of things that are nice and good about us, we have concrete undeniable indicators on which we can build genuine self-appreciation. We also come to see and understand all the unique strengths we have. Awareness of our special combination of strengths is very important because it points us to those areas in life in which it would

---

[93] See, https://whatis.techtarget.com/definition/Appreciative-inquiry-AI

be most pleasant and satisfying for us to study or work in order to these natural strengths. The old approach of trying to strengthen wh are *not* already naturally good at would be much harder and would fewer valuable results.

This is perhaps the most important insight of the strengths-ba approach or Strengths Psychology, which has become prominent than to the work of Don Clifton and Tom Rath. I was thrilled to discover thi approach, not only because it validated what I intuitively did when starting to coach any client. But it also finally offers solid research-based evidence for the fact that if we want to evolve, it's vital to recognize our strengths and then build them up. Trying to develop talents that we don't have a knack for would then simply be a waste of time. This research knocks down the belief that we can all do anything we want to and shows instead that it's way more effective to excel in life by becoming better at those things we are already good at.

The strengths-based approach

The sad reality is that instead of investing more time in areas where a child has the most potential for greatness, parents and teachers usually ignore excellence and instead focus on the perceived weaknesses. This is a totally counterproductive approach. Research shows that people have several times more potential for growth when they invest energy in developing their strengths instead of correcting their so-called weaknesses.

And yet the aim of almost any learning program, according to Rath, is to help us turn into who we are *not*, while the key to human development is building on who you already *are*. "From the cradle to the cubicle, we devote more time to our shortcomings than to our strengths," he succinctly comments.[94] Particularly noteworthy about his work is the finding that the most successful people start with cultivating their most dominant talent. Then they add skills, knowledge and practice to the mix.

Rath underlines that "having the opportunity to develop our strengths is more important to our success than our role, our title or even our pay."[95]

---

[94] Tom Rath, Strengths Finder 2.0, 2007, p.3 and p.8
[95] Ibid, p.11

...of research undertaken with a team of Gallup ...re than 10 million people in almost every country. ...n research-based consulting company, which became ...ic opinion polls conducted worldwide.

...also shows that people who have the opportunity to ...strengths every day in their work are six times as likely to be ...their jobs and three times as likely to report having an excellent ...life in general.⁹⁶ However, the vast majority of people don't have ...rtunity to focus on what they do best. Of the 10 million people ...ed, around 7 million fell short of this chance.

Rath came to the conclusion that "the epidemic of active disengagement, extreme negativity, that runs rampant in organizations, could be easily cured if managers and co-workers would focus on the strengths of people around them."⁹⁷ It is quite amazing how many different researchers and authors write about the importance of acknowledging others for what they do and who they are at this point in time. I mean imagine, we could turn so many things around at work and at home, if we would just get into the habit of giving more appreciation than criticism or blatant non-attention.

A long-term study of 1,000 children in New Zealand that stretched out over 23 years revealed that a child's observed personality at age 3 was remarkably similar to their reported personality traits at age 26. This finding is remarkable because it demonstrates that a person's talents are least likely to change in the course of their lives. Our natural talents and passions – the things we truly love to do - last for a life time, but all too often they go untapped. "Far too many people spend a lifetime headed in the wrong direction," without discovering their greatest talents and potential, says Rath.⁹⁸

It is essential that we know our strengths. Only then can we further build them up. Only then can we recognize where we could possibly best fit in, and only then can we unfold our unique potential and manifest the treasures that exist only once in this special form on our planet. The desire to actualize our potential is what self-realization is all about. It has been said by many researchers, not least Abraham Maslow, that

---

⁹⁶ Ibid, p.iii
⁹⁷ Ibid, p.iv
⁹⁸ Ibid, p.18 and p.30

self-actualization is one of the essential human needs and is thus depicted at the top of what has become known as the pyramid of needs.

In 1943, the American psychologist Maslow proposed that healthy human beings have a certain number of needs, and that these needs are arranged in a hierarchy, with some, such as physiological needs for food, water, rest and shelter and needs for safety being more basic than others, such as love, belonging, esteem, and self-actualization. Please note that ESTEEM is among our needs. Maslow emphasized the importance of self-actualization for motivation, which is a process of growing and developing as a person in order to achieve individual potential.

In fact, motivation and empowerment ultimately arise from meaning, from those things that are most valuable to us. What is precious to us is what we appreciate, what we cherish, what we are naturally drawn to, what is dear to our hearts. It logically follows that building up the motivation to start moving towards achieving a goal can only happen when that goal means a whole lot to us at our core and is not superimposed by the norms of society or religious dogma. Coaching assists very well in figuring out what we value most and, therefore, love doing most and how to integrate doing more of that into our daily life and into our work.

Developing my magic toolbox

Like most coaches, I have experimented with a variety of exercises, on myself and on my clients. Most self-help books offer large number of exercises for various purposes and the internet offers zillions of others. For me, and for most of my clients, the HeartMath exercises have produced the best results. These exercises are simple and easy to integrate into a busy life. They are based on decades of rigorous research, which proves their effectiveness to significantly reduce stress while enhancing vital energy. I mean, honestly, how good is that? Who wouldn't like to feel less stressed and have more energy at their disposal?

I discovered that flanking the HeartMath system with coaching is amazingly effective. The reason is that once we feel more at ease, everything opens up. There seems to be more space inside as the constrictions in our muscles and nervous system relax. We literally expand. There is also an enhanced capacity to think and focus, as the prefrontal cortex opens after having been shut down due to an overactive stress response mechanism. And perhaps most importantly, there is more vital energy to follow through with taking the desired actions. When we are running around with our batteries on empty, we have no energy to feel sufficiently motivated to do anything on top of the absolutely required minimum just to keep going with our heads held low.

Especially teenagers like to do practical exercises that place them in another emotional space than the one they have gotten used to. Once they understand how useful these exercises are and can feel the difference they make in their lives, they instantly apply them. This is one of the reasons I love to work with teenagers.

I have had a few cases where the HeartMath exercises aimed at cultivating emotions such as appreciation, gratitude or ease didn't work well. What then often did work was an exercise called *Active Love*. This exercise is presented in a book I warmly recommend, which is aptly called *The Tools*, and was written by Hollywood's most acclaimed psychotherapists.[99]

A good example for this was one of my most brilliant teenage clients, a 12-year-old girl. She had first observed me at an information day at her school, where I stood behind a stand with my leaflets and a few posters trying to raise interest for the service of Coaching in Education, which was still a totally new field in Egypt. However, most people seemed more interested in the food stalls or the clothes and accessories that were on sale around me.

I felt a bit ignored and out of place, and on that evening my dominant emotion was frustration. Assuming the role of a pioneer is not always a fun thing to do. And yet, my experiences have often showed me that taking one step forward full-heartedly always leads to lots of other things happening miraculously, even if they show up much later.

What I hadn't known yet was this: About one year later, a woman called me and said that her daughter had been pestering her for the whole past year, saying that she absolutely needed to be coached by me. Unnerved, this mother was finally ready to give in to her daughter's persistent wish. They passed by together, and I explained what coaching is all about and outlined my approach to it. They could ask as many questions as they wanted. The girl's eyes beamed, and we agreed that I would take her on as my up to then youngest client.

---

[99] Phil Stutz and Barry Michels, The Tools, 5 Life-Changing Techniques to Unlock Your Potential, London 2012

This young lady was a highly intelligent overachiever. What made her obsess with worries to the point of suffering from restless nights was the fear that she would not be able to keep her excellent grades up. She was dead scared that she could somehow run out of steam before she could qualify for a scholarship to study abroad. She immediately got the point when I explained to her that positive emotions induce a sense of ease and inner peace and on top of that allow us to perform at our best. The next session she returned with a notebook full of drawings and clippings of the things she not only appreciated but loved most about life. I was in awe.

She was a bit shy to admit that she created this stunningly beautiful book mainly because she couldn't focus during the appreciation exercise of the HeartMath system, so she came up with her own version of cultivating appreciation. "That's fantastic," I said. "Let's simply try another exercise." I pulled out a printed explanation of *Active Love*, and we practiced sending love to a person dear to us. We both chose our respective mothers.

The next week she returned with an even more shiny expression on her face and happily told me that she had first sent love to every person she had a disagreement with and it always turned the situation around. She then went on to send love to all her friends, to all people she knew who were ill, and then to all conflict or catastrophe ridden places in the world she had seen on TV. "I sent love to the whole world," she said with a huge smile on her face. Sending out love was the key this special girl needed to overcome her worries and develop a stronger belief in her own abilities. Since then she has always continued to be a top student.

Becoming a coach increased my capacity to love

Through coaching, I have come to enjoy a very warm and close relationship with nearly every single client. I have never had to force myself to develop empathy. It has been the natural result of seeing somebody I was totally focused on and curious about opening up in front of me and talking about their innermost fears and dreams. The more they opened up, the more the mutual appreciation grew, which automatically led to more and more loving feelings. One of the unexpected and most wonderful outcomes of developing into a professional coach was that I have come to deeply appreciate and even love way more people than I previously thought possible.

Sometimes, I caught myself thinking that I would have loved to have a coach just like I am now by my side at that young age. These thoughts got me wondering how much earlier I would have not only grasped but practically applied some very essential insights into how we function as human beings and how that is correlated to the way our life unfolds. The emotion behind that thought is some sort of regret that came from thinking I could have soared sooner.

I know now that I could not have done otherwise at any point in time because everything is intrinsically linked and interrelated and, therefore, it mysteriously unfolds and is choreographed in relation to everything else that's happening or ever happened. In those moments when I asked the totally irrelevant "what if?" question, I have found comfort through reminding myself that I needed to figure many things out by myself over many decades, propelled forward by curiosity about how we mature as human beings, in order to really know and deeply appreciate the worth of my experiences and the insights this process has taught me.

It might have taken me a while but what matters is that I did discover some of my main talents. And it fills me with great pleasure and gratitude that I can apply these talents now to support other people in their search for ways to live more lightheartedly. "Every human being has talents that are just waiting to be uncovered," says Rath.[100] What I like to add is that coaching is the best way to uncover and to bring to fruition our strengths and gifts. This is what makes coaching so very precious, fulfilling and beautiful. And this is why it is so worth the investment of time, energy, effort and money into the journey of becoming a Life Coach.

---

[100] Rath, p.30

Summary

A competent coach gets us to recognize the unique combination of beautiful character traits and strengths that we bring to any table. Coaching is the best way to unearth our gifts and talents and bring them to fruition. Really knowing everything that can possibly be appreciated about us is not only necessary for any form of fair self-assessment, it's the foundation for building self-esteem.

Self-esteem has been identified as a human need by the American psychologist Abraham Maslow. It's the prerequisite to any form of success in life. And it's the basis for the development of self-worth. A sense of worthiness is the antidote to the scarcity mentality that is part of the cultural narrative of the outgoing age. Many of us are consciously trying to overcome this ingrained survival mechanism, which creates a focus on the scarcity of resources and a need to compete to secure a share of them. Methods on ways to overcome abundance blockers and learn to thrive are booming on social media.

The crucial importance of only just these two issues, self-esteem and worthiness, for our levels of contentment, fulfillment and abundance in life is a good reason to start seeing a Life Coach. The urge to unfold our potential is way more than a psychological need. We are programed to actualize what we have in us, just like the seed of a flower is programed to flourish. It also gives us meaning and purpose to develop our talents. When we have the opportunity to make use of our strengths at work we are way more engaged in our jobs and way more likely to feel that we have an excellent quality of life.

Figuring out what we are naturally good at and feel drawn to do is crucial if we want to flourish. It's also one of the most essential aspects of the art of lightheartedness because doing those things we feel passionate about makes our hearts sing. So taking time out to think is really worth it.

Developing into a good coach takes a lot of time, dedication and experience. It's a journey that includes intense periods of ruthless self-reflection on one's many issues and confrontation with one's own ways of resistance and self-sabotage. It's a most gratifying process of accelerated personal growth as eventually self-acceptance as well as self-compassion emerge that go hand in hand with deeper levels of understanding and empathy for others.

When somebody asks the right questions at the right time and offers us a safe space for thinking where neither answers nor expressed emotions are judged, we become way more aware of our own capacity and power to solve our problems. We suddenly perceive ideas about solutions that never occurred to us before when we went round and round ruminating alone in our own heads.

The 'why' question is never useful to ask, because it creates a feeling of being blamed in the other and triggers resistance or shut down. By all means ask people more 'how' questions out of a sense of real interest and willingness to listen. We all carry a huge desire of being truly heard and seen.

The next chapter contains definitions about coaching and attempts to capture the essence of this art. A strong point is made for the importance of listening so deeply that high quality thinking can occur. At its end, the spiritual essence of coaching is touched upon by extensively quoting one of its major pioneers and founding fathers.

"There is only one thing on which virtually everything else in our lives depends. That is the quality of our thinking. Everything stems from this."

Nancy Kline

SEVEN

Coaching Inspires Thinking and Change

The thing I love most about Coaching is that it offers one of the very few settings which inspire thinking about what's most essential to us. The constantly chattering mind has a tendency to interfere and undermine our progress. Using our minds to think in creative and innovative ways is crucial.

In dominant materialistic and authoritarian cultures and systems, thinking is not exactly encouraged. Independent thinking is still widely seen as a potential threat to the prevailing power structures. Most people still seem to abdicate their ability to think for themselves. However, it's precisely the kind of thinking, and the quality of the questions we ask ourselves which determine the quality of our lives.

The essential art is then to learn how to use our minds more effectively for focused thinking and, otherwise, rely more on the wisdom of the heart. Once we see clearly that it is ultimately the heart that connects us to our own inherent wisdom, not the brain, it is easier to set out on a path to reach such a goal. Great coaching carries this insight home - especially if it incorporates the HeartMath system.

For a coach, the brilliant person in the room is the client. "The coach's job is to help the client discover that," says Nancy Kline[101] She points out that, "at this moment in human history, thinking for yourself is still a radical act."[102] I like radical acts simply because it's high time to take actions that revolutionize the ways we live and work on this planet. Indeed, the decision to feel well in our bodies and minds is a radical act.

We need to talk in order to think

What triggers deeper levels of thinking in most people is talking. People usually can't think of something unless they can talk about it first. "The human mind works best when it can hear itself, notice its inconsistencies, be reminded of its quality and take its time," argues Kline.[103] Coaching gets us to talk things through in a focused way until we arrive at mental clarity. From this point of crystal clear insight, we can make decisions that turn things around because they are in line with what is truly important to us. This is why coaching helps to unleash our potential to flourish. It delivers results as well as a sense of achievement. While it triggers some really good thinking, it's ultimately action oriented. That's the reason why a coaching session usually feels like a deeply satisfying experience.

A coach asks questions that get us to a place of clear understanding about what we wish to see happening in our lives. Coaching is about digging out aspirations, becoming aware of our special talents and traits and setting goals that are meaningful to us. It unearths our inner truth and gets us to claim it and live it. Coaching encourages us to stop playing small and expand. It inspires us to discover what's meaningful to us, so we can get out there and make the contribution which we are yearning for.

Coaching is based on a holistic approach of looking at all areas of a person's life or an organization in a non-judgmental way aimed at bringing out the best capabilities and strengths, while also addressing obstacles in the form of self-limiting beliefs and behaviors. In contrast, consulting and mentoring are commonly based on the old paradigm of a specific problem focus and a top down approach. The focus of coaching is on building

---

[101] Nancy Kline, Time to Think, 1999, p.138
[102] Ibid., p.34
[103] Ibid, p.59

the motivation to take fruitful actions that move us forward. It's not on analyzing past problems; the past is only touched upon if unresolved issues create obstacles to reaching a goal that is important now.

Coaching provides a safe space to explore our dreams as well as our fears. By working with a coach we can avoid the feeling of muddling through on our own. The coach is a trusted partner on our side to support and encourage us through our journey of change. Coaching assists us to find the best way to move forward by mapping out a clear path. Setting goals and committing to them gives us direction. It increases confidence by reducing confusion, doubts as well as procrastination. Coaching leads to the experience of higher levels of performance, fulfillment and joy.

Coaching is a process during which a client's definition of fulfillment is bound to change. At first, it could be commonly recognized measures of success, such as a good job that provides enough money and a certain lifestyle. Eventually, the process progresses to a deeper definition of success and fulfillment, which is not anymore so much about having more of anything, but about being and becoming. "It's not what fills the client's pockets or closets – it's about what fills the client's heart and soul. A fulfilling life is a valued life," says Laura Whitworth.[104]

Coaching is a structured conversation as well as a dance

A competent coach asks questions, listens deeply, allows for silence, reflects back what was said, probes into deeper questions, summarizes and thus encourages more reflection. These are the techniques we use while we are attentively engaging in a well-structured conversation, which usually contains four different main phases: seeing and feeling the vision and setting an achievable goal, undertaking an honest reality check, thinking big about options, choosing the way forward and defining concrete action steps. It's this simplicity which leads to remarkable results.

It's not an easy process to develop into an effective coach as it involves a huge amount of self-refection as well as the unlearning of thought patterns and reactions that are driven by the sub-consciousness. In contrast to what

---

[104] Laura Whitworth et all, Co-active Coaching, 2007, p.8

a large number of people seem to keep expecting, a competent coach is not giving advice. We simply don't tell people what to do.

We don't interrupt their stream of thinking either, which is why people can think better around coaches. That's the special thrill for the client and perhaps the biggest challenge for the coach who needs to learn to refrain from impulsive reactions arising out of the sense of knowing the solution. Leaning back, feeling into inner ease and allowing long periods of silence without feeling awkward is what inspires a client in their search for their own answers.

In contrast to a psychotherapist, a coach is required to be dedicated to assist their clients with figuring out by *themselves* what works best for *them*. Competent coaches have been trained to trust that nobody else than the client can know their unique situation and those solutions that are best suited for them. This professional codex of coaching is based on the insight that we already have too many people constantly telling us what to do, while this is usually not what gets us moving.

What is way more useful and exciting is to suddenly see a light bulb going on and realizing by oneself what would be a great way to tackle an issue, the best road to travel on the way to reaching a particular goal. "We have found that clients are more resourceful, more effective, and generally more satisfied when they come up with their own solutions. And because they chose the solution, they are more likely to follow through with action."[105]

It's in the last part of a coaching session that the client is asked to choose some of the actions they identified as options. This is also when the coach would ask them how committed they feel about taking those actions on a scale from one to ten. If the score is lower than a seven, it would be better to choose different actions, or perhaps even a different goal until the client can identify a high level of commitment to follow through with the steps they say they decided to take.

The way to assist a client to discover what would make them move forward towards more joy ultimately comes through an intuitive skill that the founders of The Coaches Training Institute (CTI) call "dancing in the moment." This requires a coach to be not only fully present but at ease throughout the session while remaining aware of the shifting themes

---

[105] Ibid, p.4

and currents and adapting when choosing questions directed at exploring deeper what has just shown up. Dancing in the moment is the coach's ability to be flexible and unattached, to stay curious about the unfolding conversation and adjust instinctively.[106]

Coaching became popular because it produces results

Coaching has become very popular over the past three decades. It has rapidly spread from the United States and UK to European countries, and to the Arabian Gulf and has reached some of the so-called developing countries with some delay. Among the globalized elite, it has become quite fashionable to take sessions with what is most commonly called a Life Coach.

Numerous top managers all over the world have understood the extraordinary value of bringing an experienced business coach on board. The CEO of one of the largest companies of the world, Google's Eric Schmidt, has publicly said that the best business advice he has ever received and put into practice was to hire a coach. It's indisputable today that coaching positively impacts any organization or business in tangible ways through creating numerous benefits, including enhanced productivity and as a result, increased profit margins.

One of the many benefits of coaching is that it creates more awareness and competence among top managers to effectively steer their organization through change by using improved leadership methods and by involving their teams to a much larger extent in decision making than previously thought possible or feasible.

Many new niches have developed as more and more coaches entered the field by offering their services under different labels, such as relationship or couple coaching, parenting coaching, health coaching, wellness coaching, spiritual coaching, meta coaching etc. However, in my experience, coaching is coaching. What counts is the level of presence, experience and competence of a coach, and not the label given to packaging the service provided in the pursuit of fulfilling the latest branding requirements. Coaching is simply the most brilliant method to assist anybody with

---

[106] Ibid, p.5

cultivating more success and contentment, regardless of their issues, age or profession.

Definitions of coaching

A lot has been written about coaching, and many individuals dream about becoming coaches. And, yet, I keep meeting loads of people in various countries who have never heard of it. So, what on earth is coaching? In view of a need to explain and also promote what coaching is about in more effective ways and to clarify why it is such a great idea to seek assistance from a competent coach, I will offer a few definitions here.

The definition most used by *The Coaching Academy* is this: "A coach gives you the professional support you need to go from where you are now to where you want to be, faster and more effectively than if you tried it on your own."

One of the best definitions of coaching I have come across is used in Myles Downey's *School of Coaching*: "Coaching is the art of facilitating the performance, learning and development of another."[107] A lot of emphasis is in fact placed on individual learning, which is essentially about becoming more acutely aware of who you are, where you are, what your destination is and how to get there.

Business coaching is by nature more specifically about achieving goals and playing a bigger game at work. Downey puts it brilliantly: "Effective coaching in the workplace delivers achievement, fulfillment and joy from which both the individual and the organization benefit. By achievement I mean the delivery of extraordinary results, organizational and individual goals achieved, strategies, projects and plans executed. It suggests effectiveness, creativity and innovation."[108]

He points out that when people achieve goals that are meaningful to them and when learning and development are part of the process, enjoyment ensues. "These three components, achievement, fulfillment and joy, are interlinked and the absence of any one will impact and erode the others. Learning without achievement quickly exhausts one's energy.

---

[107] Myles Downey, Effective Coaching, 2003, p.21
[108] Ibid, p.17

Achievement without learning soon becomes boring. The absence of joy erodes the human spirit."[109]

Joy is surely a key factor for any form of success in life, however, not many authors point out how crucial it is for delivering great results at work. Downey relates that during the programs he runs at his school he frequently asks, "What is your level of enjoyment?". Simply asking this question leads to a bigger level of self-awareness among participants. Consciously noticing it is all it takes to get slightly anxious faces relaxing into a smile.[110]

Coaching and the *Inner Game*

As this example shows, raising the level of self-awareness without falling into the trap of increasing self-condemnation is a fundamental tenant of coaching. "Awareness of what *is*, without judgment, is relaxing, and is the best precondition for change," says one of the pioneers of coaching, Timothy Gallwey, in his bestselling classic *The Inner Game of Tennis*.[111] The principles on which coaching is founded first came to prominence as the *Inner Game* and have been developed as non-directive coaching which relies on the capability of the individual to think for themselves, to learn for themselves and to be creative.

Downey, one of Gallweys' students, has called the *Inner Game of Tennis* one of the most influential books on performance and learning of the last thirty years and points out that it caused a huge stir when it was first published. It is still in print and has been followed by other titles, not least *The Inner Game of Work* and *The Inner Game of Music*. The *Inner Game* is the game that takes place in the mind of the player, and it is played against such obstacles as lapses in concentration, nervousness, self-doubt and self-condemnation, says Gallwey: "In short, it is played to overcome all habits of mind which inhibit excellence in performance."[112]

Gallwey underlines the observation that whatever we experience can

---

[109] Ibid, p.18
[110] Ibid, p.51
[111] Timothy Gallwey, The Inner Game of Tennis, 1975, p.70
[112] Ibid, p.11

only be known to us through awareness. He says that "it is consciousness which makes possible awareness of the sights, sounds, feelings and thought which compose what we call 'experience'. It is self-evident that one cannot experience anything *outside* of consciousness." He defines consciousness as "that which makes all things knowable" or "that power of knowing." Attention to him is "focused consciousness."[113]

It is precisely when the attention is so focused that we enter a mental state in which we can learn with ease and perform at our best. "The skill of mastering the art of effortless concentration is invaluable in whatever you set your mind to," he says.[114] Providing profound attention is one of the core aspects of coaching that brings a level of consciousness to the conversation, which is seldom found in the way most people communicate with each other. Whitworth puts it like this: "To be listened to is a striking experience, partly because it is so rare."[115] She points out that when another person is totally with you, leans in, is interested in every word you say, people open up: "they expand, they have more presence." According to Life Coach and author Martha Beck, the most valuable resource nowadays is "maximum positive attention."[116]

Deep listening triggers deep thinking

Kline argues that "the quality of your attention determines the quality of other people's thinking." She points out that "good attention to people makes them more intelligent. Poor attention makes them stumble over their words and seem stupid." Her conclusion: "Your attention, your listening is that important."[117]

Kline eloquently presents the outcome of years spent with observing the human thinking process and figuring out the ideal circumstances for profound and creative thinking to occur. The outcome is a simple process she calls *The Thinking Environment*. It can unleash the power of

---

[113] Ibid, p.85, p.86
[114] Ibid, p.17
[115] Whitworth, p.31
[116] Martha Beck, Finding your Way in a Wild New World, 2012, p.xiii
[117] Kline, p.36, p.37

any organization. Interestingly, it is very much in line with the essential principles of coaching.

According to Kline, a thinking environment is the set of conditions under which people can think for themselves and think well together. This environment makes it possible for people's thinking to move further, go faster, and produce brand-new ideas in record time. A fundamental part of such an environment is the absence of tension or rush. In short: it is an environment characterized by ease, quiet, equality and encouragement that removes ideas which limit our potential.

One could be tempted to assume that as human beings we are all gifted with the capability to think, which is what distinguishes us from other species, and that thinking, therefore, cannot possibly be such a big deal. However, the mind is a tricky instrument with a tendency to endlessly loop around worries and wounds. It also easily gets caught up in self-criticism. Most people, in fact, don't seem to be able to think deeply about matters that are important to them in a focused, analytical and yet detached way. Unfortunately, this is especially the case with many top managers and leaders.

"To stop, sit down and think for ourselves, especially with someone paying attention to us expertly, is worth the time it takes. It returns time to us many fold," says Kline.[118] She emphasizes that, "to take time to think is to gain time to live."[119] Paying profound attention to a client as a coach is what allows them to think freely and genuinely in the first place. It is in fact this core competency which coaches are required to develop. In other words, everything stems from listening.

Truly listening to someone with every part of our being is a skill that most of us don't usually master well in our everyday lives. While we do somehow hear dear ones, it usually remains at a superficial level of listening. Our attention span is often not very long. We easily get distracted by ringing phones, demanding kids or partners, or our own need to talk takes over. Most of us often feel rather soon in any conversation that we need to interrupt to make our own point, or to complete the others' sentences assuming that we know what they want to say. Even worse, we

---

[118] Kline, p.190
[119] Ibid, p.192

rush in with an advice we feel we need to offer to come up with a quick solution in order to feel more useful and valuable ourselves.

The sad truth is that we hardly ever really listen to each other, even though we know deep down inside how comforting it is to feel truly seen, heard and accepted for who and how we are at any given moment. Unlearning this mostly unconscious habit and keeping up the intention to improve listening skills is not an easy task. It takes motivation, determination and a lot of awareness to develop into a professional listener.

Being heard and expressing ourselves verbally are essential human needs. Most of us have a desire to talk things through to gain clarity about events or experiences we have had and the feelings we hold about them. While we talk, ideas flow out of us. Thoughts form as we speak. However, it is usually quite difficult to remain aware of what we say while we are doing the talking. When a coach, or a friend with evolved communication skills, repeats what we said in our own words or summarizes the content, we experience a moment that is eye-opening. This is when self-discovery happens. It is perhaps even more helpful when we are asked at that moment what we intend to do with this insight, and how we are going to take that forward.

"The coach listens on many levels simultaneously to hear where clients are in their process, to hear where they are out of balance, to hear their progress on the journey of fulfillment. The coach is listening for the nuance of hesitation, for the sour ring of something not quite true."[120] In short, a coach maintains a concentrated focus on the clients' goal and steers the conversation in a way that reduces distractions or looping and prevents it from dropping into each rabbit hole that presents itself. In this way, a client reaches a better understanding of themselves and their issues.

Thinking leads to self-discovery and is an essential component of learning. The other component is experiential. This occurs when a client implements insights and decisions by taking practical action steps. In this phase, the support of a coach is equally valuable. In the process of transforming those mental habits that inhibit excellence and creating new beliefs that are more in line with what we truly feel and desire, we often stumble and fall back into our old ways, which are familiar and seem

---

[120] Whiteworth, p.11

to keep us safe. This quite commonly happens towards the middle of a coaching process.

"Beliefs and patterns are so firmly ingrained that they become automatic responses to life's events," says Business Coach Kim George.[121] Instructions would do little to change those responses. A good question though could lead to unlock assumptions that limit our perspective. A competent coach could gently nudge a client forward by reminding them of their strengths to achieve their goals and the benefits of achieving them or, even better, ask an incisive question that removes the barrier in the thinking effortlessly.

Conscious transformation through learning

Gallwey argues that a coach has the responsibility of maintaining nonjudgmental focus, providing opportunity for natural learning, and staying out of the way. He points out that "there is a far more natural and effective process for learning and doing almost anything than most of us realize." This, he says, is how we learned to walk and talk in the first place. In order to discover this natural learning process, "it is necessary to let go of the old process of correcting faults; that is, it is necessary to let go of judgment and see what happens."[122] Judgmental attitudes result in tightness, which interferes with the fluidity needed for excellence, he emphasizes.

What I find particularly fascinating about the *Inner Game* is that Gallwey distinguishes between what he simply calls 'Self 1' and 'Self 2'. 'Self 1' gives instructions to 'Self 2' and tries to control it by constantly interfering with remarks, reprimands, worries, calculations, fears and blame. 'Self 1' has internalized the voices of parents, teachers and authority figures. It contains what is commonly called *conditioning* from the society we grew up in. It is characterized by tension, fear, doubts and trying too hard. It involves the conscious mental realm. It's the ego. And it creates a lot of noise, which boils down to *interference*.

'Self 2' includes the physical body, including the brain, the conscious

---

[121] Kim George, Coaching into Greatness, 2006, p.48
[122] Gallwey, p.12 and p.34

and unconscious memory bank and the nervous system. "Inherent in it is an inner intelligence which is staggering" says Gallwey.[123] The main thing that obstructs learning and creates self-sabotage according to him is that "Self 1 does not trust Self 2". His conclusion is that all it takes to diminish our performance are doubts and fears.

Gallwey came up with the brilliant formula: Performance = potential – interference. The goal of the *Inner Game* is to quiet 'Self 1' interference, so that 'Self 2' can be more fully expressed and do what it does best on its own.

It's not that 'Self 1' is unimportant or useless, it just seems that the roles we assign to it have grown out of proportion. "The main job of Self 1, that is the conscious ego-mind, is to set goals, that is to communicate to Self 2 what he wants from it and then to let Self 2 do it," says Gallwey. The main way 'Self 2' learns is through images and feelings, not through words. So the most important role of the ego-mind is to expose the subconscious mind to images of the desired results and then lean back and "*let it happen.*"[124]

Coaching assists us to transform our way of thinking as well as conditioned responses and habitual behaviors through noticing what we are thinking or doing and comparing that with what we would actually prefer doing. It helps tremendously with learning more effective ways of doing things on our way towards expansion. One of the fundamental aspects of coaching is the examination of obstacles to the achievement of goals, which mainly consist of ego-interference, as Gallwey so brilliantly demonstrated.

Overcoming limiting beliefs

The terminology more widely in use nowadays is 'limiting beliefs'. A good example for this is one more or less subconscious core belief that is at the base of our ego formation and is causing a horrendous amount of unhappiness and struggle to human beings. It is the illusion of not being good enough. Everybody is afflicted by this erroneous assumption

---

[123] Gallwey, p.40
[124] Ibid, p.48

in one way or another. At some point in time, we picked that up in our childhoods, and it seems to stick quite persistently.

This belief in our unworthiness perpetuates a mentality of scarcity. George emphasizes that this mind set destroys us from the inside out. She calls it "the greatest disease of our time."[125] This subconscious belief is triggered when the mind focuses on a perceived lack instead of embracing what we already are, do and have. How to break free from this thought pattern and replace it by a mind-set of worthiness that is bound to produce the experience of tender self-love and happiness is an essential question.

Gallwey makes a very original contribution to this question: "There is no need to fight old habits. Start new ones." According to him our inner intelligence, which resides in the body, is bestowed with the inherent capability to learn anything with childlike ease. The reason why it is easy for children to learn walking or pick up a foreign language is that they haven't learned yet how to interfere with their own natural, untaught learning process, he argues. "The Inner Game way of learning is a return to this childlike way."[126]

The importance of childlike ease for change

The thrilling keyword for me here is 'childlike ease.' As Kline points out, "ease allows the human mind to broaden and reach."[127] Ease and playfulness are essential components for children to learn. They are also essential components for us as adults to come up with deep thinking. These components are at the heart of Laughter Yoga, which is a wonderful way to cultivate childlike playfulness.

Learning necessarily precedes behavioral change. If it happens with ease, it's even better as it sinks in deeper and is more sustainable. The word 'learning' is not meant as the collection of information, but the realization of something that leads to change, be it of a thought pattern or a tennis stroke. Patterns of thoughts or actions exist because they serve a function, which is why they continue to exist. Awareness of the function is nearly

---

[125] George, p.18
[126] Gallwey, p.66
[127] Kline, p.67

impossible while we are in the process of blaming ourselves for having a 'bad habit'. "But when we stop trying to suppress or correct the habit, we can see the function it serves, and then an alternative pattern of behavior, which serves the same function better, emerges quite effortlessly," argues Gallwey.[128]

The harder we try to break a habit, the harder it becomes. According to Gallwey, trying too hard is a questionable virtue, which he counters with the seemingly paradoxical Zen approach of "effortless effort." Gallwey illustrates his point with a great example: children don't have to work their ways out of the trenches or grooves that are formed in the nervous system as behaviors are repeated. "A child doesn't have to break the habit of crawling, because he doesn't think he has a habit. He simply leaves it as he finds walking an easier way to get around." Starting a new pattern is easy, he says, "when done with childlike disregard for difficulties."[129]

So, to come back to the example of the not-enough-mentality, which is re-enforced by the materialistic culture of the old paradigm we are set to leave behind, it's helpful to remember that we have the capability of unlearning those thought patterns that interfere with ushering in a new paradigm simply by side-stepping them and deciding to believe in new ones. Questioning those limiting beliefs of the old era is a great way to go because the mind responds to questions.

A fantastic question to ask as a coach in order to focus the client on the freedom to come up with options that are based on a different belief could be: "How would you feel without the belief that you are not good enough?". Better still is asking incisive questions. The first step is to accurately identify the specific limiting assumption of a client, and replace it with the freeing one that is connected with their goal. For example: "If you knew without doubt that you are intelligent, how would you go about planning your event?".

Incisive questions are rather mind-boggling. Often people don't understand them when you ask such a question for the first time. It's necessary and useful to keep asking a question a few times. For example, like this: "I ask you again, if you knew that you are intelligent, what exactly would you do about planning your event?". In this way, the coach removes

---

[128] Gallwey, p.67
[129] Ibid, p.68

the limiting assumption of the client that they are too stupid to do what they set out to achieve by replacing it with a freeing one.

Limiting beliefs keep us playing a small game. Therefore, one of the perhaps most beneficial outcomes of coaching is increased awareness of limiting assumptions as well as our ability of formulating new beliefs. A great question to ask in this context is: "What would you need to believe in order to achieve your goal?".

This is best done with a large dose of gentleness because only then can a client recognize beliefs that limit them without giving space to the ego tendency of beating themselves up for believing these concepts in the first place. Labeling a thought, action or habit as 'bad' leads to emotional reactions that contain elements of shame, frustration, sadness, resentment or anger which lead to discouragement. It is, therefore, crucial that coaches cultivate an accepting attitude, as well as empathy and patience. These attributes create a safe environment in which ease can be experienced.

Kline defined ease as a central component of a *Thinking Environment*. "People who are at ease while someone is trying to think in their presence work near miracles," she points out. "Ease conceives and grows cymbal-crushingly exciting thoughts from the thinker. The loose, leaning-back, breathing-out, smiling, keenly attentive, confident, unrushed presence blasts lucid ideas out of otherwise impenetrable vaults of confusion and doubt. Ease is a deceptively gentle catalyst. Ease creates. Urgency destroys."[130]

In other words, an environment conducive to creative thinking and the behavioral change that can come with it is a space where it feels sufficiently safe to identify an issue that needs focused thinking, and then to open up, and allow the natural thought process of the mind to bring out the genius that is dormant within. It sets in motion the inner flow for the one who wants to do the thinking. And it is in this state of flow that we forget time and everything around us and are so naturally focused that whatever we work on happens with ease. We then perform at our best and this experience in itself becomes so deeply satisfactory that we feel a subtle form of joy.

---

[130] Kline, p.69

Flow arises from our essential nature

The "maximum positive attention" as defined by Martha Beck emanates ease because its main characteristic is stillness of the ego-mind. Harmony between "Self 1" and "Self 2" exists when the mind itself is quiet. And only then can peak performance unfolds effortlessly.[131] It is then that an individual is immersed in a state of flow, which results in greater power and accuracy.

Gallwey points out that letting go of 'Self 1' and its interfering activities is not easy. "To still the mind one must learn to put is somewhere. It cannot just be let go; it must be parked." Focusing the mind on a single object leads to a still mind. Focusing one's attention leads to concentration. Concentration is being in the here and now. To him, concentration is the supreme art. This art, he says, can only be fully developed when we are paying attention to something we really love. Assisting others to discover what makes their hearts sing is one of the most precious results of coaching.

According to Beck maximum positive attention comes from "authenticity and operating from our true nature."[132] She explains that the reclamation of our calm, present, vastly resourceful true nature requires a sustained connection to our environment and inner condition no matter what's going on through the state that she simply terms *wordlessness*. "Wordlessness allows us to see our true nature, and to heal from the violence of a thought system that cuts us apart, destroying our compassion for ourselves and others." It requires "replacing thoughts about events with authentic sensations that track whatever's occurring in the present moment."[133]

Countless authors and teachers have written about our true nature and offered a variety of explanations about who we really are as human beings at our core. What these teachings have in common is the point that our core essence can be experienced and accessed only by being fully aware of and immersed in the present moment.

The discovery of this indescribable essence is the ultimate goal of the *Inner Game*. Some call it soul, some call it higher self, others call it reality

---

[131] Gallwey, p.22
[132] Beck, p.xiv
[133] Ibid, p.8 and p.12

or truth, super-consciousness, God, divine presence, all that is, Tao, or simply the universe. Others refer to it as love, peace, joy, beauty, or the unnamable. "Those who have experienced the reality behind the label say that it is beyond names which can be spoken and beyond a beauty which can be described," says Gallwey.[134] He simply calls it 'Self 3'.

Coaching, which essentially aims at inspiring self-discovery and ultimately self-actualization, would remain incomplete if it would not also include the perennial human quest to uncover our most precious inner core. As teachers and seers have pointed out over the centuries across the globe, everything outside of ourselves is impermanent and therefore ultimately not sufficiently satisfactory to truly enchant the yearning of our hearts and souls. That's why spiritual coaching is becoming increasingly popular.

Gallwey puts it so very beautifully: "When the player of the Inner Game has searched for and found his way to the direct experience of Self 3, he gains access to the catalyst capable of finally stilling his mind. Then his full potential as a human being is allowed to unfold without interference from Self 1. He plays the rest of the game in the increasing joy of expressing with love his unique humanness, and in accordance with his own given talents and circumstances. He is free."

---

[134] Gallwey, p.127

Summary

It's indisputable today that coaching positively impacts any organization or business in tangible ways through creating numerous benefits, including enhanced productivity and as a result, increased profit margins.

The reason why coaching works so well is that a competent coach facilitates the performance, learning and development of another person. Individual learning is a central component, which is essentially about becoming more acutely aware of who you are, where you are, what your destination is and how to get there.

The human mind has a tendency to interfere with everything we do, by throwing up constant comments, criticism and worst case scenarios. Most people don't seem to make good use of their ability to think for themselves. Many face problems to focus and concentrate. Breaking free from the grip of the mind's habitual tendency to loop around negativity is an important part of character building and it's not easily accomplished. Coaching is one of the very few settings that inspires thinking about what's most essential to us.

The quality of our lives depends on the quality of our thinking. The decision to feel well in our bodies and minds is a radical act. More and more people are making decisions in favor of their own wellbeing every day. Many of them are supported by coaches.

To be deeply heard and really seen is a fundamental human need. If that is unfulfilled, a lot of frustration is the result. However, truly listening to someone with every part of our being is a skill that most of us don't master well in our everyday lives. A coach is a professional listener well worth the investment of time and money because the quality of listening is directly related to the quality of the thinking and inspiration any person can experience when truly heard.

Coaching, which essentially aims at inspiring self-discovery as well as self-actualization, would remain incomplete if the human quest to uncover our most precious inner core would not be covered. Indeed, spiritual coaching has become a niche that seems to be booming.

Ease and playfulness are essential components for children to learn.

They are as important for us as adults to generate deep thinking and inspiring ideas. We just forgot about that. A good coach, therefore, needs to feel at ease while being fully present and ready to dance with life in playful ways.

A great way to reconnect to the childlike playfulness we all still carry within ourselves is by taking up the practice of Laughter Yoga. How I discovered and fell in love with this funny way of exercise is what the next chapter is all about.

"When joy is 'busin' out all over' in you or in someone else, it can be one of life's greatest pleasures. To laugh freely from deep inside yourself can be a totally relaxing form of fun."

Jay Uhler

EIGHT

Falling in Love with Laughter Yoga

I never thought I would go into a public park with the aim of making people laugh. If somebody would have told me that ten years ago, I would have refused to take such a ridiculous prediction seriously. The passion that developed in me for bringing on laughter in big groups of people came as a surprise to myself. However, now, this is exactly what I love to do. When I don't have a laughter class or event for a while, I really miss it.

Looking back, it all seems to have been guided in miraculous ways, as if I was meant to do that - right from the moment I first heard about Laughter Yoga. Maybe it's just my mind that has become attached to a story in the attempt to make sense of it all. However, the two words that did the magic for me when I heard them first were *Happiness Facilitator*. That day does seem like a fateful day after all.

I was in a phase in my life where I was frustrated about ending up in jobs where I felt underworked, underappreciated, overpaid and mostly bored. I was feeling passionate about reading self-development and spiritual books and taking courses in various energy healing arts. Being able to cover the costs of traveling from the so-called third world to attend workshops in gorgeous cities in the West by myself gave me an enormous feeling of satisfaction and also accomplishment.

I loved the classes, the new people I met, the food we ate, the things I learnt, the late-night talks with like-minded souls, the wonderful feeling of discovering the existence of sister souls and fellow travelers on similar paths ….. all of it.

After going through the breakup of a long relationship, it can feel particularly thrilling to recreate yourself anew by developing new skills and investing time and money in your own growth. I think now that only in such stages of moving away from something painful, we are capable to muster the courage and determination it takes to go after building ourselves anew and to navigate the insecurity that comes with changing the way we live and work. When we engage in something like that, and many women do, it's in fact way more than a career change. It's *Daring Greatly*.

In spite of this thrilling feeling, I could not really see myself turning into a healer. To start with, I didn't even like that term, as it induces the image of somebody who has the power to heal you. I wasn't particularly keen to become like some of the full time energy healing practitioners I met along the way, either. The mind driven ego could perhaps not come to terms with leaving behind the more prestigious role of an international consultant that had taken so many years to reach in the first place.

Just to mention some of the rather cliché images I had in my mind: I sure didn't want to become an impoverished vegan health freak wearing baggy pants, clumsy looking shoes, fading hanging jumpers and no make-up. I also didn't want to be associated with house-wifeish practitioners who took a few weekend courses and then offered their services in studios for which their husbands or fathers ended up paying the rent. What I felt was that this was something I would probably love to do and would be really good at as an old woman.

Therefore, I was searching for something I could do that would make more sense to me and fulfill me more than the work I grew increasingly tired of doing. For a while, I was thinking about becoming a trainer for important soft skills such as non-violent communication, presentation, planning or self-confidence. However, that didn't give me the vibe of a thrill. I just couldn't see myself standing the whole day dressed in a suit trying to engage the minds of participants basically bored to death in their corporate jobs. I felt that this kind of scenario would be very tiring for my feet, back, head, heart and soul and just not sufficiently pleasant enough.

Happiness facilitator

One evening, I was sitting at a big table in a very cozy wooden house in Holland with a group of fellow participants in one of the *VortexHealing®* courses I was taking. To my big pleasure, this house had a fireplace and a Jacuzzi. And because I felt so cold I was the first one to basically run home after class and get myself into the large tub totally in awe about the hot water bubbling all around me.

On that evening, I was very relaxed after this treat sitting on my chair and pondering what to eat for dinner when two young women who shared the house with me for five days were passionately discussing the pros and cons of training versus coaching. One of them said: "Coaching moves you forward and helps you develop like nothing else. It's fantastic."

I had never heard of coaching before. The word Life Coach seemed a bit awkward to me, and yet, there was something that attracted my attention. Assisting people to develop themselves seemed so much more essential than focusing on organizational development, which is what I was expected to do at work. When I started to ask questions, I was told about the existence of a coaching school in London offering two free tester days. Attending one of these events would help me understand coaching and give me some basic techniques. This information had such a positive ring to it that it got stuck in my mind.

Back in Cairo, I checked London tester days out and booked a spot for it with *The Coaching Academy*. A few months later, I was extremely excited to fly there and arrive at the downtown hotel where the event was hosted. There were at least 50 to 70 people in the hall, of various ages, skin colors and countries, most of them dressed very well, everyone chatting away. I sat down, feeling a bit shy and yet full of excited anticipation and looked around me in awe.

A woman in her mid- fifties came, and sat next to me. She looked at me intensely before introducing herself and sitting down. Then she smiled and said warmly: "you look exactly like my little sister." I became curious about her sister and asked what she was doing in life. The lady replied that her sister had passed away and her loving expression was suddenly clouded with sorrow and pain. After I said I was so sorry about that, I insisted on asking what she had done professionally.

The answer hit me unexpectedly: "She was a successful Happiness Facilitator." I hectically fumbled for the notebook and pen in my handbag and said I needed to write that down. I did scribble it down, in capital letters, and a little voice said in my head: *"I want to do that, too"*.

Looking back, I realize that this was one of those moments that are turning points in life. It was like it had all been settled, just that I wasn't aware of it quite yet. "What on earth does a Happiness Facilitator do? How do you facilitate something like happiness?" I asked incredulously. The answer was that the sister of this lady had delivered Laughter Therapy workshops in some of Britain's largest corporations, including the BBC.

As a former reporter, this was a piece of information that impressed me immensely. *Making journalists laugh, that's it*, I thought. She had also been actively involved in an international Laughter Yoga network. I was stunned. I had never heard of Laughter Yoga either. I couldn't even imagine that a practice or technique existed on this earth which would get people to laugh and induce a feeling of happiness in them.

Even though this encounter had made such a strong impression on me, and my inner voice gave me a clear message, I postponed the whole idea of checking that out and getting into taking even more courses that would involve even more costly travels. And even though this kind lady later sent me a link to Laughter Yoga activities, there was a real probability that I could have forgotten the whole thing.

The reason was that in the meantime, I had decided to enroll for three diploma courses in the Coaching Academy and got busy with studying and traveling to London more often. However, the universe or fate, or divine guidance didn't forget the issue.

A friend of mine posted a link about activities on World Laughter Day on my Facebook wall. *There's even a world day for that?*, I thought and checked it out immediately. What I was led to with a few clicks was the website of Dr. Madan Kataria, the founder of Laughter Yoga and the courses he offers to train and certify Laughter Yoga teachers in Bangalore in southern India. My heart started beating faster, and I just knew that this was the next training I absolutely needed to be part of. After all, India is one of the places where I feel at home, and where my heart is aching to be when I stayed away for too long.

The decision to go for laughter yoga training in India

This happened at a time of my life when I was stuck in a state of deep grief. My father had passed away and I felt utterly vulnerable, fragile and alone in this world. Only a few weeks after he left this world, the January 25 revolution broke out in Egypt, and the building I worked in went up in flames. It was a time of unrest and chaos, often nerve-racking, sometimes thrilling and exciting because of the toppling of the corrupt authoritarian regime and the sense of empowerment as well as the collective hopes and dreams for the future that came with it.

Sometimes it felt plainly scary and, therefore, very tiring. The more I could see that what was happening was not going to get us into a bright place, the more exhausting it felt to go through the various stages of it all. I felt fed up and yearned for something to get me out of the emotions of sorrow, worry and raw pain. This was the state that got me to book my flight to India.

Like many others who take courses like these, my aim was to do something for myself to feel better. It's an average of only 10 percent of participants who go on to become active facilitators or teachers – be it in Laughter Yoga or Energy Healing courses. And I did not consciously intend to become one of them. However, I was nudged one more time by unfolding events. Life is often more fantastic than fiction.

Nudged forward

About six months after my return from India, I participated in a spiritual weekend retreat held by Dr. Magda Serry, an Egyptian ophthalmologist dedicated to spreading awareness about holistic healing modalities and meditation. In the middle of talking about chakras, meridians and ways to measure energies, Dr. Magda suddenly stressed the importance of laughter in the attempt to consciously raise our vibrations. She told us about a Laughter Yoga class she had attended in London and how fantastic she felt afterwards. She listed some of the scientifically proven benefits of laughter while her face was beaming.

Suddenly, one of my friends said in a loud voice: "We have a certified Laughter Yoga teacher in this room." I froze in shock. Dr. Magda's face lit up even more and she asked "who is it?" I knew I was in for a demonstration. My face turned red. My stomach churned. I wanted to sink under the table. Obviously I couldn't as that would have been even more embarrassing. So, I raised my hand and said meekly: *That would be me.*

As expected, Dr. Magda insisted that I should offer the group of ladies a session in the evening after the class, and I could not refuse. Until the designated time came, I felt very nervous. My brain tried to recall some of the exercises and explanations about Laughter Yoga, however, the proper functioning of my mind was impeded by the nervousness which was quite terrifying. I had no clue what I was supposed to do that evening.

When the time finally came, I stood in the middle of a big circle of ladies in a large empty room with fluffy carpets. I asked them to clap their hands and say "ho ho, ha ha" with loud voices. The moment they did that, some of them started smiling and giggling. And then it was like another part of me took over. This part knew exactly what to do when, and I lead a 30-minute session as if I had done that all my life. There was no thinking, just a knowing what to do next, how to give instructions, when to explain more, when to ask them to sit down and when to fire them up again. It just all flowed out of me - without me rationally knowing how.

Totally unexpectedly to me, many of the ladies turned out to be great laughers and cracked up right away. In fact, at some point, we all roared with laughter. It was so loud that the manager of the hotel came to check what had suddenly happened to this group of respectable and elegant ladies. I enjoyed the experience tremendously, and I was particularly touched by the reactions of two ladies in their 60s and 70s who walked up to me and thanked me profusely.

They both told me that they had not laughed for many years since their husbands had passed away. I got goose bumps. The feeling came up that I had received a message on the lines of: *If this is what it can do, you have to continue. What could be better than that?*

And yet, I was still too shy, and too reluctant to take action. It felt like a very scary thing to do. There was the ego that rebelled against the idea that I should go out there to offer sessions in yoga studios and become a clown, making a fool out of myself after I spent so many years working as a serious news' agency journalist, doing academic research, and work hard to make a contribution in the domain of international development cooperation, a much needed and valuable profession. The ego is terrified of any possibility of being laughed at or ridiculed, not to speak of losing status.

It was again Dr. Magda who nudged me forward. She had sent out an email asking the participants of her retreat for feedback on those parts they had liked best as she aimed at offering a compressed one-day version of it in Cairo. She told me that Laughter Yoga had come up as the number one preference and asked me to offer sessions during many of her workshops. This is how I started to lead Laughter Yoga sessions. Quite a few things needed to happen and many people needed to talk to me, nudge me, or push me to jump into it. I feel a lot of gratitude for all of them.

I used to be a very serious person. Laughter Yoga has changed me. I can crack up now and laugh about anything and nothing. When I lead a laugher session, a state of ease descends on me, joy takes over and the session effortlessly flows out. It makes me feel naturally exuberant.

Starting my classes

I gradually started teaching Laughter Yoga in centers. It has not always been an easy process, as sometimes nobody appeared for sessions or trainings that I began to promote mainly on Facebook, which often felt frustrating.

Most people feel a bit shy when they come to attend a session for the first time, just like I did. After all, it is very awkward to be told to laugh out loud for no reason whatsoever. However, most people have transformed in front of my eyes in no time. Participants generally look very different when they leave compared to the impression they made when they came in, and this is an enormously fulfilling feeling.

What I get to hear in nearly every session is a comment on the lines of "people will think that I have become crazy." In most people, there seems to be this fear of being judged as mad. This is the only thing that holds them back from laughing out loud. The conditioning that happened in childhood has repressed the spontaneous expression of joy. The good news is that years of programming can easily be cleared.

I usually tell participants at the beginning of the session that I am not going to teach them how to laugh, because we all know how to do that, but that I am going to break their inhibitions to laugh. Luckily this is usually an easy undertaking because laughter is contagious. Even when only a few people show up for a session, somebody is always a great laugher. This seems like magic to me, but that is my experience. As soon as that one person with this particularly funny way of laughing cracks up, nearly everybody starts laughing. Those who can't laugh during the first session and refuse to fake it have been rare exceptions.

I consider it a blessing to develop the skills for leading a Laughter Yoga session. This is one of the reasons why I feel dedicated and determined to train and certify many Laughter Yoga Leaders. I feel that many people have an undiscovered longing underneath to be offered a safe space where they can give themselves permission to act in ways their rational minds would normally consider silly or crazy.

In fact, the Laughter Yoga activity I love the most is exercising with a support group of breast cancer fighters that I initiated with my friend Ghada Salah Gad and the Breast Cancer Foundation Egypt (BCFE) in Cairo. This group is attended by a large group of women, mostly from socially modest backgrounds and in their fifties or upward. To our surprise, they loved the laughter exercises right from the start. Those women who had a bit of a problem to laugh freely at the beginning cracked up soon when they saw and heard so many others laughing.

We got into the habit of having a picnic in the park where we met after the laughing. Most of them brought dishes of delicious homemade food, and competed with preparing my favorite breakfast items. Most of them looked much happier after the sessions. We all chatted away happily and a lot of heartfelt bonding occurred in those magic moments in this special group of ladies.

The founder of Laughter Yoga keeps encouraging all of us who took his trainings around the world to create Laughter Clubs, where people can meet and practice laughing for no reason together, free of charge. You can find Laughter Clubs in most big cities and many towns all over this planet. Kataria also invites Laughter Yogis to spread joy by taking laughter to hospitals, orphanages, civil society organizations, even prisons, showing us the way by his own example.

Many of the problems afflicting humanity at this point in time could be solved so easily if more and more people would choose to laugh together in groups, and practice laughing at home and at their workspaces. Just imagine how much stress could be shed in schools if students could practice Laughter Yoga regularly. Just imagine how much lighter the atmosphere in hospitals could feel if more Laughter Yoga Leaders and Teachers would encourage patients to laugh with them there. Such a simple and joyful thing could change everything.

Taking laughter yoga into the Arabic media world

Over time, the media developed an interest in my activities. When I was asked for the first time to appear on the show of the popular Egyptian talk show host, Sherif Madkour, I was extremely nervous. It was an enormous challenge for me to talk about the importance of laughter in Arabic. I spent a big part of the night before the show learning expressions and popular sayings by heart. And I did manage to say a few of them on air.

For my second appearance on TV, I was invited by Abu Dhabi TV to fly to the United Arab Emirates together with one of my students, which added additional excitement to the endeavor of spreading awareness. I had to deal with deep seated fears of exposure to be able to do that. Luckily we had each other to share the anxiety and remind each other to giggle and laugh in order to shake it off. We ended up having a great time and enjoyed it like little girls.

Taking this courageous step forward, led to many other unexpected things. One day I received a phone call from the producer of the most famous Egyptian satire show called *Abla Fahita*, who tried to convince me to go on stage two days later. I was on the way to the dentist for a major intervention and was *nonchalant* about it - also because I had never heard of that show. Consulting media savvy friends I learnt that this looked like the chance of a lifetime. So, I called the lady back and agreed to come to the theater that same night to see the setting and discuss details.

When I was told that I would need to walk down stairs to the stage with a spot light appearing on my face and engage the audience in exercises while being filmed, I became very worried. Worst case scenarios of me falling down the stairs and not finding words raced through my mind during that entire sleepless night in which I asked myself what to wear and what to do. The next day I frantically went to the hairdresser, got a haircut, my nails done and my eyebrows plucked.

Then, I bought a new pair of shoes and a new outfit containing a long dark red flowing coat, all the while trying to visualize myself on that stage looking fabulous and facing a large hall of elegantly dressed people in evening robes sitting at little round tables. By doing this, I managed to calm myself down on that important day.

I even enjoyed the trip to the theater, feeling I was on the way to witness something grand. The make-up artist was fabulous, even insisting on gluing on artificial eyelashes. When I was led to sit behind the stage, waiting for the signal to my appearance, I felt happy and tickled like a little girl.

I did manage to walk down those stairs gracefully, however, the moment I stood at the edge of that stage and the spotlights went on, I couldn't see anybody and my mind went totally blank. Luckily, nobody but me noticed how nervous I was when I asked the audience with a voice that was much deeper than normal to stand up and take a deep breath.

Before I knew what was happening, it was already over. The show was a big success. A small part of it was used for a long time in the promo trailer for the *Abla Fahita* show, so that suddenly many people recognized me on the streets and asked to have their pictures taken with me. Even until today, I keep meeting people who tell me they saw me on that show.

Many TV shows followed as well as newspaper interviews and talks, including a TedxYouth talk. I am not as nervous anymore like I was in the beginning, but I am always very exhausted afterwards. Public speaking and media stunts still feel pretty scary. It has often been said that this is the biggest fear – even stronger than the fear of dying.

It is simple to see that this is another situation that I needed to keep feeling, facing and finding my way through fear. What motivates me to go through this kind of extra stress is my conviction that what we all need most to get through these challenging times well and learn to thrive is more laughter. In my own way I keep *Daring Greatly*.

My training as laughter yoga teacher

When I arrived in Bangalore for the first Laughter Yoga Teacher Training, I felt super excited. Many of the participants arrived at a similar time in the middle of the night and we all got to meet each other at the airport. I couldn't wait to finally have a real Indian meal again and, so, I convinced some of them to sit in one of the food stalls to have *dosa*. I felt I had come home.

We were a very international group with some members from Germany, Italy, France, Britain, Australia and South Africa. The team of Dr. Kataria came to pick us up and bring us to the Ancient School of Wisdom, which turned out to be a place of supreme beauty outside the city. This special place is an *ashram* that doesn't belong to any specific guru, or school of yoga and was created by a very spiritual and cultivated lady.

The feminine touch was visible at first sight even in the dark of the night. There was a big lush garden with an incredible richness of trees, bushes and loads of pots with a large variety of flowers obviously loved by large numbers of birds that made soothing sounds during the nights. Many sculptures decorated the entrances to cottages or little apartment complexes. The most surprising thing to me were signs with spiritual quotes on them - awesome visual reminders of wisdom everywhere.

The decoration of each and every single room also had this feminine touch, which allowed for simplicity while not being frugal. So, there were little bedside tables and framed prints of paintings. The large number and variety of pictures and posters of the famous and not so famous grand gurus of India that this lady obviously held in high esteem were absolutely astounding. The whole place gives testimony to the richness of the spiritual heritage of India.

The Ancient School of Wisdom

The Ancient School of Wisdom also contained a library with a stunning collection of numerous books, among them very ancient editions from diverse spiritual teachers not only from India. There were many outdoor areas where one could sit and contemplate and read, unseen by other people. And there was a kitchen cottage that served absolutely delicious vegetarian Indian food. I felt absolutely thrilled to find myself in such a beautiful place.

I had made sure to arrive a day before the start of the training to be able to settle in and not have to start this course after arriving in the middle of the night. The next day, I pottered around in my new temporary home, tremendously enjoying the discovery of every beautiful area or corner I came across. More and more participants started to arrive and when some of them organized a car to go to the next nearby village, I happily went along. We found a small village that contained a little restaurant, a few shops and tea stalls.

I discovered a tiny clothes shop that offered an amazing array of traditional Panjabi dresses and blouses stuffed on shelves that reached until the ceiling where an old fan provided cooler air. When the shop keeper sensed my excitement, he smiled and opened the plastic wrappings of many really beautiful outfits I pointed to. I came out beaming with joy over my purchase of three colorful dresses that looked on me as if I had never been wearing anything else. We all ended up cheerfully eating *Dosa* with fresh coconut curry again and drank the spicy *tschai* tea. This, I thought, was a good omen and an excellent start.

The first day we all met in a large room with many windows and sat in a circle on plastic chairs. A lot of stands showing large photos of laughing people gave our gathering a very professional air. We were also impressed by the large number of newspaper clippings and TV reports that featured the famous *Guru of Giggles*, as he was often referred to in the media. Kataria then asked us to present ourselves in the way of Laughter Yogis.

We had to say our name and laugh, then our country of origin and laugh, as well as our profession. I tensed up immediately. This felt like something very strange and scary to do. However, we all managed some more or less artificial laughter while doing this exercise and then we could laugh more and more the moment somebody else said their name, or profession. This exercise, which is a great way to reduce the identification of the ego, and break the ice, got us into our first round of cheerful laughing. We had a number of great laughers among us.

The training started early in the mornings with breathing exercises and laughter meditations followed by a large Indian breakfast and a long break. I enjoyed the long intervals between the laughter sessions. We needed that not only to feel more at ease and to ground ourselves again, but to relax our hurting face and abdominal muscles. I had never before in my life laughed so much on one single day and realized that it can actually feel tiring.

At some point, we were lying on the ground in a circle and were asked to laugh. We were rolling around, roaring with laughter, hitting the ground or our legs with our hands, tears running down on our cheeks, and we could not stop. The moment we all felt too exhausted to continue and fell silent, gasping for air, somebody started giggling again, and we all cracked up again and again. It was absolutely hilarious.

The training also contained quite a lot of theory, which alternated with the laughter exercises. Kataria made it a point that we all learn the core messages about Laughter Yoga by heart and present them standing, with full self-confidence, in our native languages. We were given ample time to train that in pairs, which turned out to be fun as well. I felt I would need to be able to talk about Laughter Yoga in Arabic, so I decided to present the text in the Egyptian dialect, which had the additional advantage that nobody could notice in case I left something out. It went really well and everybody was cheering wildly because for most of them it was the first time they had attentively listened to somebody speaking Arabic. They loved the sound of it.

We also learned facilitating the art of deep relaxation called *Yoga Nidra* and practiced talking each other with calm deep voices into this state of *yogic sleep,* which was a lovely experience. We learned about the advantages and difference of doing Laughter Yoga with children, with seniors, and in businesses. We were prepared very well to start our own classes as we were provided with soft copy samples for brochures, flyers, roll-ups, business cards and a logo.

One day Kataria asked us to write down the story how we came to Laughter Yoga. He said it would help us to gain clarity and to prepare ourselves to tell our story to our students in the future. This, he said, was an essential part of passing on our skills to others and of promoting our services to larger audiences. He gave us four hours to sit wherever we wanted and write. Below is the story that I wrote back then. It was chosen to be published on his website in an edited version.

How I came to Laughter Yoga

I owe the fact that I became interested in Laughter Yoga to my father, which is a bit of a paradox. My father was a very rational and very serious man; he was an academic with a scientific background who was widely read and traveled. He was proud of his intellectual capacity of getting to the bottom of things through critical questioning. Early on in life, I learned to be skeptical of everything and not to believe in anything blindly.

Rebelling daughters have the tendency to do things totally contrary to how their fathers live, and so it was not astonishing that I developed a keen interest in and passion for ancient spiritual teachings, mystical traditions and yoga. My father was not a happy man. He was not depressed either but he seemed weighed down by his early experiences of being a soldier during the Second World War when he was not even 17 years old. Many Germans from that generation share this heaviness, this atmosphere around them of being weighed down. I didn't want to be like that. In fact, I wanted to be totally different.

Even though I recognized the same rational mind and the same heaviness in me that were so typical for my father, I aspired to become lighthearted, highflying and joyful. While I was drawn to many things that were important aspects of my father's life, such as living an adventurous life outside of Germany and being dedicated to promote intercultural dialogue, I also wanted to have ease, fun and bliss in my life.

I first heard of Laughter Yoga during a seminar where I was told of a lady who was a HAPPINESS FACILITATOR. There was this little voice in my head that said, "I want to do that too." Two years later a friend of mine sent me a link about the World Laughter Day, and that's when I felt drawn to sign up for the teacher training without really knowing what it was all about. I had no clue that it would change my life. My purpose now is to inspire people to feel more joyful and to spread happiness. I have received many incredibly precious talents, gifts and teachings from my father, however, it is perhaps through what he wasn't that I learned the most.

Summary

Sometimes we have to read things over and over again to remember something that seems important to us. At other times, we find ourselves at a junction that turns our lives in a totally new direction in seconds, just because we heard a few words. It was a fateful day was when I first heard the words, *Happiness Facilitator*. Something inside me instantly knew that this is what I wanted to do.

A Laughter Yoga teacher training course I attended, which was taught by Dr. Madan Kataria got us rolling on the floor, tears streaming down our faces from all the laughing. I didn't know before how much I could laugh during one day alone and how exhilarating and yet exhausting this kind of exercise can feel. This training has changed my life, even though I was in need of being nudged forward to develop the courage of going out there and offering Laughter Yoga classes.

Most people seem to worry about what others might think if they saw them laughing out loud. The fear of being judged as a mad person seems widespread. It keeps us from giggling and laughing as we did when we were children. Laughter Yoga connects us to childlike playfulness, which feels very liberating.

As adults, we have nearly completely repressed our most human and most spontaneous expression of joy. This is detrimental to our health and happiness. It also prevents us from bonding naturally with other people from our hearts, and creating deep human connections through laughing together. Most people feel shy when they first come to a Laughter Yoga class. It feels awkward to mimic laughter and to be asked to burst into a hearty laugh for no reason. When we break through these conditioned inhibitions, we feel way more joy in life. It's all it takes.

Just shake off the inhibition that prevents you from laughing loud while you do the dishes or wash the laundry by setting an intention to bring on laughter at will. Fake it until you make it. Start with giggling a bit. It's that easy. It will help you to laugh while walking on a street when you see something funny and don't care one bit anymore what others are thinking.

One wouldn't imagine it, however, laughing for the sake of cultivating happiness takes courage. It's not vulgar. It's not insulting. It has nothing to do with mental illness. It's, therefore, not shameful. It's not a criminal act either. Many problems could be easily solved if more people laughed more. In spite of all this reasoning, laughing loud is still a rebellious act.

In my own way, I keep *Daring Greatly* by advocating Laughter Yoga through appearing on Arabic TV shows. In this way, I keep feeling, facing and finding my way through the fear of public speaking. My message is simple and important. We can all benefit enormously from laughing more. It's a fun way to thrive that can change the world. There's no need to get stuck in anxiety or depression. There's an easy way out that's hundred percent natural and fun. It's called *laughter on purpose for no reason at all*.

In the next chapter, you can read more about it.

"To create our own inner feel good trough deliberately producing endorphins is a basic life skill that I believe everyone should possess. It brings immediate and long-term benefits."

William Bloom

NINE

The Magic of Laughter

Laughter lightens us up immediately. It expands everything in our system. I know of nothing else that gets us out of heavy emotional states in this speed and ease. When we feel worried or sad, we contract. We literally shrink. However, just a little giggling or smiling for one minute can shift us out of it. Laughter is medicinal. It helps us to recover from any disease much faster. It heals us on many levels. It makes us feel happy and free.

A large number of authors and spiritual teachers have written about the enormous value of joy for our health and wellbeing in the past decade. A large number of books has been published and widely read on the pertinent issue of happiness. It points to the fact that a large number of people are searching for a way out of their unhappiness and the many afflictions that come with it.

While the theoretical approach based on the analysis of people's habits who feel content with themselves is very useful to create awareness of possible habit changes, a lot of these publications fall short of offering a practical way to cultivate happiness. Or they overwhelm the reader with a large amount of exercises to undertake. I have never met anybody who actually started practicing some of these exercises on a regular basis after reading a book, or who became happier by reading about joy. The flood of happiness tips that is circulating on the internet more often than not enhances the gloomy feeling that something is "fundamentally wrong" with us.

There is one person who has had the genius to create a simple and fun exercise routine that makes us happier on the spot. The Indian medical doctor, Madan Kataria, truly deserves to be called a genius for inventing a laughter delivery system he aptly called Laughter Yoga. Since its foundation in 1995, this new form of yoga has been spreading all over the world like wildfire, which is a remarkable success story in itself.

Kataria conceived the fantastic idea behind Laughter Yoga when he came across scientific research showing that the human body cannot possibly distinguish between a fake and a real laugh. The same benefits are reaped when we mimic laughter. The amounts of benefits we get from laughing for an extended period of time are astonishing.

Laughter Yoga mainly consists of light stretches, some dancelike movements, breathing exercises, clapping, chanting the mantra *'ho ho, hahaha'* in variations, as well as a mix of slightly funny looking laughter exercises aimed at inducing a state of childlike playfulness. When we laugh for a while, the main thing that happens is that the body gets flushed all over with two important components which we urgently need for experiencing better health and more happiness and which we usually don't have in sufficient quantities: oxygen and endorphins. The biochemical changes induced by the influx of these two elements shift the entire human system into a state of physical and psychological ease and joy.

All body functions are related to breathing

Every cell and tiny particle needs oxygen to function properly. One would think that simply by breathing automatically, as the body does by itself, we would get enough oxygen. However, that is not the case because most of us breathe in a shallow way, which limits our intake of oxygen. We tend to breathe even less deeply when we feel stressed. When, on top of that, we live in polluted cities, smoke, spend little or no time in nature or don't regularly engage in any form of cardiovascular exercises, we are bound to be severely under-oxygenated, which seems to be as devastating as being dehydrated from a lack of water intake.

Breathing exercises, called *pranayama* in Sanskrit, are at the heart of any form of yoga. Their primary aim is to train people to extend the time of exhalation so that it becomes longer than the time of inhalation of air.

In this way, the lungs are getting rid of residual air which contains plenty of carbon dioxide and are replacing it by fresh air that contains large amounts of oxygen. An average inhalation fills our lung capacity with only 25% of air, says Kataria. The remaining 75% (residual volume) remain filled with old stale air.

"To keep our lungs healthy and provide enough oxygen for our bodies to perform at peak levels we need to take deeper breaths and flush the stale air from our lungs," he emphasizes in his presentations. Holford and Lawson go as far as saying that oxygen is the most important nutrient of all. "It accounts for about 80 per cent of your body's make-up; it's a component of water, fat and protein; and when combined with glucose it is what your body uses to make energy."[135]

The secret to breathing deeper is to contract the abdominal muscles, thus ensuring that all the organs located in this lower part of our body are being gently moved and massaged. For many people who have become used to a shallow form of breathing involving only the chest muscles, this can feel difficult. Now take this: The easiest way to exhale longer is laughing. In fact, laughter is all about breathing out a large amount of air with each 'ha ha ha' to the point that we don't even realize how the body manages to breathe while laughing.

The German winner of the Nobel Prize for Medicine, Dr. Otto Warburg, has reportedly stated that deep breathing techniques increase the supply of oxygen to the cells and are the most important factors for living an energetic live free of diseases. He emphasized that "when cells get enough oxygen, cancer will not and cannot occur."[136]

Laughter strengthens the immune system

Laughter Yoga is a very beneficial exercise also for cancer patients. I have tremendously enjoyed doing Laughter Yoga with a large group of lovely ladies who are members of the Breast Cancer Foundation Egypt (BCFE). Profound changes have been witnessed. Many of them have

---

[135] Patrick Holford, Susannah Lawson, The Stress Cure, 2015, p. 91
[136] It is quoted here from the teacher Training Manual of Kataria's Laughter Yoga University, as the quote could not be independently established.

suffered hardships not only because of this potentially life threatening illness they feel determined to overcome, but also due to dire economic pressures. This support group has offered many of these courageous cancer survivors the only space to feel some moments of pleasure and fun. Laughing together has instilled a more optimistic outlook on their lives, and made them realize all the things they can still do, thus, reducing the common anxiety about the future, which creates additional health problems. Many cancer survivors in various parts of the world claim to have benefited greatly from laughter as a complementary option to the other established therapeutic strategy they have chosen to pursue.[137]

The *Laughter Online University*, founded by Sebastian Gendry, has published a large amount of scientific research on their website. This includes articles on the increased flow of lymphatic fluid through laughter, which apparently increases the rate of toxic elimination by as much as 15 times the normal rate. They also documented research on the stimulation of the thymus gland to produce the antibody-producing T-cells, B-cells and gamma interferon which are an important part of the body's defense mechanism, and which makes us less likely to get common coughs and colds as well as more serious illnesses. You can also find research there pointing out that laughter helps with pre-menstrual disorders (PMS) in women's cycles as it is then that the immune system is weakened and the thymus is especially active to compensate.

According to one of the articles I found there, laughter raises our levels of DHEA (dehydroepiandrosterone), which is a steroid hormone produced by the adrenal glands that creates rejuvenation. Many researchers consider high levels of DHEA a marker of health in the body. DHEA, which commonly becomes reduced with age, also has anti-aging, anti-cancer, and anti-obesity effects and can enhance mental abilities. Another study showed that laughter significantly reduces levels of inflammation-triggering cytokines in people with rheumatoid arthritis.[138]

---

[137] See http://www.laughteronlineuniversity.com/laughter-good-mental-health/
[138] The intention of this chapter is not a medical discussion of the numerous benefits of laughter, however, you can consult this website, as well as many other sources for more science based details http://www.laughteronlineuniversity.com

The endorphin effect

It has been widely understood by now that endorphins play an extraordinary role in the pursuit of happiness. They are part of a family of chemicals known as neuropeptides, which carry information around the body. Twenty types of endorphins have been discovered in the nervous system. Generally, they remove stress and pain. They relax tissue by reducing constrictions and increase biochemical fluidity. "Specifically, endorphins enhance the immune system by activating the natural killer cells (NK cells), which destroy defective cells and cancer cells," says William Bloom.[139]

"Endorphins can be produced at any location in the body and they can also flow through the whole system like waves in an ocean," says this holistic teacher, who is prominent in Britain.[140] These amino acids are naturally produced by the human body every time we experience "a moment of pleasure", as Bloom calls it. He makes the astounding statement that endorphins are bio-chemicals that can be found in all living beings, including single-celled creatures. The ability to experience happiness, he argues, is, therefore, biologically built into each one of us because a sense of internal pleasure, or enjoyment, is fundamental to good health. "Happiness and pleasure are built into the biological foundation of the human body," he emphasizes.[141]

The physical experience of pleasure, whatever its original source, say eating ice cream, jogging, enjoying a walk, having sex or playing is produced by the production and release of endorphins into the body. In extreme situations, the body is able to produce endorphins that are a thousand times stronger than chemical morphine, Bloom points out. They also work toward the healing of wounded or diseased tissues. Last but not least endorphins create "euphoria and bliss states in which people experience a deep spiritual connection with nature and the universe."[142]

When body tissue is tense, or 'frozen', the production of endorphins is blocked and the flow of benevolent energy or universal life force energy

---

[139] William Bloom, The Endorphin Effect, 2001, p.21
[140] Ibid, p.22
[141] Ibid, p.24
[142] Ibid, p.6

is inhibited. "You cannot fulfill your potential if you are stewing in the adrenal acid of anxiety and fear," he stresses. When in contrast, our bodies feel comfortable and safe, they act "like a magnet" and absorb large amounts of vital energy.[143]

The elixir of life

In a poetic metaphor, Bloom points out that endorphins can be understood as the legendary golden fluid that gives physical and psychological pleasure, health and confidence and connects us to the beauty of the universe, which the legends of many ancient traditions talked about. In Greece, it was considered as the food of Gods and called *Ambrosia*. In the Hindu mythology, it is mentioned as being made by churning the milk of the 'great cosmic ocean' and was referred to as *Amrita*. Alchemists called it the 'Elixir of Life' or the 'Flower of the Sun' which bestowed the gift of immortality.

Cultivating the flow of this mysterious essence is a strategy that builds a "deep sense of being at ease with the world, without any dependence upon other people or external circumstances," says Bloom.[144] The easiest way to deliberately produce and sustain the free circulation of endorphins in the body is to laugh as a form of exercise.

In Laughter Yoga, we train laughing unconditionally. We don't need anything funny to happen; we can in fact laugh for absolutely no reason. We neither need to be in a good mood, nor do we need a sense of humor, jokes or comedy. We just have to allow ourselves to giggle a bit and then to eventually burst with laughter. With just a bit of practice, it becomes very easy and most pleasant. After all, it's the most natural thing in the world. It's one of those universally human experiences. As little children, we did it all the time. We are made to laugh.

For me, it is not so much this miracle substance itself but the act, the sight and the ring of laughter that could constitute the elixir of life. It is then that we are in a state of oneness and, thus, add pure joy to the magnetic field. Laughter instantly changes everything to the better. "When

---

[143] Ibid, p.48, p.126, p.128
[144] Ibid, p.7

you laugh you change, when you change, everything changes." This is one of my favorite statements of Madan Kataria.

The mind stops when we laugh

One of the many gorgeous things about the nature of laughter is that the mind stops coming up with thoughts when we laugh. The human brain cannot possibly churn up thoughts while the body is laughing, not even when we fake a laugh. And when thinking stops, the mind finally gets a much needed break in order to relax and refresh itself.

The reason why this is really important is that we think an average of 80 to 120 thousand thoughts every day, and most of them are negative or distressing. The mind scans any situation for possible threats and compares incoming data to stored images and impressions of past events to come up with risk assessments. It's a mechanism aimed at protecting us and ensuring the survival of the human race. This made sense in ancient periods of history, however, it's about time to reduce the impact of this useless mental chatter that causes an enormous loss of vial energy.

What's so problematic about it is that nowadays most of us are bombarded with zillions of images just by looking outside the windows of fast moving vehicles, or walking around in malls, and looking at our various devices for extended periods of time. There is an unprecedented amount of visual data that our minds need to process every day. We are badly affected by this amount of mental pollution. It prevents people from thinking in a coherent or focused manner. The widespread lack of concentration negatively impacts our work as well as the quality of our relationships. Forgetfulness is another common complaint. Severe mental disorders are on the rise. Let's face it. Our minds are far from being in good shape.

Because we dream, our minds are even during most of the night busy. And a lot of these dreams are distressing too, because we process the images of all the information that we took in during the day. Only during relatively short periods of deep sleep is there no dream activity. However, sleep deprivation is rampant, and many people get only a few hours of light sleep here and there, which prevents them from experiencing this natural stage of deep sleep that leaves us feeling rested. In fact, a huge amount of people complains about sleeplessness. Tossing and turning in these kind of nights causes an ongoing sense of agony that is on the rise.

One of the few situations the stressed post-modern mind can get the rest it so desperately needs is when we laugh. Laughter stops the relentless thinking and suddenly there is emptiness. This sensation of spaciousness in the mind feels very relieving. It's like the whole system goes *'aaaahhhhh'*. It is in this space that bonding happens naturally. When we can't think a judgmental thought about the person in front of us, the heart can finally take over and expand.

Who hasn't heard or read that we shouldn't judge or think negative thoughts? We've certainly all heard this a gazillion times. However, most of us have no clue how to do that. It doesn't seem like an easy thing to accomplish given the sheer amount of thoughts that arise each day. After all, it is the automatic response program of the human mind to compare people it sees to itself, permanently checking if they look better or worse, richer or poorer, more or less intelligent than we are.

The mind is at the core of what is commonly called the persona, the ego, or the small self. This process of comparison and judgment feels very tiring because it is not in alignment with our hearts and souls. This automatic mental process prevents us from experiencing emotional closeness to other people. And yet, it is exactly those close personal relationships in which we feel accepted, cared for and loved that we yearn for ever so deeply because we are wired for connection.

The wide-spread suffering from overactive minds paved the way for those kinds of self-development teachings to become popular, which suggest various forms of mind control or re-programing. NLP (Neuro-Linguistic Programming) is one method that has become quite known. Using affirmations is another. Observing the mind and consciously choosing to think a positive thought when a negative one arises is something many authors write about in various forms. The Buddhist path of Mindfulness has become so popular that it is increasingly used in schools and companies. While this is surely a positive trend, it is noteworthy that these methods can feel quite tiring, usually don't sustain positive feelings over a longer period of time, and hardly offer practical tools to live in more lighthearted ways.

The ancient Indian system of yoga, often referred to as science, contains numerous meditation techniques that aim at going beyond the mind. Meditation creates stillness in the mind and is a wonderful practice that is very beneficial. It can take a long time of daily practice to reach a stage where we make the wonderful experience of transcending the mind and diving into a realm of infinite vastness of pure consciousness, sometimes referred to as *nirvana* or nothingness, where no objects, no comparison, no judgment, no ego, no mind exist.

Laughter Yoga is the only type of yoga and one of the only self-development practice that catapults you beyond the mind in seconds, right from the very beginning. No prior experience with yoga or meditation is needed. Right away you can enjoy this fantastic state which the Indian Guru Osho refers to as 'no-mind.' Plus, it simply is a most pleasant human experience to laugh together with others. It feels so deeply familiar and essentially good because this is what we did when we were little children.

Children laugh hundreds of times per day

It is obvious that human beings are wired to laugh a lot because little children have been estimated to laugh between 300-400 times per day. It's just that as we grow older, we become more and more serious and bogged down, and we start to censor laughter. Laughter becomes dependent on something funny happening. If we think a joke is inappropriate, we prevent ourselves from laughing. Laughing when we are adults has turned into a mental process that usually depends on our sense of humor. And what if many of us simply don't have a sense of humor and can't laugh about what others perceive to be funny? Madan Kataria, for instance, said of himself that he lacks a sense of humor. Laughter Yoga solves this problem, because it demonstrates beyond doubt that we can laugh for no reason whatsoever.

As adults, we also don't laugh with our bodies anymore. We stopped jumping or rolling around while laughing as we did when we were kids. We have generally become rather stiff and at best laugh tiny little repressed laughs that we ourselves find somewhat awkward or artificial. For most of us, those days are long gone where we would roar with laughter and roll around on the ground. More often than not, we only laugh for a few seconds here and there, which is neither enough to really crack us up, nor to reap the many benefits of laughter, or get us into the heart space.

The importance of childlike playfulness for enchantment

Laughter Yoga is all about allowing the inner child to come out and to play while still being a responsible and coherent grown up. Children make sense of the world and process painful experiences through play, which is more profoundly meaningful than we think. According to the American psychologist Lawrence Cohen, "the single most important skill parents could acquire" is playfulness.[145] If you are a parent, or want to become one, and are interested in creating a close bond to your child, practicing Laughter Yoga might be the best way to go for developing better playing skills.

Cohen, who specialized in play therapy and parenting, points out that play helps children to develop confidence and mastery, serves their "almost bottomless need for attachment, affection and closeness" and helps them recover from emotional distress.[146] He suggests that the best way of parenting is to join children where *they* live, on *their* terms. Play, he says, is one of the best ways to engage with children, to pull them out of emotional shutdown or misbehavior, into a place of connection and confidence.

Parents would do well to become more playful and laugh more often. "Since fun and laughs are the currency of children's play, we might need some work on lightening up a bit," Cohen argues. "When we get disconnected from children – and we do, again and again – play is our best bridge back to deep connection with them," he explains. When children are constantly told what they should and shouldn't do, they have no room to think for themselves and are forced to choose between 'resentful obedience or defiant rebellion' he says. "Playfulness helps them think for themselves, even about serious topics."[147]

Kataria and his Laughter Yoga University have developed a pilot program to include Laughter Yoga in Indian school curricula. Numerous certified Laughter Yoga Leaders and Teachers are offering laughter classes in a growing number of schools in various countries. I have been one of those who gave laughter classes in a school for a while. Many of us discovered that a large number of children in the age of around 8 to 12

---

[145] Lawrence Cohen, Playful Parenting, 2002, p.xii
[146] Ibid, p.6
[147] Ibid, p.26

can't really laugh or play anymore. Sadly, so many children across the globe are severely stressed by the growing demands schools place on them. Many suffer from bullying. And depression among little children is on the rise. All this could be quite easily and cost effectively remedied if Laughter Yoga would be practiced in educational institutions around the globe.

Connecting when laughing together

One of the playing exercises Cohen suggests is the following game: two people look into each other's eyes and see who can keep a poker face the longest time and who first starts giggling or laughing. I find this highly interesting, as the only rule in Laughter Yoga is to keep eye contact with all participants of a group session. When we laugh in a group while looking into each other's eyes, a deep way of relating to others happens naturally by itself. This is a profound human experience that aligns us with our core nature. It creates sparkles in our eyes.

Suddenly, it is as if we are flowing again with life. We are fully awake. There is awareness of the surrounding, and yet there is a natural letting go of all those things that usually bother us. The moment we laugh, none of it matters any more. We are abandoning ourselves in laughter, and at that moment we are reinvigorated on a quantum level.

What I love most about the idea behind Laughter Yoga as well as the practice is that it's simple and easy. It's a fantastic exercise to bring on more lightheartedness and happiness. You don't need to strain into difficult positions or make much physical effort. You don't need special outfits. You can feel the benefits after a single session. You can easily practice it at home just by laughing while doing household chores. You can join a Skype Laughter Club to laugh heartily with others who you don't know and don't see. Or you can join a Laughter Club and find new friends in this way.

I have found that practicing Laughter Yoga is the easiest way to reduce stress and get out of the grip of heaviness. In one of the popular exercises of Laughter Yoga, we lean back and stretch out our arms as if we would like to embrace the whole world. We let the head drop backwards, and we laugh to the sky. This exercise stretches a lot of those muscles in the shoulders, which are often tense and hardened. When we let go into that exercise and simply fake a little giggle first, something starts to feel more fluid and wide. When your muscles are at ease, you flow more with life, you resist less, you are less armored and stiff because resistance drops. Then the movements we do In Laughter Yoga become a dance and our rough edges are gently smoothed out as any sense of pain is washed away.

Effortlessly, we can shift into such superb states of exhilaration. Remember that children can have a tantrum, and before you know what happened, they can suddenly get up and laugh. We have the same capacity. In fact, this is one of the popular Laughter Yoga exercises: we bend down and scream, and then we stretch up and laugh. This game is therapeutical, because a lot of suppressed pain releases. It also helps us to remember our inherent ability to shift our mood within seconds. We have just forgotten about that. However, that playful little kid is still inside, and as we allow it to come out and have some fun, something deep and miraculous happens: Suddenly it's like we are moving to a different tune in a different realm. That's the magic and beauty of laughter.

Summary

The easiest way to deliberately produce and sustain the free circulation of endorphins in the body is to laugh as a form of exercise. It's a fantastic way to lighten up and expand. Nothing else gets us out of heavy emotional states in this speed and ease. Laughter is medicinal. Without much effort, we can shift into superb states of enchantment and exhilaration.

Laughter Yoga is the only type of yoga and one of the only self-development practices I know of that catapults us beyond the mind in seconds, from the beginning. No prior experience with yoga or meditation is needed. Right away, you can enjoy this awesome state which the Indian Guru Osho refers to as 'no-mind.'

The human brain cannot churn up thoughts while the body is laughing. Not even when we fake a laugh. When thinking stops, the mind finally gets a much needed break. It can relax and refresh itself. This sensation of spaciousness in the mind feels very relieving. And it is then that we can finally bond from the heart.

When we laugh in a group, while keeping eye contact, a deep way of relating to others happens naturally by itself. This is a profound human experience that aligns us with our souls and harmonizes interactions with each other. It creates sparkles in the eyes. Suddenly, it is as if we are flowing again with life.

We are fully present in the moment and intensely awake, when we are abandoning ourselves in laughter, and at that moment, we are rejuvenated on a quantum level.

It seems obvious that human beings are wired to laugh a lot more than they usually do, because little children have been estimated to laugh between 300-400 times per day. As we grew older, we have become more serious, and started to censor laughter. Laughter became dependent on something funny happening.

Laughter Yoga is all about allowing the inner child to come out and to play while still being a responsible and coherent grown up. Children make sense of the world and process painful experiences through play. Playfulness and laughter are the best ways to establish connections to children. Parents, as well as educators and teachers could do way better in what they do if they would take this fact seriously enough to consciously cultivate playfulness. Laughter Yoga is one great way of doing it because it's a practice that is simple, easy and effective.

"The path beyond the ordinary mind, all the great wisdom traditions have told us, is through the heart."

Sogyal Rinpoche

TEN

Enchanted with HeartMath

When I got on a plane to travel to the US from Germany, I felt as excited as one can possibly be. A long-held dream of getting to see California was about to come true. It was an incredible thrill, perhaps also because I sensed that the training at the HeartMath Institute that I felt so driven to attend, would open up a whole new world for me. This trip was one of the unforgettable highlights of my life.

I visited two lovely old friends who generously hosted me and showed me around in different areas of California. I sat by the beach in San Diego for many hours, just watching the large array of beautiful looking people with beautiful dogs walking by in front of me. The fact that I blended in better than in some other countries I visited and nobody starred at me made me feel free. I would walk up and down the beach, often stretching out my arms as if getting ready to take off, singing out loud with a big smile on my face. I felt light and happy.

Then it so happened that I sat in chic coffee shops in downtown San Francisco feeling delighted to see so much elegance and style among people walking by. I made amazing new friends who hosted me and took me on a road trip. I ended up visiting Lake Tahoe and drove through the Nevada area. Many times when I entered a diner or a pizza parlor with a jukebox, I felt that I was transported right into the middle of a movie. I just couldn't get over this surreal feeling that things tended to look exactly like in the many Hollywood movies I had seen.

The inner state of thrill I was in was definitely enhanced by the practice of the HeartMath exercises I began doing on a regular basis before the actual training started. This course was very different from any other I have ever attended because it was flanked by six one-on-one coaching sessions, which started two months before the course. Several studies have shown that trainings are way more effective when accompanied by coaching. However, until then I had not seen any organization that took these results seriously enough to actually apply them.

Thanks to the enlightening coaching component, we were well prepared, familiar with the exercises and pretty lighthearted. Through the Skype coaching sessions, I developed much more awareness of my feeling states. My coach carefully nudged me to keep expanding my awareness of my emotions and experiences with bringing on more uplifting feelings at different times of the day, by experimenting and using the exercises in different ways.

At the beginning, I felt more at ease practicing with closed eyes. While practicing the feeling of appreciation, I first brought on little mind movies, containing images of me walking on a beautiful beach with my dogs. Then I felt that my mind got bored after a while with running the same images over and over again. I discovered that sitting comfortably and looking at a bunch of flowers, or trees outside the window was what worked way better for me. It made me come more alive. Just attentively looking at trees while breathing a bit deeper and connecting to my heart automatically filled me with emotions of awe and tranquility.

I was amazed how easy it was and how pleasant it felt to practice shifting into the feeling of appreciation simply by focusing on anything beautiful around me. Before enrolling in this training, I had never even thought that it was possible to change the emotions I was feeling. The ability to willingly bring on the feeling of appreciation is very precious. Experiencing this capability was an enormous realization. It gave me a sense of liberation as I realized that I did not have to bear sad or angry emotions but could switch out of them easily. This realization is in itself very empowering.

The HeartMath Institute

The Institute is perched in a beautiful natural environment among hills, lush green and lots of different types of trees. It's located at the fringes of the legendary Red Forest, which is full of amazing giant trees that have been alive for thousands of years. Moving in a taxi along a narrow curvy road winding itself up the hill, leaving the area of San Francisco Airport behind and driving towards a little town called Boulder Creek, I looked around me, eyes wide open and jaw dropping. I was in awe.

The area of the Institute contains several little houses, one of them a cozy guest house where I was to share a comfortable room for five nights with a lovely lady from Mexico. Each arriving participant was warmly welcomed by a team member and showed to their room. We all felt drawn to explore the garden, which instilled a feeling of wideness as green grass extended quite a distance uphill leading into a forest area. Lots of beautiful little areas could be found where one could sit next to bushes and colorful flowers. An atmosphere of serenity and peace permeated everything.

All members of the Institute seemed to radiate this air of contentment, alert presence and relaxed happiness. It was obvious that they all practiced what they teach. I have never seen anything like that before – not even in some Indian ashrams where some meditation teachers considered as senior members would look grumpy, reacting vague or unresponsive to questions, or even acting in a variety of unfriendly ways to newcomers.

The training included a very large amount of scientific data underpinning the HeartMath system. We were offered the opportunity to absorb a complex Power Point Presentation that was delivered by senior members of the Institute. Delivering the entire Resilience Advantage training can take more than 10 hours, so the amount of facts that need to be explained is quite large. It was fascinating to listen first-hand to research results and anecdotes from Rollin McCraty, Head of Research at the Institute, and we could ask all our questions, which he kept answering patiently.

On top of that, we were divided into small study groups, and were trained to deliver this presentation ourselves. The thought of having to memorize all the information that was supposed to be said to further explain each slide felt overwhelming, to say the least. However, we were gently prepared by being given the task to focus on single modules, which we had to present in our mini-groups.

The team members were requested not only to listen attentively to further integrate the material, but to give each presenter feedback, based on specific rules, including expressing more appreciation than criticism. Still, there was quite a lot of tension breaking out among all of us, and at times performance anxiety took over when we feverishly read through the notes again and again ahead of our turns.

When our heads were fuming, it was comforting to know that soon the time for another tea break with delicious cookies or cakes or another fantastic meal would come along. Three times a day there was a large buffet offering lots of fresh organic salads and vegetables prepared in delicious ways. Just alone the way we were physically nourished was outstanding - beyond what anybody could expect during 'ordinary' training days, and, definitely, far beyond what is usually served in five star hotels.

We sat around large round tables, often in the garden, happily chatting away, and enjoying this special feeling of being cared for so very well. The impressive benefits of bringing on caring emotions for ourselves and others are not only theoretical research results at the Institute. Feeling and observing this team walking their talk created a most positive energy.

The group of around 30 participants was very diverse. Some of them were doctors and nurses, others worked as coaches, energy healing practitioners, trainers or researchers. They came from all over the United States as well as from abroad, which made our discussions so inspiring to the point that we were often hanging out together in the evenings. The positive emotional state we were in thanks to this amazing practice led to profound moments of bonding from the heart.

The value of scientific research

One of the things that amazed me most was that this training was designed to deliver pertinent scientific research results combined with teaching practical exercises. The numerous wisdom traditions and religions emphasizing the role of the heart and the importance of compassion towards our fellow human beings are not mentioned with one word, in spite of the fact that the research of the institute validates these teachings.

It was left to us to clearly see that science has caught up with ancient spiritual insights proving their relevance for everyday life. Now, we can calmly respond to skeptics: *this is science, not spiritual mumbo-jumbo, as you might think when you hear the word heart.*

The Resilience Advantage training addresses very diverse audiences motivating them to add more heart to their daily activities: from corporate businesses, to first aid responders, doctors and nurses, as well as schools, non-profit organizations or military personnel. When we are confronted with research which demonstrates beyond doubt that our heart rhythm is closely interrelated to our feeling state as well as levels of excellence in our daily performance, we are more likely to take this finding seriously and to start practicing the exercises. This is why there is no way around sharing some scientific research in HeartMath trainings – even if it might get slightly boring for some participants sometimes.

Many of my fellow students as well as some of our teachers became very curious about Laughter Yoga, when I mentioned it when introducing myself. They requested that I offer a taste of it. So, on the fourth day of the training during the afternoon coffee break, we gathered on the front lawn and had a blast. They were all great laughers. And, in spite of the high-frequency energy in the venue and the high level of genuine caring we were offered, laughing together still felt like a relief. Our minds got a much needed rest and we felt refreshed and giggly when we returned to class.

I felt happy to receive the permission to include Laughter Yoga in my HeartMath trainings. In the meantime, it is mentioned on their website that it is officially permitted to all certified trainers to integrate modules, or parts of them, into other training programs. I think that Laughter Yoga is a particularly good match for the HeartMath program. While this new form of yoga also reduces heavy feeling states caused by stress or depression, there's no theory that needs to be delivered. Instead of deliberately thinking thoughts to bring on emotions, it's about mimicking laughter. Allowing yourself to be goofy and silly is a needed counterpart to taking in big chunks of serious research.

As the training drew to an end, I felt like some major pieces of a puzzle fell into place. It was like I finally got answers to things that I kept putting in question and that had been bothering me about my rather unsuccessful attempts to cultivate positive thinking and focus on repeating affirmations.

It also confirmed some of my core beliefs. I felt incredibly pleased that now I had the arguments based on scientific data to back up my convictions. My mind and my heart were equally enchanted, which is exactly the alignment the HeartMath system helps create.

People expect action packed fun trainings

It has become a common expectation that trainings are supposed to be packed with action, which allows participants to interact. Many people seem to feel more unwilling to sit and listen for many hours like we used to a few decades ago. The top down approach which we had to endure in schools and universities, as well as many boring trainings we have attended, simply doesn't work anymore.

The minute there's some knowledge presented that challenges the mind, some people pull out their phones and drift off into the more colorful virtual world that is constantly provided by social media. This addiction makes it harder for trainers nowadays to get through to the hearts and minds of their audiences. Whatever the reasons are, the question is how to take this development into consideration and tailor workshops that are providing science-backed knowledge, super-useful exercises, as well as fun action.

My experience is that the human mind needs to be convinced to do something before we can develop the motivation to start actually doing any exercise on a daily basis. We also need to like what we are doing. There is hardly anything more convincing than presenting scientific research results flanked with technology that measures the heart rhythm and projects that live on a screen. It is then that widespread prejudices or misconceptions against yet another New Age method or fluffy exercise developed by some Life Coach somewhere dissolve into thin air.

I have also discovered that most people simply won't commit to doing any exercise that was presented to them in a one-time training seminar that lasts a couple of hours. Unfortunately, there is a trend in companies to demand shorter and shorter trainings from providers, because they come cheaper and consume less time. This is not a feasible approach towards something as important as reducing stress and anxiety among teams with the aim to boost their performance, productivity, and output.

The HeartMath system is best delivered in several sessions, because only then participants can share feedback that is based on real personal experience. When facts are presented in various ways, major results are repeated, a variety of exercises are practiced together during sessions that allow time to pass between them, it can then sink in that this system works. One could hear from a trainer that some effort is required to reap significant benefits, and be quite convinced about how nice that would be, and yet still not do what it takes to practice an exercise on a daily basis. Hearing from colleagues what they experience while practicing the exercises can significantly enhance the motivation to recommit doing them.

We are humans after all, and for most of us, it's not easy to do something that's good for us and stick to it. This is a major challenge. And it's the main reason why I believe that HeartMath coaching is ultimately more effective than the best HeartMath training, or that particularly this training is best flanked with coaching sessions. For companies this insight would obviously entail extra costs.

My hope is that the education sector is picking up on HeartMath with more ease. My vision is that HeartMath and Laughter Yoga will be taught in schools. Just imagine how wonderful it would be when children and teenagers are enabled to shift out of unpleasant emotions any time they want to. Just imagine how many mental health problems rampant in schools all over the world nowadays could easily be solved. The new world could easily contain children and teenagers who feel happy.

Passing it on

It keeps giving me a lot of joy to give training sessions that contain the main elements of the HeartMath system. I have delivered some trainings for corporates, and numerous training sessions for educators and parents in schools and nurseries, which were received very well. I usually include laughter exercises to fire participants up and give them an opportunity to develop more childlike playfulness.

These are also major elements within a group coaching course designed for students of the Egypt Montessori Center which offers a two-year certification course for early childhood educators in Cairo approved by

Montessori Educational Programs International (MEPI) in the United States. During the half-day sessions, several issues are covered aimed at building essential life skills pertinent to educators. Among them are self-esteem, goal setting, authentic communication, ways to deal with the inner critic, and ways to heal the inner child. Intelligent ways to effectively reduce stress by self-regulating energy levels are at the core of this training.

Most of the participants are young women who feel enthusiastic about learning all they can about Maria Montessori's unique approach to early childhood education. Next to this rather challenging two-year training course, most of them have jobs, as well as husbands and children to take care of, not to speak of having to cross large parts of Cairo, bearing increasingly chaotic traffic jams and pollution, to juggle all these demands. So, their stress levels are pretty high.

This is why they understand well how beneficial it is to be armed with effective tools that make them feel better and give them an extra edge in a profession, which is as important as it is stressful. It is usually very surprising to these participants when they first hear that the children they deal with on a daily basis automatically pick up on their emotions and are influenced by the magnetic fields their own hearts emit.

It doesn't take much of a woman, wherever in the world, to grasp immediately that learning how to create coherence in her own heart rhythm is one of the most fruitful contributions she can make to the healthy development of her child. Women are more practical when it comes to these matters. They are also intuitively more attuned to attending to the wellbeing of their children.

Perhaps this is one of the reasons why so many more women than men are interested in developing themselves. Most workshops in the area of self-development, self-care, coaching or healing in any form are mainly frequented by women. Some of them are getting increasingly tired of the fact that they can hardly share their interests, or the things they have learnt with their men-folk. I feel that men have more and more catching up to do.

A man might be mentally convinced that practicing HeartMath increases his effectiveness and helps him perform better at his job, however, this conviction alone might not be enough to induce a change in his daily habits. The idea of contributing to the wellbeing of his children also doesn't necessarily get a man off the couch. What does is chronic pain, illnesses, sleeplessness, or mild versions of depression suffered through for quite some time. At least, those are the reasons that male clients have come to me seeking support through coaching. And it is then that real progress can be first made.

Women usually don't seem to lump around that long before they are ready to seek out professional assistance. However, in these times of extremes, a large number of women are not only the main caregivers but increasingly also the main financial providers for their children. It is still so very common among women to put themselves last on the long list of people and things that need to be taken care of first. So, even though there are more women interested in seeking assistance from a coach, or a holistic healing practitioner, huge numbers of us are habitually haunted by financial worries and feel reluctant to spend any on ourselves. Especially in financially difficult times, mothers have this instinctually ingrained habit of rather coming up with the means to send their children to a coach, instead of seeking help with enhancing their own parenting skills and developing ways to model a joyful life.

Observing these tendencies got me to a place of tailoring training workshops which emphasize the logic behind prioritizing our own wellness. In view of the dire consequences of self-neglect and the amount of heavy emotions related to it, it's important to be introduced to methods that are real game changers. Actively inviting more lightheartedness into our lives creates big breakthroughs. Observing that in oneself and in others is incredibly thrilling.

Summary

It's easy and pleasant to practice shifting into feeling appreciation simply by focusing on something beautiful around you, such as a plant or a painting, while slightly slowing down your breath.

Before enrolling in the resilience advantage training of the HeartMath Institute, it had never even occurred to me that it was possible to change the emotions I was feeling. The ability to willingly bring on any uplifting feeling is radically liberating.

We don't have to bear heavy emotional states for long periods of time but can switch out of them within minutes. With practice, it becomes easier not to feel that badly affected by people acting out their dramas around us. This is indeed empowering.

It doesn't take much of a woman, wherever in the world, to grasp that the ability to create coherence in her own heart rhythm is one of the most fruitful contributions she can make to the healthy development of her children and loved ones.

Trainings are way more effective when accompanied by coaching. One reason is that a coach ensures that lessons learnt are implemented and carried forward in a bigger process of change at work.

Most people won't commit to doing any exercise presented to them in a one-time training seminar that lasts a couple of hours. It seems to me that even less people would start practicing exercises just because they read how beneficial they are in a book. Prove me wrong and go to the last section of this book, pick one or more of the exercises outlined there, and do them!

There is a trend in businesses to demand short and shorter training formats from providers, because they come cheaper and consume less time. Something as important as reducing stress and anxiety among employees in order to increase their effectiveness and maximize output cannot be achieved through short and boring off the mill training sessions. It's about time to rethink and revolutionize the way training courses and workshops are delivered in companies and other sectors.

The HeartMath system can only be effective when the exercises are practiced. To ensure motivation to practice among participants in trainings, it is most effective to deliver the various modules in several sessions. Only then participants can share feedback based on their own experience. When facts are presented in various ways, major results are repeated, and a variety of exercises are practiced, it can sink in that this system produces remarkable results.

One-On-One HeartMath coaching sessions are well worth the investment. You can read more about the enormous impact emotions have on our system and how they affect every aspect of our lives in the next chapter.

"It's time for more heart on the planet. As people learn how to manage their emotions from the heart, then a new intelligence and understanding can emerge"

Doc Childre & Deborah Rozman

ELEVEN

The Power of Positive Emotions

The emotions we feel directly influence our heart rhythms, and that rhythm produced by our heart determines just about everything else. All our religions, wisdom traditions, and mythologies talk about the heart as the seat of the soul and the doorway to the spirit. For ages, a lot of emphasis has been placed on cultivating heartfelt feelings, like compassion, gratitude, forgiveness and love. Most of us just haven't known how to do this.

At the present time the mind has taken the front seat for most of us, and the intelligence inherent in our hearts as well as the power of our emotions is still widely ignored, or underestimated. One thing is for sure: the importance of a harmonious heart rhythm for our wellbeing, success and quality of life cannot possibly be overstated. Rigorous research undertaken by scientists of the Institute of HeartMath over more than two decades has proven that emotions are the primary drivers of the human physiology.

Heavy emotions lead to increased disorder in the heart's rhythms and in the autonomic nervous system, thereby, adversely affecting the rest of the body. In contrast, positive emotions create increased harmony and coherence in heart rhythms and improve balance in the nervous system.

The reason why it's so simple to consciously create such a tremendously important change is that the brain associates a smooth and coherent heart rhythm with feelings of ease, joy, appreciation, security or wellbeing.

In a nutshell: The heart rate variability pattern, as they scientifically call it, informs the brain how the body feels. HeartMath research has shown that shifting our attention to the physical area of the heart, combined with slightly slowing down our breath and generating a positive feeling is a quick way to create smoothness and balance in the heart rhythm.

A direct link exists between emotions, brain-function and heart rhythms which can be measured and displayed by cutting-edge technology developed by the institute in California. This technology demonstrates on a screen what happens to the heart rate rhythm when we focus on feeling any uplifting emotion, such as appreciation or gratitude. A heart rhythm pattern that was chaotic and jagged emerges as a pattern that becomes wavier, more flowing, with less edgy ups and downs, right in front of your eyes, when doing such a simple exercise, within minutes. When that happens, everything in our body goes into synchronicity and we perform at our best. Even better, resilience builds up.

The HeartMath® System — a science-based way to reduce stress & anxiety

There's so much genius behind the HeartMath system that most people feel fascinated when they see it happening on a screen. Inventing an effective way that enables people to cultivate balance in this central organ in their body, and on top of that, proving beyond doubt that this produces great physiological, mental and emotional results is a pretty mindboggling thing to do. The explanation of the numerous benefits this practice generates could fill many books.

Through the HeartMath exercises, we can develop a calm yet upbeat and alert emotional and mental state. This leads to more inner strength and resilience in the face of any form of adversity, including crisis or diseases. These techniques were developed for busy people to use on the go. They are successfully practiced by management teams of top companies, as well as Olympic athletes, first aid responders, doctors and nurses as well as military personnel and students in the U.S. and around the world.

Over five million people have transformed their stress in this way. This in itself is a remarkable achievement, accomplished by a comparatively small team of inspired individuals living and working close to Silicon Valley, right at the fringes of the Red Forest. What makes this a unique approach to transforming stress, anxiety or depression so effective is the fact that the practice re-patterns and re-structures our inner emotional landscape so that healthier perceptions, feelings and attitudes become a more automatic and familiar way of being.

HeartMath research results demonstrate clearly that a big part of the stress we suffer from is related to the amount of negative emotions we feel, which reduces the proper functioning of major systems and depletes the amount of vital energy available to us in the body. It follows logically that the key to stress reduction and more inner balance needs to aim at reducing the negative reaction patterns to draining emotions by increasing those emotions that nourish us. This can be done easily through practicing simple exercises regularly that access the power of the heart.

This is a big deal because depression and anxiety are epidemic

When we worry a lot, then the rhythmic patterns that this emotion creates in our body - not only in the heart but also our respiratory, digestive and hormonal rhythms, as well as patterns of muscular tensions and facial expressions- become so familiar that we don't feel comfortable when we're not worrying or anxious. The brain keeps shifting to anxious thoughts and feelings as this is the known path which creates the least resistance. It becomes a default mode. The brain simply considers the familiar to be more comfortable. This is how anxiety becomes a habit, an automatic response to stressful thoughts and feelings.

Without effective intervention, anxiety or other draining emotions can become self-perpetuating and self-reinforcing, write Doc Children and Deborah Rozman. "The way to interrupt this cycle is to introduce dynamic new patterns and to reinforce them until they become familiar, thus establishing a new reference pattern. Once a new reference pattern becomes stabilized, your system will strive to maintain a match with this new baseline."[148] This is important in view of the fact that depression is now one of the most disabling conditions in the world.

Depression is commonly classified into three types: low-level depression (dysthymia), major depression and bipolar disorder. Numerous types of anxiety disorders have become very common too, including: generalized anxiety disorder, obsessive-compulsive disorder, panic disorder, Phobia disorder, Post-traumatic stress disorder, etc. Anxiety keeps the body flooded with stress hormones that drain vital energy, which is one of the main reasons for chronic fatigue.

Its intensity varies from unease, worry, strong fear to panic attacks. It could last for a short or a long time. Anxiety makes us feel impatient, irritable, more self-judgmental and prone to explosions of anger, which then often leads to feelings of guilt and consequently depression. What makes matters even worse is that anxiety often propels addictive behaviors, such as abuse of alcohol, drugs, food, shopping, sex or doing anything in extreme ways.

Anxiety often becomes chronic. Most people don't know how to release anxiety. Some techniques have become quite popular, such as visualization, mindfulness meditation or various relaxation methods. However, many of them are only temporarily effective and wear off quickly because the underlying causes have not been addressed.

The same goes for popular psychological treatments, including cognitive behavioral therapies (CBT), that aim at helping people to take a more rational approach towards thoughts and better control their reactions. It is based on the tenant that emotions always follow thoughts and that, therefore, by changing our thoughts we could gain control over our emotions. Childre and Rozman emphasize that, "too often CBT does not release or transform the underlying feelings of anxiety."[149]

You can't release or turn emotions around with the mind

Researchers explain that emotions can be triggered by thoughts, however, emotional processes can operate at a much faster speed than

---

[148] Doc Childre and Deborah Rozman, Transforming Anxiety, 2006, p.7
[149] Ibid, p.4

thoughts. They can also arise totally independently from the cognitive reasoning process. In fact, emotions often occur due to unconscious associations based on memories of events, or beliefs we were raised with. For example: If we became ill from eating something, the smell of it makes us feel nauseated even much later in life. "Or if you were raised to believe that people of a certain race or culture are violent and untrustworthy, then just seeing a person from that culture can trigger fear, even though your rational mind knows better."[150]

Childre and Rozman point out that feelings and thoughts are separate, yet interacting functions, which communicate through two-way neural connections between the cognitive and emotional centers in the brain. Science has shown that the neural connections from the emotional to the cognitive center are stronger and more numerous than vice versa. This is a fascinating fact which deserves to be given more attention.

Most therapeutic or self-development approaches, including coaching, focus on changing thought patterns and challenge underlying beliefs or fears by turning them around into positive statements and affirmations. Childre and Rozman succinctly put it like this: "The theory is that if you change your thoughts and beliefs, then your feelings will change. But this is not always the case. Feelings and emotions become habitual and often have a life of their own."[151]

This finding is interesting for several reasons: It shows that the widespread concept that emotions are always preceded by thoughts is erroneous. It helps explain why therapies or practices that focus entirely on controlling or re-programming the mind don't work for many people. It explains why emotional attitudes can disrupt the thinking process and get to dominate thinking. It also shows why the attempt to keep strong emotions under control through thought alone seems like a waste of time and energy. What is different about the HeartMath solution is that it addresses emotions directly.

Childre and Rozman emphasize that people can't just turn emotions around with the mind or clear deeply ingrained feelings or beliefs that haunt them from incidents in the past. "You can't pray, affirm, talk or rationalize feelings and beliefs away. You have to restore your missing

---

[150] Ibid, p.5
[151] Ibid, p.15

connection with your heart," This kind of transformation, they argue, requires a different power of intention which has to be drawn from the heart.[152]

Emotional self-management is empowering

The HeartMath solution empowers people to take responsibility for their own emotional energy management, which leads to the unfolding of heart intelligence. "Until the emotions are regulated, even the most helpful insights cannot be translated through the nervous system and integrated into people's attitudes and lives. Transforming stress, anxiety or depression effectively happens through *resetting your patterns and regridding your emotional response system.*"[153]

Much of the research underlying the HeartMath approach is based on measuring *heart rate variability* (HRV), which measures the time elapsing between heart beats. It is an important indicator of the functioning of the autonomic nervous system. The autonomic nervous system is regulating our hormonal system, immune system, digestion, elimination, sleep and nearly everything that occurs automatically in the glands and organs. A healthy and well balanced autonomic nervous system is vital for health and wellbeing.

Most commonly, however, the two branches of the autonomic nervous system, the Parasympathetic which slows the heart rate and the Sympathetic, which fires us up, are far from being in any kind of balance. This is partly why we experience so many ups and downs in life. The argument that we should forget about balance because life is messy and we live in an up-side-down world is very familiar to me.

Living in a super chaotic city like Cairo, I have sympathized with this idea for a while. I thought it was kind of impossible to create more balance in my 'outer' life when everything seemed to be about learning the skills to surf the cross currents and navigate the constant flux in order to keep floating with my head held high and not drown in the madness of

---

[152] Childre and Rozman, Transforming Depression, 2007, p.7
[153] Ibid, p.14

it all. I still think there's something to this badass argument, and yet, like everything else, it's a matter of perspective.

What changed the way I feel about creating inner balance now is the deeper understanding that the common condition of utter imbalance in our nervous systems creates havoc in the body, which, among other things, leads to a shut-down of our thinking abilities or our immune systems. Yes, it's that dramatic what a 'normal' stress response, commonly referred to as 'fight or flight' does. Even the digestive system can be shut down for anywhere between six to twelve hours. This, I think, is a strong point for consciously building more harmony in our heart rhythms.

What makes the heart so important?

One of the facts I find most fascinating about the HeartMath research is that the heart is the largest source of electromagnetic energy in the body. An electrocardiogram (ECG), commonly used in clinics, shows the electrical signals produced by the heart. Every time the heart beats, it produces electricity. Take this: The heart produces 40-60 times more bio-electricity than the brain.

According to basic physics, where electricity is produced, a magnetic field is created. The heart produces a magnetic field that extends over 3-4 feet, or around one meter, all around our bodies, 360 degrees. And this is only what can currently be measured by an instrument called a magnetometer. It is most probable that it extends way further than that, and just can't be measured yet.

The brain also produces a magnetic field, however, it's way smaller than that of the heart. It radiates only one inch, not even three centimeters, away from the head. In contrast, the electromagnetic field of the heart penetrates every cell of our bodies and extends into the space around us carrying and emanating a whole lot of information about us.

This magnetic field we emit changes according to how we feel. When we feel negative emotions, it produces a range of waves that are erratic and incoherent. When we experience emotions that are commonly associated with the heart qualities dearest to us, like affection, appreciation, or gratitude, a more harmonious, or coherent, range of wavelengths are broadcasted. So, whether we are aware of it or not, like it or not, the emotions we feel make an impact on everything and everybody around us.

Our electromagnetic fields, which are not the same as the aura which some people gifted with clairvoyant skills can see, are sending out data on our feelings in the same way as a mobile phone or TV set does. We pick up on the fields of others and are constantly influenced by them. Science can now explain why we can instantly feel good around some people or in some places or feel immediately repelled.

Another little known fact is that the heart has its own complex nervous system that operates and processes information independently from the brain or the nervous system. It has been termed "heart brain."[154] This understanding comes from research in a field called Neurocardiology. The heart's nervous system contains around 40.000 neurons, or sensory neurites, which detect a large number of processes and sends this information to the brain.

In fact, the heart sends far more information to the brain than the brain sends to the heart. Imagine that this research result has been known since the late 1800s and was largely ignored. What makes this piece of information important is the fact that the neural signals which the heart sends to the brain affect brain centers involved in decision-making, creativity and self-regulation. This is how important the heart brain is.

The heart has also been classified as a hormonal gland. It produces a hormone called atrial natriuretic factor (ANF), which among other things reduces the release of the stress hormone cortisol. That means that the heart interferes on its own when too much stress hormones are produced by the nervous system. It was also discovered that the heart produces the pleasure inducing substance dopamine and secrets the love or bonding hormone oxytocin, which are still widely considered to be released only by the brain. "Remarkably, concentrations of oxytocin in the heart are as high as those found in the brain."[155]

The research undertaken or gathered by the HeartMath Institute validates what the ancient Egyptians knew all along about the importance of the heart. It's time to honor this knowledge by understanding that the

---

[154] HeartMath Research Center, Science of the Heart, 2001, p.4
[155] Ibid, p.6

heart is the quint essential force to actively engage in becoming more lighthearted.

Life is dead without emotions

Emotions have often been called humanity's 'universal language'. We all feel the same kind of emotions, just at different times and in varying degrees. Emotions allow us to feel the taste and texture of life. Emotions are what makes life juicy and worthwhile. They fuel our actions and move us forward. Without them, life feels boring and meaningless.

We all experience emotions that uplift us, as well as those that feel unpleasant and create a nagging sort of emotional stress that drains our energy. Usually, we oscillate between those poles. The most common response to those emotions that feel painful is that people try to push them aside or distract themselves in all possible ways so they manage to ignore them.

Numerous psychologists have attempted to classify emotions into different categories and identify a small number of core emotions. Most people are more aware of those emotions that make them feel miserable, in spite of the widespread attempt to shut them out. Sooner or later, they reach a point where they, "feel sick and tired of feeling so miserable," as one of my clients put it. So it might be useful to name those emotions that seem to be a part of the experience of joy. They contain appreciation as a core element, as well as gratitude, enchantment, enthusiasm, fascination, contentment, acceptance, expansion, fulfillment, peace and bliss.

A great way to look at emotions has been presented by the American Psychotherapist, Tara Bennett-Goleman. She argues that emotions are a force that can either separate or connect us: "The road in life forks at every moment, with one part leading toward confusion, separateness, and entanglement, and the other toward clarity, connection, and mental freedom."[156] In fact, a lot of research has shown that happy people engage in communicating with fellow human beings wherever they are, which makes them feel appreciated and connected. Feeling connected is a major aspect of joy.

---

[156] Tara Bennett-Goleman, Mind Whispering, 2013, p.8

Bennett-Goleman beautifully describes deep levels of connection she has witnessed or learned through communicating without words with horses: "In horse whispering, this deep connection is called 'joining up', and we cherish it in our lives whenever and however it occurs. In those moments, any sense of separateness dissolves and it's like we are one being, replete and perfectly in a shared cocoon. There's an invisible link." She points out, that 'joining up' is an experience of our interconnection and 'natural relatedness.'[157]

Such genuine connections can arise when we feel a genuine bond with another being. However, they can also happen spontaneously in any number of ways – for instance, through creative absorption, dancing, from being in a state of awe about the beauty of nature, or in meditative immersion. Bennett-Goleman points out that "when we shift into such a flow of being, we embody a pattern that connects." What happens in those moments is "a deep sense of wellbeing, security, and receptivity pervades our hearts." It brings out our positive qualities, allows us to perform at our peak and opens ourselves to a deep resonance with others.

In contrast, the patterns of disconnection interrupt this flow of being. "In these disconnecting patterns, we may find ourselves feeling insecure, holding to distorted views, acting in self-focused or dysfunctional ways, and tuning out." She points out that these patterns create a "fog of bewilderment moving through the mind" creating disconnecting emotional patterns and obscuring clear awareness.[158]

As much as people are longing to feel connected, one of the factors that leads to isolation and a sense of separation is stress. "When people are overloaded with stress, it's hard to connect with anything or anyone, whatever they believe," Childre and Rozman emphasize. This alone, they say, can lead to depression.[159] One of the most painful results of anxiety and depression is that it makes us feel so disconnected to everyone and everything.

Disconnection is a result of the fact that so many people have been conditioned to shut down feelings as a defense mechanism when emotional distress seems to have become too much to bear. The fear of feeling painful

---

[157] Ibid.,p.6
[158] Ibid, p.8
[159] Childre and Rozman, Transforming Depression, p.6

emotions is very wide spread. It leads to separation as well as avoidance strategies that are unhealthy and ultimately increase our problems.

Avoidance of emotions comes with a hefty price tag

The American psychologist Jay Uhler points out that early on in life we have learned from our families of origin that some emotions were deemed 'good' and others branded as 'bad', which usually leads to the experience of confusion and inner conflicts in life. Uhler emphasizes that most people grew up in what he calls the 'Hurtful, Frightening Family' where the articulation of positive emotions was shunned. Expressing fear or pain was also not accepted, even though there was a large amount of both bottled up inside family members who engaged in never ending conflicts. "In the Hurtful, Frightening Family affection is seldom or never expressed. There is fear of physical or emotional contact. There is an avoidance of emotional connecting for fear of being hurt."[160]

Uhler argues that people who cannot allow themselves to experience and express negative feelings usually cannot express the positive ones either, as the repression may get generalized to all feelings. The issue with repressing emotions is that they don't leave us alone and hang around, just waiting for any chance to be felt and unleashed. "Feelings are like gas," says Uhler. "The more you try to repress or stifle them, the more pressure they develop until they burst through the constricting container."[161]

"These repressed emotions often rule our perceptions and decisions without our being aware of it," point out Childre and Rozman.[162] "Repressing feelings creates a free-floating anxiety, and you feel anxious without knowing why," they argue.[163] People who carry a whole lot of bottled-up unpleasant emotions feel very heavy. They are like walking time-bombs. The trigger could go off any moment, and they then explode. When anger that's been habitually repressed over a long time bursts open, it could be dangerous.

---

[160] Jay Uhler, How to make friends with your feelings, 1993, p. 36
[161] Ibid, p 199 and p.20
[162] Childre and Rozman, Transforming Depression, p.16
[163] Childre and Rozman, Transforming Anxiety, p.17

According to Childre and Rozman we live in "a worldwide environment of anger" that exerts a magnetic pull drawing people into reactivity.[164] One of the main problems we face when these darker feelings have become dominant in our emotional landscape is a state of emotional density can build up that filters out the pleasant emotions. The sparkle we used to feel in certain situations, the inspiring moments, and the satisfaction we derived from the small things and the daily activities have left. The thrill is gone.

When anxiety or sadness take over, even those experiences that felt like a reward before don't elicit a joyful response anymore, leading to a chronic feeling of dullness. And as the emotional connection to others is gradually reduced or lost, people plunge into a 'dead zone.' I think it is no coincidence that many films shown lately on international TV channels feature zombies with gruesome looks and horrible details. A large amount of people walking around in the streets staring at their mobile phones seem to be totally unaware of and unresponsive to their immediate surroundings. Too many people seem to be imprisoned in an advanced state of zombification.

What is so shocking about this is the obvious lack of connection: connection to self, to others, to the environment, to the planet, to spirit. The reason I find this so shocking is that universal emotional needs of human beings include the need to care and be cared for, which is expressed and experienced through connection and affection. It seems that the epidemic of stress cuts more and more people off from opportunities to satisfy their natural needs and human desires.

It is remarkable how many people across social strata and professions are utterly unaware of the emotions they are feeling. "Most people who suffer from anxiety have problems admitting their feelings," explain Childre and Rozman.[165] When I ask participants in my workshops to name some of the feelings they felt over the past month, their faces usually go blank. At the most, they can identify anger or sadness. Therefore, I find it quite useful to check out lists or maps of emotions, drawn up by various authors. The one I find most inspiring is a nuanced list of feelings we feel when our needs are satisfied or when they remain unsatisfied. It

---

[164] Childre and Rozman, Transforming Anger, p.11
[165] Childre and Rozman, Transforming Anxiety, p.49

can be downloaded from the website of Marshall Rosenberg's Center for Non-Violent Communication.[166]

Highly interesting is also the Map of Consciousness developed through muscle testing by the psychoanalyst David Hawkins. He attempted to prove that thought patterns and their corresponding emotions present themselves in consciousness as an attitude that creates an energy field which is measurable. "In the field of psychoanalysis, positive attitudes are called welfare emotions, and the negative ones are called emergency emotions," points out Hawkins.

He goes on to say that chronic immersion in emergency emotions results in physical or mental ill health and a gross weakening of one's personal power.[167] Interestingly this categorization is in line with that of the HeartMath Institute, which distinguishes between nourishing and depleting emotions. This distinction is helpful because we can easily figure out whether an emotion feels warm and giving or cold and draining.

Hawkins points out that all that is really necessary to overcome negative attitudes is a sincere desire for change that leads to a decision point. "All that is really necessary is to expose oneself to a high-energy field and one's inner attitudes will spontaneously begin to change," he emphasizes.[168] The HeartMath approach seems to go further as it demonstrates that we have the ability ourselves to elevate the energy field we emanate by choosing to feel a nourishing emotion. Their observation is that regular practice for several weeks creates a new baseline of habitual emotional responses. That means that mental-emotional attitudes transform quite easily by feeling our way into more high frequency emotions. Obviously, this requires awareness and acceptance of the whole range of feelings we can go through in a single day.

"If you do not experience your feelings, then you have learned that your feelings are unacceptable, and you have blocked them from your awareness, or numbed them out," says Uhler.[169] He adds that we are only in control of our lives to the extent that we are able to be aware of and deal

---

[166] Marshall Rosenberg, https://www.cnvc.org/Training/feelings-inventory
[167] David Hawkins, Power vs Force, p.225
[168] Ibid, p.225
[169] Uhler, p.20

with our emotions. Facing the feelings and becoming conscious of them is the only way to get out of the dead zone and come more alive.

The idea of owning up to our emotions makes many of us feel exposed and vulnerable. However, once we admit to ourselves or somebody else that we feel anxious, we start diminishing the power of anxiety over us. Plus, it's only then that we can take one step further and counterbalance or neutralize the disruptive effects that emotional processing has in form of lots of thoughts and feelings churning in the background which don't allow us to think clearly. It's then that we can remember to do an exercise to shift out of it.

"We cannot have joy in our lives, until we deal with our pain, anger, fear, and helplessness," Uhler stresses.[170] 'Befriending' our feelings, as he calls it, is the way to go. The Indian sage Osho puts it this way: "Once you have learned to face your misery, you start becoming joyful, because in the process of facing it the misery starts disappearing and you start becoming more and more integrated."[171]

One of the exercises of the HeartMath solution is to take a few minutes in which we breathe a bit deeper and focus on the heart, allowing ourselves to feel any unpleasant emotion in the heart and then imagine that it dissolves and eases out of our bodies. This practice makes you feel less helpless and more in charge – especially in times of acute stress or illness. It is about feeling the feeling, accepting it and then shifting out of it with intention.

Pursuing happiness is counterproductive

The reason why so many people are seeking happiness is that so many people feel miserable. "Rarely can you find a human being who is not miserable. It is so rare that it almost seems unbelievable," says Osho.[172] He stresses that the desire for happiness simply shows that "you are not happy right at this moment." This one of the reasons why the ultimate aim behind any goal people pursue is happiness. Whenever I ask any coaching

---

[170] Uhler, p.217
[171] Osho, Joy, the Happiness that comes from Within, 2004, p.48
[172] Ibid, p.39

client for the reasons behind the desires to get a promotion, to lose weight, to get married, or whatever it is they are setting out to accomplish, the answer is about the expectation of happiness the achievement of that goal would bring.

It's strange that there seems to be a widespread tendency among people forgetting that they could choose feeling happy in the first place. Why pursue goals that are unlikely to make us happy and ignore the fact that we can go for joy directly? It's puzzling to me to see that most people don't seem to be aware that they can choose to feel happy at any given moment.

University Professor Raj Raghunathan points out that, according to his research, it simply doesn't occur to most people to ask for happiness in surveys as an answer to the *Genie Question*, which allowed them to name anything they wished for. "The fact that people forget all about happiness when responding to the Genie Question *unless* they are reminded of it is quite consistent with findings on something called 'medium maximization'."[173] Medium maximization refers to the tendency to forget about the end goal that one wants to achieve, and to pursue, instead, the means or mediums to that end goal.

This seems like an excellent explanation for the bizarre situation of many people who seem to keep seeking happiness by chasing goals in the expectation that this would make them happy in spite of plenty of previous experiences showing clearly that this approach doesn't work. Happiness or joy - terms used intermittently here - remain elusive as long as we keep seeking outside of ourselves.

"It is from inner space, the unconditioned consciousness itself, that true happiness, the joy of Being, emanates," says the bestselling author and popular contemporary spiritual teacher Eckhart Tolle.[174] What we keep forgetting is what Osho puts beautifully: "Joy is the very stuff the universe is made of. But you have to look straight-on, you have to look in the immediate. If you look sideways, then you miss it."[175]

The seeking itself obstructs any possibility of finding it, because happiness exists inside us, right at our core, in the heart. "Seeking is the very

---

[173] Raj Raghunathan, If You're so Smart, why aren't you Happy?, 2016, p.34
[174] Eckhart Tolle, A New Earth, 2005, p.236
[175] Osho, Joy, the Happiness that comes from Within, p.42

Lighthearted

basis, the very fabric of suffering," says the spiritual teacher A.H. Almaas.[176] Osho states it like this: "If you pursue you will find unhappiness."[177] Tolle says it equally succinctly: "Don't seek happiness. If you seek it, you won't find it, because seeking is the antithesis of happiness."[178]

Osho makes this point very clear: The moment we desire happiness, we have moved away from the present. "Just stop seeking," he says, "and you have found it – because seeking means an effort of the mind, and nonseeking means a state of relaxation. And happiness is possible only when you are relaxed."[179]

In order to feel more relaxed, it is useful to let go of the identification with suffering and unhappiness, which the mind keeps replaying. This attitude was planted into us as we grew up, and we were forced to do things we never really wanted to do, in ways of upbringing that instilled a lot of sadness. That in itself, according to Osho, is not natural. Tolle also points out that unhappiness covers up our natural state of well-being and inner peace, which are the source of true happiness.

What gets us to the state of happiness has to do with the ability to drop the frenzy of constantly engaging in countless activities or paying attention to the incessantly thinking mind, which keeps pulling us into zillions of useless thoughts, and go within instead. Joy can never be found outside of ourselves because we can't get out there to get what we are. It's about uncovering, or allowing, of that to come forth and shine through what is already there.

Discovering happiness is about leaning back, encountering the inner space of consciousness, or appreciating something intensely and then relaxing into the beauty of the feelings that arise automatically. This is essentially what spiritual teachers in every culture down the ages have been preaching. It's just that most of them have either sternly prescribed strenuous disciplines and practices that seemed impossibly difficult to follow or didn't elaborate much at all on ways to get us there.

One of the reasons I find it highly interesting to live on this planet at this very point of time is that various ways to cultivate emotional

---

[176] A.H. Almaas, Diamond Heart, Book Four, 1987, p.23
[177] Osho, idid, p.20
[178] Tolle, ibid, p.96
[179] Osho, ibid, p.32

fulfillment and happiness have been extensively researched during the past decade. Positive Psychology is a new approach of psychology that doesn't focus on the analysis of mental illness as this discipline mostly has done since its beginnings, but instead it focuses on the attempt to research those habits and attitudes of people who report feeling content. In a nutshell, it's about gaining understanding of the central elements that help us nourish and cultivate happiness.

According to Martin Seligman, a pioneer of the psychology of happiness and human flourishing, we can experience three kinds of happiness: 1) pleasure and gratification, 2) embodiment of strengths and virtues and 3) meaning and purpose. Seligman provides a mental 'toolkit' to achieve what he calls the 'pleasant life' through inspiring people to think constructively about the past, gain optimism and hope for the future and, as a result, gain greater happiness in the present. He argues that without the actualization of our unique strengths and the development of virtues towards a bigger end, the human potential tends to be whittled away by mundane, empty pursuits of pleasure. The meaningful life, according to Seligman, includes investing oneself into creative work which creates a greater sense of purpose in life and accordingly, a greater sense of happiness. The interesting keywords for me in his research are *feeling invested* and *flow*.

Flow feels meaningful and joyful

Let us first look at the concept of flow. Highly happy people habitually dive into the state of flow. Most of us have had glimpses of the experience that the psychologist Mihaly Csikszentmihalyi has called flow. It's an experience in which we are so immersed in what we are doing that we lose track of time and are fully present in the moment. Time seems to both speed up and slow down. People who experience flow reported that they were totally absorbed into the activity at hand so that they had no extra mental capacity to evaluate their own performance. So, there's no mental chatter to distract, no ego disruption, but intense one-pointed mental focus. This means that we are in a state that can be characterized by presence, being fully here, aware, wide awake.

Osho points out that happiness just happens simply because it is always with us. What is needed to experience it is absorption that leads to a state of mindlessness or egolessness. "Perhaps that's why you call it 'happiness' – because it *happens*. You cannot manage it, you cannot manufacture it, you cannot arrange it. Happiness is something beyond your effort, beyond you. And could occur just by digging a hole in your garden, if you are totally absorbed in the activity – if the whole word is forgotten, including you – it is there."[180]

The absorption in a task, whatever this task may be, stops the background noise of the mind and leads to inner stillness and space. There is a sense of being fully alive. Neither the immediate surrounding matters, nor are past and future of any concern. Tasks just get done effortlessly. There is a sense of ease, as actions just flow out seemingly by themselves. Self-focus and importance we usually give to time are suspended. And that is when inspiration can happen. Tolle describes it this way: "When you negate time, you negate the ego. Whatever you do, you will be doing extraordinary well, because the doing itself becomes the focal point of your attention. Your doing then becomes a channel through which consciousness enters this world. This means there is quality in what you do, even in the most simple action."[181]

Being in the moment of doing is very important to achieve flow. In fact, the importance of this kind of intense presence at the very moment is emphasized by most contemporary spiritual teachings. This quality of presence allows an experience of beingness. "Whatsoever it is, be here now – and a tremendous revelation is waiting for you. The revelation is that nobody can be unhappy in the here and now," says Osho.[182] Right in this moment, unhappiness is impossible. This is an important revelation. Once we deeply grasp its implications, it might be easier to become more aware of the degree of our presence or absentmindedness in any given moment.

Because we are not present, the world we live in is a place of suffering, Almaas emphasizes. "What makes it a place of fulfillment is that we are present in it. For fulfillment is nothing but the fullness of our presence."[183] Tolle points out that we cannot be present unless we become friendly with

---

[180] Osho, ibid, p.33
[181] Tolle, ibid, p.265
[182] Osho, ibid, p.41
[183] Almaas, ibid, 34

the present moment. When we are in a state of flow, we feel naturally enchanted with what we do.

The state of flow connects us to a realm of timeless bliss. This state is not as elusive, esoteric or mysterious as one could be tempted to think. It has often been attributed mainly to people who engage fully in activities they like, such as writing, painting, designing, or sports. Flow states also occur when we are challenged to stretch our capacities and grow. The desire to build expertise or master a task seems to be essential to experiencing high levels of flow states.

The first time I became consciously aware of this state was when I set myself the goal of swimming 1000 meters quickly. Half way through, I would often feel that I couldn't go on, but when I pushed through in spite of pain in my shoulders or arms, there it was. Only the next breath when coming up from the water counted, my mind went blank, and the entire mental focus, as well as sensory impressions, were directed on the present move, and the next one. The body suddenly seemed to move with more ease and grace, and the feeling of the water around me and the act of swimming became filled with a joyful quality that wasn't there before. A big number of athletes regularly experience flow states.

Flow happens when we stretch beyond something that we perceived as a limit. At the same time, and this might seem like a paradox at first, "the desire of worldly success gets in the way of doing well in almost any domain," says Raghunathan.[184] Flow occurs when we forget about extrinsic rewards and focus totally at the task at hand. And that allows us to make the most progress, he points out. According to his research, flow is a critical determinant of both happiness and success.

The definition of success that the globalized economy and media are promoting is creating a huge amount of performance anxiety and stress on people because it is focused on what we have and not on how we feel, what we contribute to the greater good and who we are. The human needs for esteem and meaning have become thwarted as they have been associated more and more with material possessions, which might give us some prestige. However, that is usually devoid of real esteem received from others. It is usually out of touch with heart intelligence and spirit and, therefore, remains empty and ultimately disturbingly unsatisfying. "Don't

---

[184] Raghunathan, ibid, p.68

let a mad world tell you that success is anything other than a successful moment," says Tolle.

His definition of a successful moment is noteworthy: "There is a sense of quality in what you do, even the most simple action. Quality implies care and attention, which come with awareness. Quality requires your Presence."[185] This is exactly what flow brings about. And that can be experienced by anybody. Equally remarkable is the fact that everyone, universally, finds flow to be meaningful and satisfying. This finding, says Raghunathan, suggests that the desire to be absorbed or "to get lost in flow" is a fundamental human need. He concludes very matter-of-factly that, "pursuing flow is a far better approach for enhancing not just short-term and long-term happiness, but also success, than pursuing extrinsic rewards."[186]

Flow is available to all, no matter the age, economic or health condition, which is a truly amazing fact. It means that flow can also be experienced by people suffering from stress, anxiety or depression. While the desire for happiness and the thought of having to engage in activities that promise more of it might often be super stressful for people faced with these challenges, the extraordinary state of flow can be naturally and easily accessed even when we feel utterly miserable. And, most significantly, it shifts us out of it. Flow is the solution to some of the most prevalent problems we are currently facing as human beings living on this planet.

The good news is that the state of flow can be easily brought on and cultivated by practicing HeartMath exercises for only a few minutes. HeartMath was founded by Doc Childre in 1991 to help people bring their physical, mental and emotional systems into balanced alignment – a state not only referred to as being in flow but also as 'the zone', or coherence. When the heart rhythm is coherent, all our systems go into synchronicity with that kind of harmonious balance, and the experience of flow is the natural result. This is what enables us not only to perform at our best, but to feel emotions of contentment and joy.

These emotions are delightful because they are in alignment with spirit. They feel deeply nourishing and rewarding in themselves on an

---

[185] Tolle, ibid, p.270
[186] Raghunathan, ibid, p.72

individual level, while they also create a major impact on everything around us. Marianne Williamson points out that, "in order to move ourselves – and our civilization – into the next phase of our evolutionary journey, it's time to re-enchant ourselves."[187] Re-enchanting ourselves and those around us contributes to the most needed kind of change. Childre and Rozman express it beautifully: "The hope of the twenty-first century is that people will recognize that emotions are the next frontier to be understood and managed for personal, social, and planetary peace and quality of life. It starts with you."[188]

---

[187] Marianne Williamson, The Age of Miracles, p.23
[188] Childre and Rozman, Transforming Depression, p.17

Summary

Emotions are what makes life juicy and worthwhile. They fuel our actions and move us forward. Without them, life turns into a dead zone. Most people aren't aware yet that they can choose to feel happy at any given moment without having to reach any other specific goal first.

A majority of people spend more time in the range of heavy emotions than in the array that feels light and good. A big part of the stress we suffer from is related to the amount of negative emotions we feel.

Emotional processes can operate at a much faster speed than thoughts. They can also arise independently from the cognitive reasoning process. Emotions often occur due to unconscious associations based on memories of events, or beliefs we were raised with. This is why thinking positive thoughts or repeating affirmations often doesn't produce results.

When we worry or feel depressed a lot, the patterns that these emotions create in our body and facial expressions become so familiar that we don't feel comfortable when we're not anxious or depressed. The brain keeps shifting to what has become a default mode. The only way to establish a new baseline is to introduce dynamic new patterns and to reinforce them until they become familiar. Shifting into uplifting emotions several times a day is a sure bet.

Our electromagnetic fields are sending out data about our feelings in the same way as a mobile phone or TV set does. We pick up on the fields of others and are constantly influenced by them.

Joy can never be found outside of ourselves. It's about uncovering, or allowing, that to come forth and shine through what is already there. One way to cultivate it is to become friendly with the present moment. This gets us out of the often habitual resistance mode and delivers us to a state of acceptance.

The state of flow is not elusive, or esoteric and not reserved to artists or athletes. Flow is available to all, no matter of the age, economic or health condition. It can be experienced by people suffering from stress, anxiety or depression. The thought of having to engage in strenuous activities that promise happiness is often stressful for anxious or depressed persons.

However, the state of flow can be naturally accessed even when we feel utterly miserable. And, most significantly, it shifts us out of feeling bad and into feeling enchanted.

Flow is the solution to some of the most prevalent problems we are currently facing as human beings living on this planet. The good news is that the state of flow can be easily brought on and cultivated by practicing HeartMath exercises for only a few minutes.

Our mental-emotional attitudes can be transformed quite easily by feeling our way into high frequency emotions. This requires self-awareness and self-honesty. These are some of the qualities that are naturally cultivated when we practice meditation. And this is what the next chapter is all about.

"Object consciousness needs to be balanced by space consciousness for sanity to return to our planet and for humanity to fulfill its destiny. The arising of space consciousness is the next stage in the evolution of humanity."

Eckhart Tolle

TWELVE

What I Love About Meditation

I used to have rather rigid definitions of what meditation is. That was around those times when I mediated regularly, every morning in fact. I started it as soon as I was 18 years old. There have been phases, even periods, stretched out over many years, when I was an ardent meditator, sitting in silence, not to be disturbed, with my eyes closed and going into inner observation mode.

At those times, I felt that meditation was what held me together, helped me to keep on going. I didn't need to force any discipline on myself. There was this knowing that without the meditation before the day would start getting busy, I would not get through it very well. And so I just mediated. At other times, I didn't.

Now, I am unsure how to best define meditation. It's an experience of an intimate encounter with our level of presence or absence in the moment, with our thoughts and the gaps between them, with our way of breathing, our arising feelings, our pain, our neurosis, as well as an encounter with that space where there is peace, where there is bliss. It feels different for everyone. It has to be experienced in various ways also to be able to know what meditation is about.

Even though so many people write about it, the experience of deep meditation cannot be described well in words, because the realm of meditation opens when thoughts are left behind and, therefore, it can never be really captured by the thinking mind. Even if we might be tempted to think we have understood intellectually what meditation is, if we hadn't experienced those indescribably beautiful and blessed moments where everything feels light, wide, and free, then we cannot really grasp even the most poetic descriptions of this state.

I also feel hesitant to draw lines between various meditation styles, or recommend any technique in particular. I can only narrate my own story with meditation. And this story, I feel, is best told by describing what I enjoy about meditation now, and then adding glimpses of past events that led me to this stage.

I have become one of those people who pick and choose among various delicious items on the menu. Eclecticism is the luxury of this crazy postmodern time we are in. We can allow ourselves to be like butterflies, flattering free in an abundant field of flowers, partaking in the best nectar from here and there. And the unique bouquet of experiences we have made and skills we have developed is so enriching because there is such a large variety. Over are the times were there was only one brand of spiritual, religious or healing practice in town.

I don't stick to one discipline or routine anymore. I just simply can't. That time has somehow come to an end. So I mix and match, like many of us do. I don't get up at dawn to do my practice. And I don't believe that I need to battle my ego, or fight against my mind. Also, I don't buy into the widespread idea anymore that we need to urgently improve ourselves – preferably in painful ways so we can gain more.

I believe that life is meant to be cherished and enjoyed. Life is about having fun, about enthusiastically embarking on adventures. It's about enjoying the ride, basking in the glory of the moment when the sun comes out from behind the clouds. It's about learning to celebrate and rejoice and feel the beauty and mystery in every moment.

I don't believe the ancient teachings stating that 'life is suffering'. Looking around us, we find huge amounts of people suffering, but does that mean that life per se has to be like that for everybody? More importantly to ask: why should we keep on believing this opinion? After all, it's not that we are helpless to the point of being out of control. There is a lot we can do to lighten up and melt down some of the individual and collective suffering. One of these ways to alter our perception is meditation.

Heartfulness meditation

My favorite kind is the Sahaj Marg system of Raja Yoga, now more known as Heartfulness Meditation. I sit with my back upright and my legs folded and observe my breath first for a little while. Then, I practice a relaxation exercise to soften my muscles a bit – simply by becoming aware of them and asking them to relax, as it is practiced in *Yoga Nidra*, which is the relaxation exercise of any classical form of yoga. Similar to hypnosis, one can also imagine a white light entering from the feet and relaxing all the muscles in the body. Once comfortable and relaxed in the sitting position, I focus on my heart region, thinking the thought that divine light exists in my heart. That's all that there is to it.

I love the simplicity of this school of meditation. This path promotes meditation on the heart in the morning and a clearing of impressions from the heart region in the evenings, as well as a prayer for spiritual elevation. Another core feature is devotion to the master, or guide, and trust in the lineage of masters he represents.[189]

The heart deserves the biggest focus in meditation. This has been postulated by many spiritual paths and teachers, but now we can also come to this conclusion based on the findings of the HeartMath research. The focus on the existence of divine light in the heart draws me inward more than repeating a mantra, which is an exercise that can become quite boring to the mind. This subtle thought of light without the attempt to actually see any light has a special appeal to me.

I also like this idea very much as well as the feeling of yogic transmission of energy, which is called *pranahuti*. It's an ancient practice which was apparently lost in human history. In Sanskrit, *prana* means life-force and *ahuti* means offering, so *pranahuti* means 'offering of the life-force'. Kamlesh Patel, also known as Daaji, the fourth spiritual guide in the lineage of Sahaj Marq, describes it this way: "*Pranahuti* refines and purifies the energy field of a human being, what we call the subtle bodies or

---

[189] For more information see, https://heartfulness.org/in/

vibrational bodies. These subtle bodies include the intellect, the ego, the thinking mind and consciousness. As a result, consciousness expands and evolves."[190]

Daaji oversees Heartfulness centers and ashrams[191] in over 150 countries, and guides thousands of certified trainers who are imparting this transmission free of charge. These trainers can be called upon to meditate together, also over long distances. While it was needed to make an appointment before, now an App has been created to facilitate the connection with trainers. A Heartfulness session is now literally just a click away.

What resonated with me was the insight that our hearts are in dire need of purification because of the numerous layers of images and impressions that have been accumulated and stored there. This is a concept that is also central to Sufi teachings where the heart is said to be covered not only by layers of dust but also by a number of veils.

I enjoy these 'sittings' with meditation trainers. Often, I feel much lighter afterwards. Sometimes, I can feel energies swirling around my heart region. Sometimes, there is a sense of deep peace and comfort that comes in towards the end of such a session.

After I took quite a few courses in various energy healing arts, I felt that these transmissions of yogic energy feel similar to an infusion with the energies used by various energy healing arts. It's like a wave of high frequency energy pouring in which seems to know exactly what it needs to do with any system. After all, *chi* or *ki* is also translated as universal life force energy, or divine consciousness.

I have meditated regularly in this way for around fifteen years, and I lived in what was then the main ashram of the organization for two years, which I will describe in more detail below. One of the many things that changed since then is that I don't believe any more that we need to close our eyes and sit still for up to an hour to meditate. I have experienced some of the most blissful states of witnessing consciousness flowing through me while giving energy healing treatments to others.

---

[190] See the interview with Daaji on this site: https://www.collective-evolution.com/2018/01/02/7-things-to-know-about-pranahuti-yogic-transmission-a-global-guide-to-heartfulness-meditation/
[191] Sanskrit word for a hermitage, or meeting place of a spiritual community

On top of that, I have discovered the enormous joy and release that happens in Laughter Yoga meditation. Sitting together in a group of people and doing an exercise where we are laughing out loud for absolutely no reason as long as we possibly can is a tremendously freeing and precious experience. And because you can't think when you laugh, this exercise absolutely deserves to be called meditation. The longer I did it, the more I discovered that Laughter Yoga is a deeply spiritual practice.

Gazing into nothingness

Apart from laughter meditation, I have come to tremendously enjoy gazing into the space around me instead of all the existing objects, which is basically focusing on emptiness, on nothing. That spaciousness around us is normally in the background of our awareness, and it can quite easily be brought to the foreground. I have first come across the term 'space consciousness' through reading Eckhart Tolle's books. However, I was too carried away by the very beautifully crafted sentences, so that it remained mainly an intellectual delight.

What really brought home the message about the importance of noticing nothingness were two things: a simple explanation together with an easy guided meditation by Frank Kinslow, a chiropractic physician and clinical spiritual counselor. The founder of the *Kinslow System of Quantum Entrainment* was inspired by Tolle and developed simple and effective techniques. The title of one of his books struck a chord and developed nearly into some sort of slogan: *When Nothing Works Try Doing Nothing*.

"You don't have to synthetically generate your awareness like you do with a positive emotion," says Kinslow. "When you are awake you are aware naturally and without any effort."[192] This common everyday awareness, he argues, is all we need to look past the thoughts and notice that there is nothing behind them. The word 'awareness' simplifies the matter to me, in contrast to the word 'consciousness', which is more complex and therefore feels like something ultimately inexplicable.

Obviously, there are different degrees, or shades, of awareness. "If we think of awareness as light, then the different kinds of awareness represent

---

[192] Frank Kinslow: When Nothing Works Try Doing Nothing, 2010, p.9

different intensities of light," explains Kinslow. The purest level of it is nothing. Kinslow relates that he has guided hundreds of people from all walks of life and origins to become instantly aware of the nothingness that can be observed between the gaps of thoughts. In contrast to what many spiritual schools and teachers say, it can be experienced most easily, he stresses. That's basically all it takes to connect to our essence.

This is how he describes it: "Well, as it turns out there is something in the nothing. The something that is in nothing is awareness. Not awareness of something like the moon or an apple. This awareness is awareness of nothing. This is what I call pure awareness. Pure awareness is the ground state, the basic stuff of all created things."[193]

Pure awareness is always there, however, the mind gets bored of it quickly, because it contains neither objects, nor energy. Therefore, Kinslow recommends that after 2-3 minutes of noticing the stillness of nothingness with closed eyes, we should shift the flashlight of awareness on the feelings we feel. There will be some sense of wellbeing, such as "a sense of lightness or expansion, a feeling of silence or peace." For reasons that are not clear to me, Kinslow calls these emotions "Eufeelings." He suggests watching them arise with easy attention for some minutes with closed eyes, and then opening the eyes and continue observing these feelings while looking at objects as well as the space between them.

I realized that gazing at the space between things around me, infused me with those feeling states Kinslow describes in an effortless way. Especially outdoors, when intentionally looking at the space between trees, for example. It also works well when I am at home and look up from any activity and become aware of the space between me and the other end of the living room. Just looking into that spaciousness, and not being distracted by the beauty of any of the objects in the room, connects me again with this special energy or awareness of bliss. The more I practiced this easy exercise, the more instantly refreshing it became.

For quite a while, there was a guided meditation available on Kinslow's website which really put me in touch with space consciousness. It started by being asked to sit comfortably, to close your eyes, and become aware of different parts of our bodies, such as the hands and the feet. Then the instruction was given to feel the space beyond the arms, for example, and

---

[193] Ibid, p.13

then to feel the space all around the body, then the space in the room. And then this awareness of space was extended beyond the roof of the house, and above the city, and further and further into the sky. I was amazed how easy it was for me to feel that spaciousness, and how good it felt to become aware of it.

Now I know that becoming aware of pure awareness is an absolutely lovely feeling. It's super easy to bring on. It doesn't need long hours of meditation to eventually be blessed with an experience of transcending the thinking process and experiencing that indescribable dimension of pure awareness.

Like many people, I believed that it's difficult to reach that state, and that it's like some sort of blessing that was rarely given. I had to go through many different experiences during many years of my life - with and without meditating - before something suddenly gave way that had felt like a locked door over numerous years, before I could really get a taste of the dimension of thoughtlessness.

The struggle to start meditating

When I was 15 years old, I wasn't impressed at all with what was going on in school. Living in a small town in Germany made me feel like an outsider. I had no sense of belonging, and my heart was aching from the intense longing of returning to Egypt, where my family had lived before. I felt uprooted and misplaced. I enrolled in various courses in a government subsidized program for popular adult education. In this way, I learned to sew and color textiles and I took my first yoga class. Yet, none of this really satisfied my heart, which felt very unhappy and heavy.

My emotional landscape started to shift only after meeting two young men who were meditating. I was fascinated - not in a romantic way - it was as if my soul responded. This terrible feeling of being alone and misunderstood gave way to the hope that some people existed somewhere with whom I could share my aspirations and dreams. These two tall and skinny men had already finished high school and had done work instead of going to the military. They were bright, funny, relaxed and lighthearted, like nobody else I had met in Germany. I was looking forward to our meetings at the ice cream parlor. Their presence felt nourishing, refreshing and comforting. This is how I became more and more interested to figure out what meditation is about and how on earth they were doing it.

The idea of sitting in silence and focusing on a *mantra*, or sacred sound, was very appealing to me. The many benefits of meditation I heard about from my new friends sounded amazing. And these guys were walking their talk. They were following a system developed by the Indian Guru Maharishi Mahesh Yogi called *Transcendental Meditation*™. Inspired, I decided to visit their candle-lit center in Cologne, where I was received warmly by one of the meditation teachers. At the end of the talk, she told me that before I could be initiated into meditation, I needed to bring her an approval signed by both of my parents because I was not yet 18 years of age.

Well equipped with brochures and booklets, I returned home in an elevated state to tell my mother all the details. She was sympathetic to this new idea of me meditating. Probably, she hoped that it would soothe the unease I felt about having to live in Germany. In the evening, however, I was in for a big surprise. My father simply refused to approve without even looking at the brochures or giving me any explanation. Never before had he prevented me from enrolling into anything. He had always encouraged me to go for anything I was interested in and to freely express my opinions and take and stance, even if he seriously disapproved of them. Suddenly he said no, and that was that. He just couldn't stand the thought that I might lose my mind by following any Indian guru. Sadly, he didn't have the gift to explain his position or talk about his fears. Instead he stonewalled.

I felt deeply disappointed, helpless and at the same time enraged. I simply couldn't see why there should be anything wrong with meditating. It felt humiliating that I wasn't allowed to do what my heart and soul yearned for. My parents argued vehemently that night, and a frosty atmosphere crept into the house and prevailed for quite a while as my father stopped talking. It was the first serious disagreement and rift I experienced in the relationship with my dad, causing me to feel like I had suddenly lost quite a big chunk of the deep respect and admiration I had held for him.

The pain of not belonging

While in the bigger scheme of things this incident might appear ridiculously irrelevant, for me it felt as if something in my spirit was insulted. I could not have articulated it at the time, but it took on such a tragic note because it shook the one thing that had been most important to me until then: my sense of being supported and understood by my family. Many times we had moved countries, which left me feeling alone, different, and awkward. We didn't have close contacts to the extended family, and so we shared the sense that it was ultimately my parents, my brother and me against the rest of the world.

The feeling that I didn't belong anywhere was intensely painful. I don't think my parents realized how deeply uncomfortable that was, because they were born and raised in one place that kept feeling like home to them. What had somehow buffered the sense of fragility and unhappiness that came with feeling like some sort of an alien, and which I kept hidden deep inside like a dirty secret was the unshakable feeling of belonging to my family. Overnight, this feeling basically vanished into thin air. What appeared in its place was rebellion.

The very next day I defiantly announced that the moment I turned, 18 I would start meditating anyway. In the meantime, I got busy with rebelling. I cut off my beautiful long hair, dyed the short rest of it blue and wore blue lipstick. I walked to school barefoot, wearing a long gypsy style skirt I made myself together with heavy ankle bangles from Egypt. This is how I found out that it was forbidden to enter the school without footwear, which I found utterly ridiculous and returned home fuming. I started to do all kinds of crazy things, but luckily not liquors and hard drugs.

I dedicated myself to exposing teachers who made racist comments in the school magazine, and I started sympathizing with leftist, feminist and environmentalist thinking, engaging in fierce debates with whoever was willing to talk politics with me. In this staunchly Catholic and conservative small town, the bad ass side suddenly appeared and gave me the negative pleasure of talking and acting in provocative and aggressive ways.

Starting with transcendental meditation

When I turned 18, I didn't wait long to return to that TM center. We set an appointment for the initiation, and brought along a piece of fruit, a white piece of cloth and a flower, as requested. It was explained to me that this was a symbolic gesture to honor the Hindu tradition of students providing for the needs of their guru. On that auspicious day, I received a mantra and was requested to say it with a low voice to ensure that I pronounced it correctly, and after that keep it silent, like a sacred secret. I was instructed to sit comfortably, breathe easy and focus on the mantra whenever the mind would be drifting or wandering. We meditated together for 20 minutes. I was asked to come back a few times, and start the practice on my own. There was nothing spectacular about this initiation ritual. It was subtle, simple and beautiful.

This is how it came about that I started meditating in a regular and dedicated manner, twice a day for 20 minutes. After all, I had been waiting for the time to be able to do that for what felt like ages. In the meantime, we had moved to another city, and I had been elected as the head of the student union in a high school of my own choosing. Soon I discovered that practicing meditation gave me more energy, and a sharper mental focus.

With this energy, I could do many of the activities I was engaged in with more efficiency and ease. I felt good about doing the practice and enjoyed the feeling of peace that would arise seemingly by itself. When I got up in the morning, I was actually looking forward to meditate. I didn't talk about the fact that I started meditating with anyone, as I sensed that nobody around me was interested in spiritual issues. I just did it silently, for myself.

One part of this strong motivation was probably also about proving my point to my family. When I finished high school and moved away from home, I couldn't get myself to meditate anymore. In hindsight, it has become clear to me that over decades my meditation practice was strongly influenced by the people closest to me and the particular circumstance I had found myself in. I would be so affected by these two elements that I would actually stop or start meditating.

It took a lot of strength to stand up against my family and follow my spiritual aspirations, even risking a breakdown of my relationship to my father. This gave me the courage to stand alone. As painful as it was, it taught me that I could stand up for my values and aspirations. In the long run, it showed me that if I could stand alone at that young age, I could do it again. Standing alone is terrifying. And yet, I consider it one of the most essential lessons for maturing and evolving.

Turning my back on meditation

Once I was done with high school, I was lucky to receive a scholarship to study Italian for three months and got entirely carried away by the thrill of living in one of the most beautiful towns in Italy. I made friends, and tremendously enjoyed eating fancy pastries and drinking cappuccinos in coffee shops around the university in Perugia. Having lunch and dinner at the student's canteen was another highlight. Even the food they served in canteens at universities in Italy is absolutely delicious. For the first time in my life I was wearing heels, put on make-up and gained weight. These things were suddenly way more fascinating than sitting alone in meditation.

After that stunt, I spent six months in Egypt doing social service at the SOS Children's village and learning Arabic. I had a wonderful time there and deeply connected with many of the orphans living there, as well as some of the women who were employed to play the role of substitute mothers. Even though I felt quite fulfilled, there was a lot of restlessness because I couldn't figure out what to study and which profession to choose through which I could best contribute to making a difference in this world.

When I finally decided to enroll in university in Berlin and study philosophy and mass communication, I got immersed in figuring out how to live on my own in a big city that had such a degree of anonymity that I never bumped into anybody I knew by accident. I felt lonelier than ever before. My boyfriend, an outsider in his own way, was the only friend I had. We used to talk about everything for hours. He saw me and accepted me the way I was. It was the first time I felt entirely accepted by anybody, which kept me in this relationship for many years even though it wasn't always going that well. The thought of losing him, which I knew would have to happen one day because I wasn't interested in getting married and settling, was utterly scary. Unfortunately, this gifted young man was not interested in spirituality one bit. Looking back, I realize that this was one of the factors that led me astray from the practice of meditation that had been so precious to me.

It took many years and a miraculous string of events for me to find my way back to meditating. I fell in love with another man who was not only radically rebellious but also spiritual. He talked to me about raja yoga and introduced me to one of his friends who initiated me into Heartfulness Meditation. It was as if I had received the key that helped me develop the ability of dealing with all that was to come when I nervously boarded a plane to Bahrain where I started a new job which catapulted me into what at times felt like a different planet. I can honestly say that without holding on to my morning meditation practice I would have suffered a nervous breakdown right from the start.

Stepping into the world of ashrams

Around a year after I was expelled from Bahrain, I traveled to India with the aim to live there for a while. From all the exciting journeys I experienced, this was the one that affected me most deeply and changed the course of my life. From an earlier visit, I knew the *Babuji Memorial Ashram* on the outskirts of Chennai, which was at the time the main ashram of the Shri Ram Chandra Mission mentioned above.

I had in my mind to stay there only for a brief visit, leave my luggage safely stored, and venture to the coast in southern India to find an affordable little cottage to rent by the beach where I could retreat from the world to write. Little did I know that I would end up staying at this rather unknown place for two entire years.

When I arrived in India, I was limping. I had sprained my ankle stepping down from a ridiculously high side walk while I was in Egypt preparing myself for this big trip further east. My foot was swollen and walking was so painful that I postponed my departure. This made me recognize how afraid I felt of going on this journey. I could feel the fear creeping up on me, and yet I knew that this was the road I really longed to take and that I would not want to miss out on it whatever the response of my body was. So there I was, quite freaked out by my physical pain mixed with emotional panic and doing it anyway, which I'm really glad I did.

I will never forget how it felt to arrive at the big gate in front of the ashram and to limp my way down the paved path through a lush garden leading to the meditation hall. It was actually only a few days before my 35th birthday. The hot and humid weather of southern India hit me hard. Sweat was running down my back and my legs and left large stains on my beautiful Indian clothes, which I felt acutely ashamed of. And yet, in spite of all this, there was this special feeling of peace, and a sense of tremendous relief that I had never experienced before, nor even thought possible.

It was like a heavy burden suddenly lifted – as if the fears, the tension, the trauma around having been expelled from Bahrain, and all the accumulated stress of working for nearly three years as a reporter in the Persian Gulf region dropped off. I finally felt safe. I felt that nobody would ever harm me in this place. It felt like coming home. And the only thing I wanted was to stay.

The master, as everyone called Sri Parthasarathi Rajagolopalachari, was on a trip to America at the time of my arrival. The ashram was rather empty. Most of the people I met found it very bizarre that I arrived at a time when the guru was not around, and couldn't understand that I didn't seem to mind at all. In fact, most visitors to the ashram came specifically to see the master, especially the ones coming from abroad. I was quite comfortable that I didn't need to think about what my relationship to this master was, or whether I actually wanted to become a disciple of any guru in the first place. His absence gave me the time to figure out my next steps.

The first time I had seen the master was in a hotel room in Munich. He didn't look anything like I expected an Indian guru to look like. Shariji, as he was lovingly called by his followers, was tall, muscular, cleanly shaven, and, most surprisingly, he was wearing jeans, with a purple polo shirt and Birkenstock sandals. He had worked as a business man and looked like one to the point that one could have been tempted to think that he just came from playing a match of a golf.

He sat on a little sofa in a rather small hotel room, crammed with people sitting on the floor around him, who eagerly stared at him, trying to soak up his energy. The only things said fell into the category of small talk. I was introduced to him, he looked at me and asked me to sit down. A few other people were introduced, he asked a few questions, looked around, remained silent for a while, then made a few remarks on the weather. That was it. Before I knew what had happened, the audience was over and Shariji was off to another place, other people pushing and pleading to get a glimpse of him. I was utterly unimpressed.

His Master, lovingly referred to as Babuji Maharaj, was the kind of guru who had the looks of one. He was skinny, seemed frail, had a white beard and seemed to curl up in effortless ease in any sitting position. In the photos I had seen of him, his eyes seemed to look either directly into mine, or straight into infinity. These photos stirred something up in my heart. Somehow, it seemed to have been Babuji I was feeling so eager to encounter. However, he had passed away long before I had heard of him.

When I first met Shariji, I was in my early thirties, and felt eager to succeed in my profession, to explore the world, to expand my horizons and my freedom. Living a self-determined life as an independent woman was one of my core values. Given the amount of repression, violence and slavery, so many women currently living on this planet suffer from, the incredible opportunity to choose what I wanted to study to what and where I wanted to work, and how and with whom I wanted to spend my time felt like a huge privilege. I certainly didn't have in mind to reduce it in any possible way – especially not in order to follow another patriarchal belief system, based on male-dominated interpretations of ancient Eastern spiritual teachings and traditions. That's how I saw it back then.

Settling close to the ashram

Surprising to myself, within one week after arriving at the gates of the ashram, I rented a new and totally empty apartment close to it. This again led to raised eyebrows. Some of the followers of the master with whom I got to talk to said that I would have needed to have his permission to stay in the area. I felt that was rather strange. However, I was diplomatic enough not to give a Western style speech of freedom of choice, but to reply with spiritual terminology that ultimately united us because on some level it made sense to all of us. What I replied was that it must have been him in the first place who inspired me to come and then instilled the desire in me to stay.

What I gladly followed was the advice of some elders to write a letter to the master. It took me a while, because I found myself pouring my heart out to him in eleven typed pages, which I assume he would never read. Some of the righteous people one always seems to find in religious or spiritual organizations, protested when they saw the large envelope I dropped into the letter box. I was told about the existence of a rule to stick to only one page. However, I felt that this letter was the beginning of a breakthrough for me, and that it, therefore, absolutely needed to be delivered, whatever the rules said.

I wrote about all troubles tormenting me: the fears, the incidents that I couldn't forgive myself for, the feelings of failure and shame – it took the form of one big confession. While writing, floods of tears were released and I ended with beseeching the master to teach me how to love. That's all I wanted. I felt miserable about not being able to love unconditionally. I wanted to really experience and know what love is - to be in love with existence, to be aware that I am made of the energy of love. "*Oh master, teach me how to love,*" is something I often found myself saying internally, or writing in large letters in one of my many diaries ever since.

In and around that ashram, I have received glimpses of love and peace that were so wonderful that it's difficult to find words for them. Suddenly, there would be waves of that indescribable energy that seemed like a breeze from another realm - especially during the second year of my stay when I moved to a cute little cottage behind the ashram. Again and again, I was showered with bliss descending on me in most ordinary moments – such as when washing my clothes or watering plants. I had never known this feeling, neither was I familiar with that word prior to my settling there, even though I had visited and met the master in this very ashram before.

For four years, I had meditated regularly, however, it was only in the group meditations in this ashram during which I came to know how absolutely elevating deep absorption can feel. The discovery that I could completely go beyond the chattering mind was wonderful. It was such a realization that it was possible to step out of the mind, to have no thoughts at all for quite a long time. I often felt it was incredibly liberating just sitting on the floor of an improvised meditation hall with a corrugated sheet metal roof.

Sometimes, I observed my thoughts, sometimes that felt uncomfortable, sometimes my legs or back started hurting, and there was a strong urge to move. I figured out that if I changed my position it would not become more comfortable but that I would just keep on fidgeting and the focus on the physical pain would grow during the rest of the meditation. Therefore, I forced myself to sit still for the entire time. Only much later I realized that this in itself was a precious training. Not many people can sit without moving for one hour. If the body is motionless, it helps the mind to settle down too.

Sometimes painful thoughts kept ruminating in my mind and I couldn't find a moment of inner peace. At other times, I could feel very irritated with people coming late in noisy ways, coughing or sniffing constantly or even snoring loudly around me. While watching my own indignation or anger, this one hour in the meditation hall could stretch out endlessly. And yet, I hardly ever missed out on a group meditation during those entire two years. Whatever happened, I just loved being there.

Coming out of meditation at the end, I sometimes felt I came back from somewhere far away where my spirit had flown to, and I had absolutely no clue where I had been during the meditation. It was like losing track, losing any chance of creating a story, like a black out. There was no conscious awareness of what had happened whatsoever, as much as I would try to retrieve it. However, it felt refreshing and uplifting, and, therefore, I knew I hadn't been sleeping.

And, sometimes, there was full awareness of my body sitting where it was, while there was no sense of pain in it, no awareness of the other people around me, and no thinking. In these precious meditations, I became aware that there was only infinitely vast and free wideness. There was not a single thought, no objects to focus on, no light, no forms, no sense of time, just colorless, somewhat greyish-bluish-whitish space. I felt like flying in that wideness and yet there was no me to fly. There was no sense of being separate from it, rather floating in it, immersed by it.

I didn't fully realize back then that this encounter with nothingness was what deserved to be called a most meaningful realization, partly because nobody around me explained to me what was going on, and I hadn't yet read any descriptions of this state in any books. I just felt that all was very good, and that I was simply having a more profound meditation than what I had experienced before.

Immediately after group *satsanghs*[194] in the morning and evening, I briefly jotted down some observations about the meditation in a diary.

---

[194] Satsang derives from the Sanskrit words *sat which means* being, essence, or reality and *sanga* which means association. The word refers to fellowship with others who share similar spiritual aspirations, as well as fellowship with Truth, or with the Divine, in meditation.

Sadly, for me now, reading these diaries is not very enlightening at all, even though I have carried them with me around the world and kept feeling that they are among my most precious possessions. I wrote things like, "many thoughts today, felt very restless", or "was totally absorbed", or "I felt peaceful and calm and just observed my thoughts and feelings." I didn't analyze what I had felt and had just accepted what came up without giving it much afterthought.

Only when other meditators talked about the things they experienced that could sound like they had been on some sort of astral trip during which they saw colorful lights and received messages, I started to feel that there might be something I kept missing. It is this kind of comparison that leads to strange judgments of the mind, and the feeling creeps in that somehow one doesn't really get it right. The mind is tricky and takes pleasure in instilling a sense of inadequacy.

Encounters with the master

The master liked to sit by one of the beaches in Chennai just before sunset. He wouldn't announce when and where he went if he would go. And he didn't talk much when he was there. On those days, when some people suspected he might be by the beach in the afternoon, many would jump into *rikshas* and take long trips across the whole city to the two beaches where he could be and searched for him. Only on very few occasions, I went along with this wild chase. Most of the time, I felt that I needed to do my work apart from the spiritual practice which consisted of writing a book about my experiences in Bahrain. I never found a publisher for it and went on to re-write it into a doctorate dissertation.

I also felt sometimes that the master would prefer to be left in peace, which might have been one of these projections. Privacy is not something any guru can enjoy. I often felt profoundly sorry for him being bothered by so many people who constantly wanted his attention, his blessings, his prayers, his advice.

One afternoon I was among a large group of people sitting around him on the sand by the beach. It was one of the very rare occasions where I actually asked him a question. Most of the time the questions I had in mind just melted away when I was in his presence. However, on that day

I said: *I don't see anything in meditation after all these years. Most people seem to see colors and have adventures. I never do and I wonder if there's anything I do wrong.* Shariji Maharaj smiled and attentively looked into my eyes. It felt as if his glance saw right through me. "It's a blessing that you don't see anything," he finally answered with what felt like an unusually strong emphasis. "When you see things, there is distraction, it becomes an experience and you attach meaning to it. Most people seek only spiritual experiences, and then the ego becomes attached to that." That answer made a lot of sense, and it was the validation of my form of practice, which I needed at that point.

Many years later, when I attended courses in energy healing arts, other moments arose when I would again feel somehow inferior to other students because I couldn't see neither auras, nor angels, or anything else. When I pondered whether I should take up specific courses to develop my psychic sensing abilities, I remembered this answer. The main thing for me about meditation and spirituality has remained the same: to ignore the mind, open the heart and become aware of this pure awareness. For me, there's nothing that could be more precious than that.

In an ashram, the central focus of everyone is on the master. And what many people seem to love most is to talk about their encounters with him. This was one of the things that bothered me from time to time. Unlike any other relationship I have ever engaged in, the relation to the master remained mysterious to me. I just couldn't define what was happening, as it was outside all boxes that can be labeled by the mind. All I can say is that a high frequency field is attractive and pulls you in so that a mysterious relationship develops by itself.

I didn't practice thinking of him, or drawing him into my life, or my heart, in any way, as some recommended. I hardly ever made an effort to see him, and never sat in front of his office for hours on end like many people did. I acted quite nonchalantly about my relationship with the master and didn't realize what a blessing it was. Over time, little magical moments stringed up together that created unexpected shifts in feelings, as well as unforgettable memories.

One day, I was sitting on the back of a motorbike of a neighbor who gave me a lift to the ashram, when I saw the master sitting in the front a small car approaching us. When I saw him, I felt a pang of happiness, and waved my hand enthusiastically, like a little girl. And he waved back in exactly the same manner. This gesture opened my heart, and the whole day I felt very bubbly. I observed myself feeling like a teenager secretly in love with somebody who suddenly discovers that the feelings are mutual. My heart was humming on the lines of *he waved to me*.

For a while, we simply waved to each other from far. One day I entered the ashram from the gate in the back and saw Shariji sitting in the garden surrounded by a group of people. When I saw him, a big smile appeared on my face and without thinking what I was doing, I started waving frantically to him. Again, the master did exactly the same thing while the jaws of some conservative aspirants dropped. As unspectacular as it sounds, and as silly as it might appear, these waving experiences opened my heart and an inexplicable love for him developed and deepened in this way.

The master often stayed up until late in the night, and he usually retreated for an afternoon nap. After that, it seemed to me that he often had a grumpy expression on his face – as if he didn't really want to be where he was but would have preferred dwelling in higher realms with his beloved master. The only thing he seemed to like talking about was in fact his master. That's when he seemed animated and his face was glowing with love. Sometimes, he gave me an impression of being tired, stern, and overloaded with carrying so much pain from all of us. Guruji, how I called him internally, was certainly not looking like a lighthearted happy man. His bliss, I somehow sensed, or rather assumed, had a different quality, a different tone to it.

The more I read the more I grasped that the ocean of bliss is just another stage in an infinite spiritual journey. In Sahaj Marq teachings, it is said that one needs a very capable master to get beyond that stage, because we become all too attached to the lovely feeling of bliss. My master, I felt, moved beyond it. I sensed that he was internally highly developed beyond what I could grasp, or what appearances he or the organization he worked so hard to further develop could reveal.

On the outside, he didn't show or express that very well. Shariji said of himself that he didn't like to give speeches. He was not an eloquent talker. His speeches could turn into stern criticism of superstitious beliefs, the divisions among brother and sister human beings through the caste system, empty ritualistic worship, or corruption. He would urge us often to stop participating in any form of corruption by stopping to bribe anybody - even it meant extra visits to the post office to get your phone line back on, etc. At that time, I liked his harsh criticism of the dysfunctional aspects of society and politics.

It was clear in many ways that Shariji was not particularly fond of what he saw happening around him, and yet he carried on doing what he did, tirelessly traveling all over India as well as to the United States and Europe. He encouraged the building of more ashrams, and he was listening to countless people's suffering. He led powerful meditations wherever he went, which cleared layers and layers of accumulated impressions so that we would feel lighter as our hearts and souls were filled up with light.

Whenever any of us at the ashram would feel tense or really worn out, we would attribute it to this kind of intense cleaning. It wasn't always easy to bear. In fact, life in an Indian ashram is not a piece of cake as one might be tempted to imagine. One thing was the relentless heat and humidity. I only had fans and no air-conditioning system, which stopped many times a day due to repeated power cuts. I had no warm water and ate the most basic food consisting of variations of rice and lentils.

Despite the basic nutrition, I actually really enjoyed eating in the ashram. The act of eating while sitting in silence on the ground felt nearly like a sacred act and the food felt more delicious to me than anything I could have had in any restaurant. I didn't even see the necessity of getting myself fruits or taking supplements that would have been available in any nearby pharmacy. And I tremendously enjoyed living in a small cottage with a tiny patch of earth around it that I turned into a garden. Looking back, I feel amazed how intensely I enjoyed these basic conditions for two years without ever getting seriously ill.

A few days before the master would come back from any trip, we usually felt as if we had been thrown into a huge pressure cooker. I often experienced headaches, stomach cramps or diarrhea – a bit like a so-called healing crisis can feel after an intense energy healing session. Once he was back, it felt like the ashram transformed into some sort of buzzing atomic power plant. The energy would feel so strong that it often affected us physically, as if a different energy ran through our veins washing, or rather purging, out everything that was not in alignment with it.

Visitors who were unprepared and not used to this kind of high frequency energy and its relentless intensity of releasing blockages would often become sick. Agreeing to a process of emptying out our cups is one thing, going through the process for years is another. At times, it made me feel raw with unnamable inner pain that boiled up like festering blisters. Often, it was so tiring that it felt like a vacation when the master left the ashram to go on another tour.

Other than transmitting light to our hearts and purifying them, the master was very dedicated to build a large meditation hall in the ashram in Chennai. He tirelessly engaged in the progress and walked over the building site, discussing with architects and encouraging volunteers who arrived from all over the country. Thanks to their enormous physical effort, the construction of the splendid hall, as well as a large area for dormitories under it, was finalized in practically no time.

Shariji often spoke about fulfilling our duties – be it as students, householders, husbands or parents. Even though this was not really one of my core values, and I believe the whole concept of doing things out of a sense of duty belongs to the outgoing age and ought to be replaced by more inspiring mental constructs, I could see where he was coming from. This charismatic and special man had dedicated his life to serve his master. He simply saw it as his duty to do what he had been requested to do by his guru. Sometime before he passed away, he was quoted as saying that he had never felt as if he was a master. The only master he saw was Babuji Maharaj.

I couldn't help but feeling a lot of compassion for him because I felt how heavy this burden was on him. Some of those aspirants who served the master - be it as some sort of bodyguard or through preparing his meals, driving him to places, or sleeping close by while he traveled – had the vibes of people one would instinctively avoid under all circumstances. They often looked gloomy and dark. It was striking that they never smiled and continuously seemed to be in a bad mood. Many of them certainly lacked basic good manners and hardly ever showed kindness to anybody, which was repelling.

I often felt that many people in this place took their meditation practice with a seriousness that didn't really serve the higher purpose of it all. There was a tendency towards living an ascetic life that could border on austerity. As much as I resonated with a purist practice that didn't contain rituals, or mantra chanting, I felt that the absence of joy was glaring.

When I came back to the ashram many years later, after I had discovered Laughter Yoga, I clearly felt that it would be a most beneficial practice to add in order to lighten up those aspirants who became stiff and dogmatic in their practice, and therefore remained hard-hearted. On the other hand, many of the Laughter Yogis I encountered have demonstrated a lack of the depth that comes with profound spiritual aspiration and regular meditation practice, and many of them would definitely benefit from a exercising silent meditation on the heart. This is one of the reasons I believe in the importance of mixing various methods and styles of spiritual practice, not just in yoga, to further enrich them and multiply their wonderful effects.

It struck me that there was some sort of mysterious teaching in what we perceive as darkness or lightness. "Where there is a lot of light, there is a lot of darkness," the master said once. We definitely had to face quite a lot of darkness – our own, as well as that of our brothers and sisters in the organization - when we aspired to get close to him on the physical plane.

The master was aware that there was a lot of envy arising among us the moment somebody started relating that they had seen the master, or spent time with him by the beach, or in his office. "Oh I missed that opportunity," was the common thought that would creep in. Or worse: "why her and not me?" In that regard we were feeling and acting like children, jealous when the attention and love of the mother goes to the brother or sister, always suspicious that the other one got more. We all wanted to sit by his feet and have the chance to open our hearts by talking to him and simply have him and his attention for ourselves. How thirsty humans feel for love becomes glaringly obvious in the entourage of an evolved spiritual teacher.

Many times he used to remind us that he gave his attention to those of us who needed it the most. "If your neighbor called a heart doctor to come to his house, would you envy him?", he asked in several of the speeches he used to deliver after leading the group satsangh on Sundays in Chennai. These reminders were necessary for all of us. And while I also would have loved nothing more than the chance to sit with him alone and just talk, I felt very blessed to spend a lot of time in his ashram and attend the meditation sessions - whether he was out of town or at the beach or even in his office in the middle of the ashram, seeming so unreachable because he was always swamped by visitors with urgent demands. He would also tell us that many of us going about their days, or sitting in silence in the ashram, received many more blessings from him than those who sat with him in his office.

So many blessings

One night, I was suddenly wide awake before 4 am in the morning and felt I urgently needed to go to the ashram right away. I had no clue why and didn't question the urge to get dressed and start moving. It was still pitch dark and so I walked very carefully in slow motion over a large open and uneven field as I could hardly see the ground in front of my feet. My idea was to head for the cafeteria and see if I could get hold of a tea. Turning around a corner in the ashram, I saw the master coming towards me, accompanied by only one of those disciples who were permanently around him. He had his walking stick with him and sternly looked far ahead of him.

I stood there, feeling very surprised to the point of being somehow dumb founded, folded my hands in front of my heart, lowered my head and said "Good morning master." He said "good morning", lifted his walking stick, pointed it right at my heart and continued walking. Nothing else was said. No words were needed. I stood there for a quite a while, trying to digest the sudden surge of energy that had exploded in my heart and ran through my whole system. *Boom*. That whole day I felt like I was in a maze and at the same time fully alert. I had no words to describe what happened other than: he pointed his stick at me and something changed. I didn't know what had changed and what he did, or what was done through him, but some work had been done on my heart. I was sure of that even though I couldn't figure it out.

Like everyone else around me I liked it very much when he looked at me. It infused a lovely feeling. There is a passage in Arabic spiritual songs that refers to this desire to receive just one glance from a man of God: *Nasra ya maulana*. This is why I sometimes went along with many others to receive the master at the airport when he returned to his home in Chennai from yet another trip. He was constantly and unpredictably on the move, like many sadhus and gurus in India throughout history. The master would walk by, scanning the crowds, looking at most people, usually with a serious expression. Sometimes his face lit up, he would smile, stop to shake a hand and ask a question, or put his hand gently over the head of a child that was held up towards him in the hope that it would be blessed. When he looked into my eyes, some part in me felt nourished and deeply satisfied. Just one glance is all it took. I went back home feeling foolishly happy. *He looked at me.*

I am not sure if it's the ego's insatiable desire for recognition or the soul that rejoices when it's finally recognized by a highly developed fellow soul. I can't tell. Maybe it's both. After all we are both the personality and the soul, which carries the divine spark, the manifested and the unmanifested. And in both of these aspects a strong desire was ignited that kept growing: to see the master and be seen by him. That's what we were all basically longing for.

I didn't know then how much I would continue to miss him and that one day those encounters with my master would feel like the most precious moments of my life. At some point my savings ran out; I was broke and needed to return to the world of work. Otherwise, I would have never left that wonderful place. Leaving the ashram and not being able to lay my eyes on my master anymore was among the most difficult things I have ever done. Moving from this field of special bliss to a mega city felt like being expelled from paradise. Once again, I needed to learn to stand alone.

This time round the lesson was about finding the master internally. It also had to do with dropping that part of the personality that wanted to remain identified with the seeking and the attempting of living up to defined standards of how life should be lived as a devotee. It sounds simple, however, it's been a very difficult lesson to learn. As I dropped the formal practice some years after leaving India, and broke free to discover other very valuable ways to become more lighthearted, I eventually developed more awareness of and more reliance on my own inner teacher.

To end this chapter, I would like to further illustrate this point with a quote from Sogyal Rinpoche, who beautifully expresses the rare blessing that is inherent in a relationship with a master: "The inner teacher, who has been with us always, manifests in the form of the 'outer teacher,' whom, almost as if by magic, we actually encounter. This encounter is the most important of any lifetime."[195]

I have visited other ashrams and encountered a number of other enlightened masters over the years. However, I never felt any deep attraction to them, or resonance with them. When my master passed away, there was an acute sense of loss as well as guilt that I hadn't visited him more often, and hadn't stuck to practicing his teachings. The longing to feel surrounded again by his miraculous field of bliss increased. What I realized only then was that sacred places and awakened beings carry a distinctly different energetic imprint. The energy they generate is not the same.

Guruji has remained my one and only master. When I finally came to the ashram again it was like a pilgrimage to say farewell to him over a year after he passed away. I sat in front of his picture in the meditation hall and suddenly floods of tears ran down my face, and I cried for a long time as my heart was opening in sudden pangs of adoration and love for him. I felt his presence very strongly and could even hear his voice talking to me.

No other place on this planet feels as splendid and as home to me like his little known ashram in a suburb of Chennai. It looks tiny now, as it has been surrounded by huge, ugly office buildings that are a part of the booming Indian IT industry. The contrast couldn't be bigger. And yet, the moment I step into this small enclave that keeps generating such a tremendous amount and quality of light and love, I feel elevated to magnificent heights of lightheartedness.

---

[195] Sogyal Rinpoche, The Tibetan Book of Living and Dying, 2017, p.138

Summary

There were times when I felt that meditation was what helped me to keep on going. I didn't need to force any discipline on myself. I just meditated. At other times, I didn't.

Meditation is an experience of an intimate encounter with our level of presence in the moment, with our thoughts and the gaps between them, with our way of breathing, our arising feelings, as well as an encounter with that space where there is peace, where there is bliss.

It doesn't need long hours and decades of meditation practice to transcend the thinking process and experience the dimension of pure awareness. I believed that it's difficult to reach that state, and that it's like some sort of blessing that was rarely given. It took me a while to discover that the realm of thoughtlessness is easy to access and that it generates subtle high frequency feelings. Nothingness can be observed with open eyes by focusing on the space between things.

One of the special features of Heartfulness meditation is yogic transmission of energy, which is called *pranahuti*. It's an ancient practice that was lost. This 'offering of the life-force' refines and purifies the subtle bodies. As a result, the heart softens, plus consciousness expands and evolves.

When students are ready, teachers have a tendency to appear. In some ways, they are reflections of the inner teacher who has always been with us, and help us to become more aware of this source of guidance inside out hearts. The encounter with an enlightened spiritual master teacher is considered a huge blessing in all ancient wisdom traditions. In the East, it is generally seen as the most important encounter ever. It is the love that develops in the student's heart for the teacher that accelerates spiritual attainment.

When we become a part of a spiritual lineage or organizations, a group identity imprints itself on us. We also tend to take on roles, just as we did in our families of origin. Identifying with the seeker, follower or student and trying hard to follow rules and routines can make us forget that life is about having fun and enjoying the ride. It's not so much about discipline as it is about learning to rejoice by feeling the beauty and mystery of it all every day.

When there is not enough shared joy in a spiritual place, or any lifestyle for that matter, it might be time to move on and remember the inner courage to stand by ourselves and in our own truth. We can allow ourselves to be like butterflies, fluttering free in an abundant field of flowers that all contribute to our awakening. Years of absorbing, learning, practicing different modalities, eventually lead to a level of accumulation and integration when something suddenly seems to seep deeper into our cellular structure and we can go with the flow more often.

In the next chapter, you can read more about lightheartedness induced by meditation. Some light is shed on various types of meditation, and the crux on academic research on meditation.

*"To meditate means to be there.
To be there with yourself."*

Thich Nhat Hanh

THIRTEEN

Meeting your Self in Meditation

Meditation is a delight and a purpose in itself. To simply be present with yourself and for yourself feels very pleasant. Meditation - in the way of Heartfulness - definitely makes you feel more lighthearted. "The gift of learning to meditate is the greatest gift you can give yourself in this life," says Soygal Rinpoche.[196] It's a gift to cherish, to bask in - without the hope or expectation to get an extra payoff.

It's not an activity to undertake with the aim to gain anything. This seems utterly counter-intuitive or even non-sensical to the common post-modern western mind, which needs to be convinced of tangible benefits that make anything worth doing. However, meditation cannot be done. It's essentially about non-doing. It's about allowing ourselves just to be, and to witness whatever arises in the form of thoughts, emotions or sounds around us. It's a practice of effortlessness that dispels heaviness.

It's an appointment with our higher Self, as well as an attempt to get to know the workings of our minds and perhaps be blessed with a glimpse of what could be felt in between or behind the many thoughts that cloud our perception of pure consciousness. It's like taking time to sit on a balcony, comfortably and calmly on a rather cloudy day, patiently resting and yet

---

[196] The Tibetan Book of Living and Dying, 2017, p.68

ready to get a glimpse of the sun that could suddenly emerge from behind the clouds.

There's nothing spectacular about it. While meditating, most people don't get to see bright lights, don't receive messages from angels or get to perceive shiny celestial beings, nor do we suddenly hear heavenly music and are welcomed to enter paradise. In fact, when some people talk or write about meditating, they really mean listening to recorded voices of teachers who ask them to imagine all kinds of things on those lines; I feel that they missed the whole point of meditating in the first place.

The popularity of meditation is unprecedented. Zillions of ways to meditate exist. In Buddhism alone, there are countless methods of meditation. Osho presents a large range of ways to meditate in a whole book published on the issue. In one way or another, these practices all aim at training a variety of mental habits, and they also produce distinctively different outcomes. This is one of the findings of the analysis of research on meditation undertaken by Goleman and Davidson. They point out that there is "a tsunami of meditation research," with around 1,000 studies being published per year.[197]

While it is a good thing that we live at a time where we have the opportunity to experiment with such a large variety of meditation techniques, this development also causes a lot of confusion and ultimately frustration. It, therefore, seems in order to shed some light on various types of meditation, and the crux with academic research on meditation.

Goleman and Davidson distinguish between two different meditation paths: "the deep and the wide." According to them, the deep path prevails in a pure form in ancient lineages, mostly practiced by yogis and monks in Southeast Asia. There is a second level of the deep path, where some traditions have been removed and adapted in forms more palatable for the West. The wide approaches further remove the spiritual context of meditation practices and water them down to render them handy for the largest number of people. "The current vogues of mindfulness-at-your-desk, or via minutes-long meditation apps, exemplify this level," they point out.[198]

It's certainly great that more people have started to engage themselves

---

[197] Daniel Goleman & Richard J. Davidson, The Science of Meditation, 2017, p.78
[198] Ibid, p.3

in various meditation exercises that are part of the wide approaches. Also, a few minutes of meditation here and there are certainly better than nothing. "Five minutes of wakeful sitting practice is of far greater value than twenty minutes of dozing," remarks Rinpoche.[199] By all means, whatever practice contributes to reduce the widespread human heaviness, or increase relaxation in these times of super stress is absolutely great.

Meditation is part of a larger spiritual context

The problem I see happening with the attempt to water down ancient practices and remove them from their original spiritual context is that instead of the clearly defined purpose that is being pursued in traditional paths, such as liberation or enlightenment, the post-modern meditator is prone to seek for and expect results, such as a payoff in the form of altered personality traits and behaviors as proof for spiritual progress being made.

This predicament is also ultimately underlying the approach of Goleman and Davidson who set out to analyze high quality research for scientific proof that repeated practice of meditation induces lasting embodiment of positive traits, such as patience, kindness or presence, or even character transformations at the higher levels, leading to equanimity and compassion kept up under all circumstances. As psychologists, they obviously need to define parameters and are therefore fixated on analyzing outcomes and benefits of meditation. It's definitely a positive contribution to widen the scope of traditional psychology by researching human personality traits and outcomes of personal growth, which exceed the range traditionally thought possible within the limits of this particular science.

However, it is bound to be an ultimately materialistic approach to something that is a deeply spiritual practice. The assumption on which they base their research is that meditation is a tool to foster "such beneficial fixtures of being."[200] I find the term 'fixture' as in 'installation' or 'game' rather irritating in this context. As mentioned above, the practice of meditation is best unburdened with expectations to improve one's personality.

---

[199] Rinpoche, ibid, p.3
[200] Coleman and Davidson, p.46

Character building is in fact something that is promoted and encouraged by yoga teachings as well as Buddhist teachings as the first steps on a path, long before a practitioner is even introduced to the practice of meditation, and there are special exercises designed for that purpose. The personality first has to be well developed and fine-tuned, according to these traditional teachings, so that we can then eventually go beyond it and eventually transcend the grip of the ego. While this practice doesn't have anything to do with meditation per se, wisdom is impossible to attain without a refined and well-tuned character.

The Buddha has taught that the ignorance of our true nature is the root cause of all suffering. And the root cause of ignorance itself is our mind's habitual tendency to distraction. He realized that the key to end the mind's distraction "is to bring the mind home to its true nature, through the practice of meditation."[201]

If this understanding or approach is missing, it can happen that the personality or the ego is strengthened, which defies the whole purpose. Apart from that, it is difficult to believe that a watered-down meditation practice, which is largely devoid of the spiritual insights it is originally meant to deliver, can lead to lasting character transformations. These states, or traits, have been described by enlightened people from the East and the West as a by-product of the process of awakening and self-realization, and not as a purpose in itself. These kinds of benefits are traditionally even encouraged to be dedicated to worthy causes, such as world peace, or the enlightenment of all human beings, and not to be held out as further trophies of the ego to keep it motivated to sit down and mediate in the first place.

Sogyal Rinpoche states it very clearly: "The purpose of meditation is to awaken in us the sky-like nature of mind, and to introduce us to that which we really are, our unchanging pure awareness which underlies the whole of life and death." [202]

---

[201] Rinpoche, p.58
[202] Ibid, p.60

What meditation is and isn't

It might be helpful to establish what meditation is not. Lying on the floor and listening to a recording of a so-called guided meditation is not meditation but a relaxation and visualization exercise. It fills the mind with more sounds, images and stories, with the aim to focus it on something other than itself.

Ancient Eastern teachings tell us that one of the essential aspects of meditation is purification of the mind. This emptying out of the mind happens when we observe thoughts without getting entangled in them. It eventually leads to thoughts slowing down, so that the original nature of the mind can become a conscious experience.

To ensure that the mind is and stays alert, a sitting position with a straight spine is commonly recommended. I prefer sitting on the ground on a flat cushion, folding my legs into the half lotus position, while leaning my back against another cushion. My experience is that changing my position when it becomes uncomfortable doesn't help, but only brings up more body sensations and thoughts of discomfort. So, taking the time to find a spot and a position where we can sit still with a straight back and yet feel sufficiently comfortable is important.

Most meditation schools I have come across recommend choosing the same time and the same spot for meditation to assist the body to become used to sitting still, which is an important component in the attempt of stilling the mind. Most of them advise meditation before dawn and at the time of sunset. It is also advised to start with 10-15 minutes and then slowly extend the time of meditation. Many schools recommend 20 minutes; others don't consider anything under an hour to be sufficient for a beneficial meditation practice.

Again, if we can't get ourselves to get up before dawn, we can meditate at any other time. And if we can't meditate always at the same time, or feel bored with sitting always in the same spot, that's fine too. The important thing is to meditate and to enjoy it, and not to burden ourselves with a lot of rules and paraphernalia.

Other than some authors recommend, who seem to like complicating matters, it's important to state clearly that we definitely don't need to light incense or candles, set intentions for every meditation, take a hot bubble bath to meditate in, invoke angels to descend, surround ourselves with crystals, or pray before meditating. However, if it helps to create a little personal ritual to feel our inherent connection to the realm of the sacred, so be it.

In any case, let's remember that meditation is a simple and natural practice, not a ritual, not a substitute for a religious belief, and not a cult either. The more time we spend on the preparation and the more fuss we create around it, the less time we have to actually meditate, and the less ability we develop to simply sink into a meditative state wherever we are.

Meditation is also not about daydreaming or drifting off into unknown realms. It's about becoming more acutely conscious, not less. This is why it's basically useless to meditate after the intake of drugs or alcohol. That's something else, like a relaxation exercise, that might have its time and purpose, but it doesn't deserve the term meditation. Contrary to what some people claim, these substances don't sharpen the mind to its highest possible level of attention and awareness, they make it rather dull. Substances don't lead us to go beyond the mind through transcending it; they instill a feeling of no-mind, because we dropped under the realm of the mind. "Instead of rising above thought, you have fallen below it," says Tolle.[203]

Transcending the mind

Meditation is not about controlling the mind, it's not a concentration exercise either. While one of its benefits includes improved clarity and better mental focus, meditation for me is not an activity where we mechanically repeat a mantra or stare at an object. 'Bringing the mind home' involves effortlessly observing the gaps between thoughts and diving into them. This is what going beyond the mind means.

It sounds simple, however, for some people it feels like torture when they become aware of the huge amount of negative thoughts popping up the moment they would sit down to meditate. This, it seems, is the main obstacle for many people. The Indian guru, Shri Ram Chandra, pointed out repeatedly that the thoughts themselves don't disturb us but that we

---

[203] Eckhart Tolle, A New Earth, 2005, p.229.

feel disturbed by them. "The thoughts don't meddle with you, rather you meddle with them," he stressed.

Babuji Maharaj, as he was lovingly called by his disciples, often said that the way to get rid of thoughts during meditation involves being unmindful towards them and to treat them as uninvited guests. "Thoughts during meditation are just like children playing in the road. When your attention is not towards thoughts, they are wholly ineffective and are of no value," he said.[204]

Witnessing and yet gently ignoring our thoughts in order to eventually go beyond them, just like ignoring the sounds of playing children, is a beautiful practice in itself. It lightens the strong habitual grip of identification with the content of our minds. We are way more than what happens in our minds. This is one of the precious realizations that meditation practice brings home.

The issue of transcending the mind by becoming aware of "space consciousness" is at the core of the teachings of Eckhart Tolle. He argues that our lives are so out of balance because the dimension of object consciousness is the predominant reality for too many of us. "Most people's lives are cluttered up with things: material things, things to do, things to think about." Being trapped in the dimension of form, means being trapped in the egoic state. According to Tolle, this over-evaluation of form and the unawareness of the dimension of inner space is the cause of our suffering. He argues that "when the dimension of space is lost or rather not known, the things of the world assume an absolute importance, a seriousness and heaviness that in truth they do not have."[205]

His prescription is to balance object consciousness with space consciousness. "At the heart of the new consciousness lies the transcendence of thought, the newfound ability of rising above thought, of realizing a dimension within yourself that is infinitely more vast than thought," he says.[206] According to Tolle, this ability of going beyond the ordinary state of mind can by cultivated by focusing on the space around us, and the space between and behind objects.

---

[204] Shri Ram Chandra Mission, Meditation, Chennai, 1997, p.53
[205] Tolle, ibid, p.227
[206] Tolle, ibid, p.22

Alert inner stillness

This is how he explains how that happens: "Space consciousness means that in addition of being conscious of things – which always comes down to sense perceptions, thoughts and emotions – there is an undercurrent of awareness. Awareness implies that you are not only conscious of things (objects), but you are also being conscious of being conscious. If you can sense an alert inner stillness in the background while things happen in the foreground – that's it!"[207]

This 'alert inner stillness,' is what we can rather easily become aware of in meditation. Tolle calls it "the joy of being." It can be found in meditation, and yet meditation is not a prerequisite for discovering it or focusing on it. According to Tolle, formal meditation "is no substitute for bringing space consciousness into everyday life."[208] I think this is a remarkable distinction, because we are not usually aware of that spaciousness in every meditation.

As far as we take time to sit down and allow ourselves to experience some stillness, be it in the form of meditation, or by focusing our awareness on the space around us, it should be something that pleases us, something we like. While Rinpoche said that meditation is the greatest endeavor we can possibly undertake in this life, he also tells his students to make their approach to meditation as joyful as possible, in richly creative ways. "In one sense meditation is an art, and you should bring to it an artist's delight and fertility of invention," he stresses.

"Become as resourceful in inspiring yourself to enter your peace as you are at being neurotic and competitive in the world," says this remarkable teacher.[209] There's no use of forcing yourself to engage in something that doesn't make you feel good. So, if it's not pleasant, if it doesn't feel smooth and nurturing most of the time, either try another style or ditch it and instead do something else to become more lighthearted.

---

[207] Ibid, p.228
[208] Ibid, p.246
[209] The Tibetan Book of Living and Dying, p.84

Mind the gap

Meditation is a space where we gently bring the mind back again and again on something we focus on. This something should be of a most subtle nature. In the ordinary mode of the mind, we perceive a non-stop stream of thoughts popping up. However, in meditation we discover that this is not the case, because there are gaps between our thoughts. In these gaps, the underlying consciousness can be found. In these gaps is revealed what Buddhists call 'the nature of the mind'.

"The work of meditation is to allow thoughts to slow down, to make that gap more and more apparent," says Rinpoche.[210] What appears then is beautifully described this way: "A primordial, pure, pristine awareness that is at once intelligent, cognizant, radiant, and always awake. It could be said to be the knowledge of knowledge itself." This, he says, "is in fact the nature of everything."[211]

Tolle has spoken and written eloquently about observing the thinking process in order to discover and widen the gap between thoughts. "The 'Mind The Gap' warning so familiar to passengers on the London Underground turns out to be universal advice of enormous import and urgency," says the author Jon Kabat-Zinn in the preface of Rinpoche's book. Indeed, I have grinned many times at the unintended effect of this repeated warning blaring all the time from the speakers in the London Underground, which reminds us of a deeply spiritual meaning as well.

It is in meditation that we can observe whatever thoughts and emotions arise and allow them to pass like the wind pushing away clouds or rising and settling waves in the ocean. There is a distance that is created from the ongoing noise in the mind simply by watching it and letting it be, without trying to influence it by struggling against certain thoughts, trying to change them or think more positive or following down the paths that thoughts keep inviting us to enter - like little rabbit holes in which we tend to get lost a lot. "The secret is not to 'think' about thoughts but to allow them to flow through the mind, while keeping your mind free of afterthoughts," explains Rinpoche.[212]

---

[210] Ibid, p.78
[211] Ibid, p.48
[212] Ibid

The role of an enlightened master

Traditionally, it has been assumed by all Asian approaches and schools that it is the grace of an enlightened master alone, which can deliver the student to reach the spiritual heights of enlightenment. While this belief seems perfectly natural to most Asian spiritual aspirants, the concept of following a guru doesn't go down that well with many in the Western hemisphere where personal independence is a core value.

Since a number of European countries broke free from cruel fascist dictatorships, numerous people questioned the role of the churches during those dark times and distanced themselves from what increasingly felt like outdated and dogmatic belief systems imposed by institutions whose integrity started to be put into question. Democratic and leftist forces, as well as the peace, environmental and feminist movements strongly promoted that people stop blindly believing in authoritarian and patriarchal concepts and start thinking for themselves in order to form their own opinions and stand up for their personal convictions. In this climate, personal freedom has become a core value shared by many, making it difficult to accept philosophies based on the idea that spiritual progress should be tied to the ability of unconditionally loving and ultimately surrendering to a spiritual teacher.

Rinpoche puts it this way: "Many people in the West are suspicious of masters – often, unfortunately, for good reason. I do not have to catalogue the many dreadful and disappointing cases of folly, greed, and charlatanry that have occurred in the modern world since the opening to Eastern wisdom in the 1950s and 1960s. However, all the great wisdom traditions, whether Christian, Sufi, Buddhist or Hindu, rely for their very force on the master-disciple relationship. And so what the world needs urgently now is as clear as possible and understanding of what a real master is, what a real student or disciple is, and what the true nature of transformation is that takes place through devotion to the master, what you might call 'the alchemy of discipleship'."[213]

As remarkable as this 'alchemy of discipleship' is for a large number of students, including Westeners, who wrote extensively about this special relationship to their masters, it has remained a touchy subject in the West.

---

[213] Ibid, p.137

So what are gurus expected to do? The role of a spiritual master is to direct the attention of the disciple to the realm of pure consciousness. Figuratively speaking, masters are pointing their fingers to the moon. It is up to the student to get the message and fix their attention on the moon or to get emotionally attached to the finger pointing there.

Among the expected tasks of a master is to awaken the inherent wisdom of the disciple. It has been said in many ancient scriptures that a master is like a mirror, reflecting the pure consciousness that is our real nature. They also reflect back to us all those entanglements, and ego obsessions that obscure this pristine awareness from prevailing in our direct experience.

Spiritual awakening is not an easy journey. Again and again we are confronted with the neurotic ways of the rational mind, and our resistance to lighten up in the form of the many persisting unhealthy habits and addictions. From this perspective enlightenment usually looks like an unreachable state, a promise held out to us that is realized only by very few people.

It's in these moments of heaviness or despair that it feels very liberating to have an inner conversation with a master. It's tremendously comforting to know that you can ask for help from the master you chose to guide you through the darkness and to feel that your plea has somehow been heard. A master gently pushes us onwards by bestowing the blessing of releasing some unfavorable condition we have become stuck in by transmitting doses of light that purify our hearts.

Rinpoche expresses it beautifully: "Not only is the master the direct spokesperson of your own inner teacher, he or she is also the bearer, channel and transmitter of all the blessings of all the enlightened beings. That is what gives your master the extraordinary power to illumine your mind and heart."[214] This capacity of a guru to illuminate our hearts is part of the attraction, or inward pull, that many people have experienced in the presence of enlightened masters. Just to be in the high frequency energy field of a guru is considered a major blessing in most traditional spiritual teachings. The growing scientific understanding of the magnetic field of energy that is generated and broadcasted by the human heart offers an explanation for this phenomenon.

---

[214] Rinpoche, p.139

As outlined before, the HeartMath Institute has presented solid evidence that our heart rhythms affect those around us. It is, therefore, perfectly logical that the heart rhythm of a person who manages to sustain extraordinary high levels of coherence at all times because they dwell in the realm of space consciousness would create a magnetic field that transmits feelings of harmony, inner peace or bliss to everybody and everything around.

Those who are receptive to it can consciously recognize this shift in their feeling state. This transfer of energy would also explain why many people who have carried urgent questions with them and sought to be in the vicinity of a master to ask them these questions can often not remember them when in the presence of the guru. The mind chatter melts away, and amid the waves of bliss permeating the seekers heart, the question suddenly seems completely irrelevant.

Do it yourself

I believe that a major characteristic of many people living in the Western hemisphere is to do things by themselves and not to rely anymore to such a large extent on maintenance people, experts, or a hierarchy of clerics. This approach to life as well as religion has taught us a lot, got us very far in many ways, and freed us of from the shackles of dependencies of many sorts. This is not only a valid experience if it comes to home repairs, it also goes for the discovery of the spiritual realm.

Some of us might feel drawn to a particular guru at some point in life and discover that this could be the most significant relationship they ever had. There might come a point when some might feel that they need to move on, or not. Others might never even ponder the possibility of becoming a disciple of any teacher. But it doesn't really matter anymore and this feels like one of the huge advantages of living at this specific time. In most periods of history, spiritual teachings were secrets passed on to a handful of initiates in traditional lineages. Fortunately, today, this is not the case anymore.

In fact, there are many examples of people who did not practice any spiritual practices and woke up one day and found themselves on a very lighthearted level of self-realization. Tolle himself is a prominent example for that. Another is the bestselling author and teacher Byron Katie who was trapped in a serious depression and suddenly had a radical moment of awakening that changed her life in such a profound way that she never experienced suffering again.

She realized on a deep level that when she believed the painful thoughts her mind would churn up, she would suffer. If she wouldn't, she was feeling well. Katie went on to develop what she calls "The Work" – a razor sharp method of inquiry that cuts through the tendency of believing stressful thoughts, which run our lives if left unchecked. She travels the world to make this work accessible to growing numbers of people.

I am sure that there are many more people at this point in time who are experiencing advanced stages of spiritual awakening. It's just that many of them have probably not ventured yet into becoming publicly known. For most people, it seems to be more of a gradual process, however, some people wake up just like that. I have come across quite a lot of material, most of it written by mediums channeling messages from spirits, that various factors and constellations of this particular time are assisting, or rather nudging, us to raise our vibrational levels and awaken. This is another indicator for me that the era in which we had to depend on a lineage of masters to increase our chances of enlightenment has come to an end. In the new cycle that has already begun, circumstances for awakening seem much more favorable.

So the question is not so much about whether or not we choose to enter a relationship with a guru, the question is whether we are willing and motivated enough to take time for ourselves to sit in stillness so we can enjoy our inner treasures. The most valuable gift we can give ourselves is time to get in touch with our inner hearts, that space where peace and bliss abide. "If we really want to experience life to its fullest, change must come from within," says Gaur Gopal Das whose lighthearted motivational speeches have become popular among millions of people. Das is an Indian spiritual teacher, and lifestyle coach, who is a monk of the International Society for Krishna Consciousness.

Inner change revolves around the quality of our thoughts and feelings, as well as the state of awareness of our own essence, which is pure consciousness. What we are up against is not only our own resistance but an increasing amount of distraction as mainstream culture and media promote hectic, noisy and often violent forms of constant entertainment. "In a world dedicated to distraction, silence and stillness terrify us; we protect ourselves from them with noise and frantic busyness. Looking into the nature of our mind is the last thing we would dare to do," says Rinpoche.[215] Going within with delight to uncover lightheartedness so we can evolve to higher dimensions of consciousness really means *Daring Greatly*. It's ultimately the most rewarding way of daring.

---

[215] Rinpoche, ibid, p.53.

Summary

The most valuable gift we can give ourselves is time to get in touch with our inner hearts, that space where peace and bliss abide. Going within to evolve into higher dimensions of consciousness is the most rewarding way of *Daring Greatly*.

Inner change revolves around the quality of our thoughts and feelings, as well as the state of awareness of our own essence. Spiritual awakening is not an easy journey. We are up against a whole lot of resistance to lighten up in the form of the many persisting unhealthy habits and addictions, as well as increasing amounts of distraction from a noisy world.

A relationship with a spiritual master of caliber can be very helpful, as they have the capacity to illuminate our hearts. Just to be in the high frequency energy field of a guru is uplifting. The growing scientific understanding of the magnetic field of energy that is generated and broadcasted by the human heart offers an explanation for this phenomenon.

In most previous periods spiritual teachings were secrets passed on to a handful of initiates in traditional lineages of masters. Fortunately, today, this is not the case anymore, which is one of the huge advantages of living at this specific time. So, we really don't need any gurus anymore, and can have the courage to stand alone and learn from different schools and teachers.

Witnessing and, yet, gently ignoring our thoughts in order to eventually go beyond them, just like ignoring the sounds of playing children, is a beautiful practice in itself. It lightens the strong identification with the content of our minds. We are way more than what happens in our minds. This is one of the precious realizations that meditation practice brings home. It's a practice of effortlessness that dispels heaviness.

The question is: are we willing and motivated enough to take time for ourselves to sit in stillness so we can discover the joy of being? There's no use of forcing yourself to engage in something that doesn't make you feel good.

If it's not pleasant, if it doesn't feel smooth or nurturing most of the time, try another meditation style, or ditch the practice altogether. Then meditation is not for you at this point in time. No big deal. Simply do something else that sets you on the path of becoming more lighthearted.

"It's alright to have a good time. That's one of the most important messages of enlightenment."

Thaddeus Golas

CONCLUSION

Just bring on Easy Peasy

You can experience your present reality on much deeper levels of ease and joy simply by raising your energetic vibration. The frequencies you vibrate on have little to do with the thoughts you think. It's the emotions we feel that make all the difference. That's the rocket fuel that can lift us up to higher states of lightheartedness. "It's hard to believe, but changing the content of your mind does nothing to change your vibration level," says Thaddeus Golas[216]

He points out that, "we always have the experiences and perceptions appropriate to our vibration level." One of the many reasons why the level we vibrate on is so important is that we perceive everything differently once our vibration rises. When we are in love, everything seems to be wonderful. "Our level of consciousness decides what we see," says the late American psychiatrist and spiritual teacher David Hawkins.[217]

A leap from a lower vibrating field, which is characterized by various layers of contraction, to a higher harmonic frequency requires expansion. This can happen only in a relaxed and open feeling state. It cannot occur by pushing. It comes with allowing relaxation and exuberance. "You are at the level of consciousness that has the greatest pleasure and ecstasy you are capable of accepting," points out the American writer Golas.[218]

---

[216] Thaddeus Golas, The Lazy Man's Guide to Enlightenment, 1972, p.36
[217] David Hawkins, Power versus Force, 2013, p.253
[218] Golas, ibid, p.45

In the age we are currently in, we are about to leave behind a central tenant that was given to the value of hard work and tireless efforts. My great grandmother used to say that there is nothing more difficult to bear than a number of good days. This widely known German saying implies that doing nothing is impossible and that when there are good days, the bad ones are sure to come. It is just one example for a worldview that expresses resignation to harsh circumstances or misery and, thus, keeps perpetuating them.

Nowadays, some of the famous coaches keep hammering in similar belief systems by emphasizing various rather difficult efforts we should commit to in order to overcome mediocrity and achieve greatness. This contemporary reinforcement of old beliefs has made it even more difficult for many people to conceive the idea that experiences of pleasure are important for our health, our sense of safety, as well as for the possibility of evolving our levels of consciousness. Allowing ourselves more ease while still pursuing personal growth is indeed a big shift. This is what leads to lighthearted thriving.

Relaxing is not an easy thing to do. As absurd as it sounds, however, it takes practicing. It has a lot to do with letting go of the urge to struggle or control. It's also connected to feeling that we are good enough. It's about letting go of the thought that we need to be doing many things to improve ourselves. Without being relaxed, it's not possible to feel happy. That means that the one skill to develop in these frantic times is ease.

Huge numbers of people don't seem to know anymore how nice it feels to ease up because they don't seem to know how to relax. And the things most of us do habitually to unwind aren't relaxing at all, such as watching TV, getting hooked up on social media, running around in shopping malls or hanging out somewhere to get high or tipsy. These things add a whole lot of visual and emotional impressions to our systems that need to be processed.

What we often do unconsciously in what has commonly been called 'spare time' is adding more toxins and more stress. A lot of the recreational activities many people engage in before or after long office hours can also look and feel rather like another dose of self-punishment, such as driving the body too hard in tough workouts. For tired bodies and tense muscles, this is not a gentle thing to do.

Most of the time, most of us are in a state of more or less chronic anxiety, worry or stress. Ease is a state that many people have difficulty to recall as a feeling in their bodies. While this is the new normal, we do well to remember it's not our natural state. As mentioned before, even the organism of an amoeba is equipped by nature to produce endorphins – which is a neuropeptide triggering feelings of relaxation and pleasure.

"Most of us accumulate stress every day, which manifests in our minds as anxiety and in our bodies as tension," say Holford and Lawson.[219] At this point in time, the human species in general seems to be rather addicted to the stress hormone adrenalin. Relaxation, and the ease in our muscles and nervous system that comes with it, doesn't seem to be very popular. Non-doing is widely judged as laziness, and in cultures where sloth as in big laziness is considered to be one of the deadly sins, it just doesn't sit well with us. It's certainly not something spectacular to post on Facebook.

What most people don't seem to know yet is that feeling safe comes from feeling well physically and emotionally. This is how important relaxation is. It instills a feeling of pleasure and safety. Feeling safe is the antidote to fear. We all have a strong longing to feel safe, especially in this era of epochal change and upheaval. Feeling safe comes when we feel relaxed in our bodies and minds. Period. The surest way to trigger a happy chemistry in the body is to enjoy something. "You must have a pleasurable life to feel safe," says William Bloom.[220]

Enjoyment and pleasure ease the toxic tension frozen in our bodies and expand us. "Every time you linger in pleasure and truly appreciate it, you do something immensely good for your health."[221] It's as simple as that. All too often we expect our bodies to function and don't look after its needs for rest, comfort, play and our own positive attention.

Awareness of the body

One of the problems is that we have not been taught well to be aware of our bodies. It seems that we don't really inhabit them well with our

---

[219] Patrick Holford, Susannah Lawson, The Stress Cure, London, Piatkus, p.98
[220] William Bloom, Feeling Safe, 2002, p.36
[221] Ibid, p.38

awareness. We tend to forget the body while we are doing what it is we do in life. Most of us seem to become aware of the body only when some parts of it start hurting. Pain is in fact a wake-up call to start taking more tender care.

I have come to realize that not many people I met in Egypt can relate to the word 'ease', much less connect to that relaxed state. The way to explain ease when someone never consciously experienced it, is to ask them to smile. Not in an artificial or cold way, but rather by allowing a warm smile to appear on your face. A smile immediately relaxes the tension, not only in our facial muscles, but in our whole body as well as in the mind. This is the reason why the experience of laughing together extensively in a group is so important because it induces this wonderful state of ease.

Ease is much more than thinking or feeling that something is easy. Ease comes with a physical experience of relaxation and feeling good in our bodies. This is when we can more easily accept and appreciate who and how we are. Ease can happen when we take time to enjoy a bubble bath in a tub, or a massage, or a swim in the sea.

Ease also comes from going through a lot of difficult experiences and realizing that we have always come out well on the other side. It comes when we develop trust in our ability to bounce back from distress. It comes when we know it will for sure because it happened to us many times before. Then we can trust that in due time we can rise up again like the metaphorical bird phoenix from the ashes to soar.

If we want to feel safe, we need to learn the practice of steering our bodies away from the impulse to produce loads of chemicals and hormones of fear at the slightest distressing moment and instead actively stimulate the production of the pleasure chemistry. It's a repetitive process to be done over and over again. It's not a practice we do a few times, and that's it.

Becoming more lighthearted is a process that involves not only the mental, emotional and spiritual dimension, but also the physical body. It is a spiritual attribute of lightness felt in the heart and generated by high frequency emotions, and yet, tensions and toxins do accumulate in our bodies. The many knots in our muscles or joints are often terribly painful reminders that it might benefit us immensely to ease up. Joy can only arise in a relaxed state.

The starting point is to take a few deep breaths and focus on the breath moving from inside. The key skill is to pause a bit and notice. We can easily feel the body from within and scan it from top to toe, feeling its aliveness, and daring to feel its pain. Most of us shy away from this ancient Asian practice which nowadays has become popular in the form of mindfulness, because it seems unpleasant to feel the aching parts. However, the awareness of what hurts, where, in which way, actually feels comforting and often reduces the pain. At the same time, the practice allows us the conscious experience of feeling how little moments of pleasure sink into the body and create a beautiful flow of endorphins. It's elating by itself to realize this.

Our bodies need our attention, just like a child craves for attention. Neglecting the body leads to the body acting up – like children do. "If your mind ignores the body, your body will feel abandoned and will tense up, blocking benevolent chemicals and energies," explains Bloom. He underlines that when people dislike their bodies, it's like living with "a constantly disapproving adult", which is a recipe for fear, tension and anxiety.[222]

The mind can easily integrate a new attitude of a loving parent towards the body, who fully accepts and sympathizes with all the inner imperfections and distress. We can actually develop the habit of doing that, even if we didn't grow up with particularly loving parents. This is the major challenge of growing up: developing into a mature adult capable of parenting ourselves in all the ways we would have wished to be taken care of as kids.

Checking in with how we feel inside is part of the beautiful attitude of self-compassion. It's also a good way to emotionally disengage a bit from unpleasant events or people around us. This minute of intense attention to our body reconnects us again to our own center of strength. In these situations, the body has enough trouble dealing with low frequency energies coming in, and doesn't need to be aggravated by the mind getting lost in running anxious thoughts. Instead of being overwhelmed and creating a toxic chemistry, you can send a message on the lines of: "Hello lovely body, I'm sorry that you are going through distress now. I am sending you some nice feelings now, so you can be okay again." Tender self-talk together with friendly feelings creates an immediate shift.

---

[222] William Bloom, The Endorphine Effect, 2001, p.61

To recover a strong sense of energetic security, it is also very helpful to become aware of the ground beneath us, because our bodies need the electromagnetic field of the earth to thrive. When we lose the sense of connection to the earth, it can create a feeling of instability and weakness. So taking a walk, and consciously feeling our feet on the ground, or sitting on the ground and leaning our backs against a tree, or lying on the floor and feeling it's texture, are easy ways to restore the feeling of connection to nature the body craves. Simple activities like these restore the flow of benevolent energies.

Floating in the sea

The element of water helps me sense on a deeper level what letting go and flow feel like. Swimming in the sea, or soaking in a hot bubble bath seems to miraculously melt down muscular tensions and with that the stored armor of self-protection and resistance to what is. Floating in salt water is a great way for me to effortlessly rejoice. When the body floats in water, cradled by waves, it feels weightless, embraced and free. This, for me, is the perfect experience of ease and lightheartedness.

It is then that I feel truly part of the environment. Something in me expands, and I feel aligned with my natural inner element. Like a child, I can jump in the waves, feeling tempted to giggle for no reason or even to laugh out loud, tremendously enjoying all kinds of movements in the water, or imagining an existence as a fish or a mermaid. It is then that the otherwise often abstract notion of oneness suddenly makes perfect sense. The water that is flowing around me is also flowing around and through every being around me at the same time and somehow connects us in mysterious ways.

Water has been used as a symbol for emotions. It definitely has the quality to dissolve the heavy ones and enhance the uplifting ones. There is no way to carry anger or sadness when I am caressed by the warm waters of the Red Sea. It has a rather mystical quality to it too, perhaps, because it feels somehow ancient to the point of being primordial. All life on this planet has started in water. This is where we emerged from. Maybe this is why it feels so fundamentally comforting. Besides, our bodies consist to a huge percentage of water. Seeing to it that these liquids can be in a harmonious state and flow gently like little waves seems to be essential for a profound sense of wellbeing. The feeling creates the healing. For the self-healing mechanism to be functioning well we need to relax.

More comfort in the body

Cultivating more ease in our bodies allows us to feel more comfortable in our own skin. There's a lot of talk nowadays, especially in caching circles, about self-development starting beyond our comfort zone. This approach doesn't take into account that it's imperative to allow ourselves first and foremost to feel comfortable in our own bodies. That's way more important than putting on comfy clothes, which many of us love to do, because our health and wellbeing depend on it. So creating more comfort by feeling appreciation or sending a smile into the body is a foundation for the ability to then courageously face events that at first might feel uncomfortable to us.

We all know that drinking sufficient amounts of fresh water and sleeping enough are as vital for our bodies as a diet that contains a lot of fresh vegetables and fruits. We help our bodies to rejoice and function better when we stick to a way of eating that is nourishing and feels good to our individual system. We also know that there are many things we do that are detrimental to our health and that we would feel way better if we managed to drop these habits.

It's precisely the fact that these things are known to us, and the mention of them reminds us of our feelings of shame about some of our laziness, addictions, or dysfunctional daily habits, which is bound to lead to a big build-up of resistance. It is not questionable that healthy food is good for you, and that a competent nutritionist can help enormously with changing your diet in order to reduce inflammation in the body and make you feel more energized and lighter. However, when we are stuck in resistance, we do what we can do and appreciate ourselves just the way we are. In those situations, it's great to remember what even nutritionists say: emotions are primary food.

The award winning Indian medical doctor and passionate advocate of the ancient holistic system of healing called Ayurveda puts it this way: "Anger, greed, pride, jealousy, hatred and frustration are the enemies of good health. Study after study, with longer periods of observation, has repeatedly identified the above traits as the most important risk factor for illnesses. They are more important than all other biochemical parameters like sugar, blood pressure, or cholesterol."[223]

This quote confirmed to me what I have always instinctively felt: our emotional state is the most important factor influencing our health and wellbeing. I used to get the shudders when opening books that talk about all the items that should be dropped when starting a healthy diet. I would definitely close any book the moment I came across any remarks aimed at encouraging people to drop all their addictions. Some of our bad-ass behaviors have become very dear to us to the point that they often seem impossible to leave behind. It's a big step when we realize that dropping a dysfunctional habit might make us feel better, but it's not the one most important factor for enhancing our wellness. We can very well cultivate joy while we continue with eating pizza, smoking cigarettes, drinking wine, watching TV or whatever it is that we are seemingly unable or unwilling to drop.

So, if you are the couch potato type, don't go into a stress reaction because I am not at all suggesting that you go to the gym, stand on your head or do anything difficult that scares you at this point. By all means, stay on your sofa, and really enjoy it. If you love watching TV, do that and enjoy it. If you love dancing in the house, do more of it and enjoy it. If you love to read, curl up and enjoy diving into a good book. Do more of the things you enjoy and realize consciously the pleasure that this gives you. Shifting your emotional landscape first by bringing on more enjoyment and allowing yourself some pleasurable moments on a regular basis makes it much easier to then follow through with goals you would like to achieve.

My experience has shown me many times with myself and with clients that when we take one step towards feeling more lighthearted, others follow miraculously. A little change of habit can create great results. Taking the physical approach is what many people seem to be drawn to first. If that is the case for you, remember that for a tense body and overwhelmed psyche it's very pleasurable to allow yourself a massage. Just lying on a massage bed and being rubbed all over with aromatherapy oils and their fantastic smells sure feels like heaven to me.

---

[223] B.M. Hedge: You can be healthy, New Delhi, 2017, p.112

I mean who doesn't have hard shoulders, aches in the neck, or the lower back, or the knees from sitting too much in front of computers and in cars? We carry so many aches and pains while pushing through our everyday lives, most of the time trying hard to ignore the warning signals of a body that is tired. Feeling how certain knots release, noticing how some muscles seem to become longer, sensing how pounds of tension seem to drop off, creates calming of nerves and comforting emotions.

Massage has become very popular all over the world because it's such a pleasant experience to feel lighter. The reason why I enjoy massaging others is because I love to be massaged. This is why offering this experience to another person feels very pleasant to me. It's precisely because my body seems to need massages to release deep seated stress symptoms that I chose to add Wellness & Massage Therapy to the range of things I do for a living. Having a massage regularly is part of maintenance of our body, as well as an effective strategy to prevent feeling worse in the future.

When there is a lot of tension in muscles all over, driving the body harder by going for a work-out is not such a good idea. I have seen a lot of clients who did that a few times and ended up feeling so much pain, that they finally chose to come for a massage. In spite of their condition, many of them ask for a hard sports massage. The conditioning that there can be no gain without pain seems still very widespread. My approach – especially in these cases – is suggesting a gentle treatment that is relaxing and nourishing. The gentleness feels reassuring to a body that is tight and hard as a result of too much stress and neglect. When we soften into ease, blockages can be removed and the vital life force energy can flow unobstructed. It's only then that healing can start happening.

My suggestion would be to find a form of moving your body that you like and promise yourself to seriously engage in that. Whether it's swimming, walking, yoga, hiking or dancing is not that important. It's the level of joy while doing these activities that creates a shift in your physiology. Allowing our bodies to move more joyfully is what it boils down to. Even the term 'work-out' feels counterintuitive to me. It defies the purpose if it's about work again. If there is more pushing, it's going to backfire. However, if that's what you truly enjoy, go for it. Emotional and physical delight is the compass, the North Star. It points the direction to navigate chaos and consciously co-create a new era.

Longing for paradise

In many of the highly evolved ancient cultures, pleasure was held in great esteem and placed in a sacred context. Egyptian temples were not only places for worship, but for sensual delights such as music, dance and physical treatments with oils. Goddesses of love were worshiped in numerous cultures before the advent of monotheistic religions. Followers of these religions went to great lengths to destroy this part of our heritage. However, the legacy of a sunken paradise has lived on through oral history.

A good example is Dilmun, the legendary land of love where the Gods dwelt, which is referred to in the epics of the Sumerians, as well as ancient Egyptian texts.[224] Not much is known about what has been described as a lost island paradise, where sensual enchantment and love seem to have been a central characteristic. The fascination with a magical island in faraway waters was kept alive during the various kingdoms of pharaohs in Egypt. It is actually still an important part of the collective human narrative not just in Egypt. The longing for a promised land, a just government and well-being for all people shape myths and legends all over the world. Through stories handed down over generations in diverse places, including India, Iran, Japan, Mexico and North America, just to name some places, we can follow the mythological traces of an ideal society that was deluged by heavy floods.[225] The most famous of the many apocalyptic accounts are those of the sunken continents of Lemuria and Atlantis.

The Garden of Eden that these legends point to can be interpreted as a metaphor for oneness and innocent joy that doesn't know about opposites, or time. Life on earth, which is subject to the laws of duality, began with the loss of this original innocence. Many mystics have pointed out that it is thinking, which by nature operates in the realm of duality that obstructs the experience of love and oneness. Paradise can only be realized by the heart when the mind is silent and a great inner stillness appears.

In our daily experience, oneness consciousness and feelings of unconditional love feel very much out of reach to most of us. Many people seem to think that they have never really experienced true lasting love, and

---

[224] Michael Rice, Search for Paradise Land, Essex, 1985, p.122
[225] Rand and Rose Flem-Ath, Atlantis. Der Versunkene Kontinent unter dem Ewigen Eis, Munich, 1977, p.97

these thoughts bring up a large array of painful emotions. Love has become such a huge concept and expectation that somehow we tend to shy away from what we are most longing for. However, if we take a good look at some of its components, it becomes clear that loving as a daily reality can quite easily be attained. Appreciation, caring or compassion are some of the core elements, and they belong to those tender feelings available to us the moment we remember to bring them on.

While we practice shifting into uplifting emotions it's wise to remember that we have inherited many patterns of lingering at the heavy end of the emotional spectrum. We all keep forgetting that all those feelings of shame, guilt, resentment or rage are not only destructive for our own bodies, but also for the universe at large. This is how the Indian sage, musician and founder of one of the first Sufi[226] orders in the West, Inayat Khan, puts it: "When the wind blows and storms rage and bring destruction, this is seen as a mechanical act of nature. But it is not merely a mechanical phenomenon; it is directed by humanities feelings, by its intense feelings. Feelings become huge life forms. Like a battery they give power to wind, storms, floods and volcanic eruptions."[227]

Becoming aware of the storms, we unconsciously co-create is essential. It's equally important to stop beating ourselves up for feeling so many heavy emotions. That's just how it is. What matters is to keep going with our various attempts to shift out of them - one at a time. Self-compassion comes with practice. It arises once we realize that, "when the heart is out of tune everything goes wrong; it makes the whole atmosphere out of tune."[228]

Khan has succinctly pointed out that for Sufis spiritual culture is all about the tuning of the heart. Like a music instrument, the heart needs to be tuned to a certain pitch of vibration that resonates with its natural tone and purpose – a pitch that allows us to feel the ecstasy of life, he says. When sympathy, kindness, compassion, gentleness, gratefulness and appreciation are not there, then the heart is like a loose string on a violin.

---

[226] Sufism and its different schools or paths have widely been considered as the mystical part or branch of Islam, however, this way of thought and practice is much older than Islam, or Christianity for that matter.
[227] Inayat Khan, The mysticism of sound and music, 1996, p.200
[228] Inayat Khan, The Art of Being and Becoming, 1982, p.159

Khan underlines that the heart quality has immense power. If it's lacking all inclinations that drag any person downward will appear and bring a person down. "As long as the heart is not tuned to its proper pitch, one will not be happy."[229]

Whether we desire to feel more joy, or are longing to make a positive contribution to this world, it is the condition of our own hearts that requires to be changed first and foremost. "Better conditions can only be brought about by the individual who realizes that it is the development of the heart that can accomplish this, and nothing else," stresses Khan. The key to sustainable change individually and collectively is in the tuning of our hearts to a humane vibration and harmonious rhythm.

This tuning of our hearts happens each time we are consciously willing to ease up and start to emit any of those emotions that feel like a refreshing summer breeze. With every pleasant emotion we generate, we create more serenity. Over time we become aware that the years of remembering, learning, navigating, reading, relaxing, meditating and tuning have all contributed in some strange way to bring about a tipping point, where things suddenly feel and flow more smoothly.

It's as if a new subtle pattern has finally seeped out from our hearts and sunk deep into the core of our cellular fabric. The process is as easy as tuning any instrument again and again. In order to play it well, it simply needs to sound so harmonious that listening to its sound creates delight and even rapture. Feeling light at heart relieves every atom of our bodies and minds from the disharmonious frequencies of heaviness and discord. This is the way how our hearts can finally stop being at war, and we can create peace within. It's what we as stressed individuals living in a world of distress need more than ever before. Lightheartedness raises us up to higher octaves and spheres of harmony and joy.

---

[229] Ibid., p.155, 157

EXERCISES

EXERCISE ONE

Appreciate & Accelerate Growth

Step 1

Make a list of all the turns and twists that led to unexpected and exciting opportunities which this special time of change and turmoil has offered you already.

Take a few minutes to allow images or memories of some of the adventures you have lived through to come up in your mind.

Remember the good times. Write down some beautiful memories to behold.

Step 2

Look back at your life and become aware of where you were twenty, or ten years ago.

- What have you accomplished?
- How have you changed?

Write down your major achievements, all those things that happened that you can possibly be proud of.

Step 3

Remember the difficulties, the pain and the major challenges you have been through, not to relive them or soak in self-pity, but to ask yourself the most important questions:

- What have I learnt from them?
- Where have I arrived (did I arrive) because of these experiences?
- What is it that I feel drawn or even nudged to do because of this?
- Where does this want to take me?

Step 4

Promise yourself to keep unlocking your inherent potential for joy, which automatically expands you into a more exuberant and healthy version of yourself.

EXERCISE TWO

Embracing Change

Step 1

Sit down and take a few deep breaths. Allow yourself to become aware that the winds of change ultimately always work in your favor. Out of this insight, set the clear intention - like setting the sails of a sailing boat – to navigate gracefully to wonderful new shores.

Step 2

Write down all the beautiful character traits you have, all the nice things that you already have and do, which you can possibly appreciate.

Step 3

List all the things you dream of doing when you successfully ride on the new waves. How can you assist with bringing on a new era?

Step 4

Lean back. Relax. Take some really deep belly breaths. Close your eyes. Feel the aliveness that flows through your body and around it, the aliveness that you are.

Feel the preciousness and worth of this universal life force permeating you and everything and everybody around you.

Step 5

Visualize all the abundance, possibilities, and adventures rolling into a life you love to live.

Step 5

Bring your awareness to the emotions you feel when you think these thoughts and see these images. Keep your eyes closed and allow yourself to bask in the beautiful feelings that emerge.

EXERCISE THREE

Raise Your Vibration

Step One

Close your eyes and take a few deep breaths. Hold out both arms in front of you, palms facing each other. Feel the inner side of your hands. Become aware of all sensations in them, of their aliveness.

Step Two

Slowly move your palms against each other. Keep the maximum focus on the palms of your hands.

Step Three

Repeat the exercise and become aware of all sensations

At some point, you might feel that you can't move the hands closer to each other – as if a ball of pressed together energy would sit there and prevent you from bringing the palms of your hands to touch each other. Or you might feel a sensation of tingling in your hands, or a feeling of cold, warmth, or even heat.

Step Four

Stretch out your hands, palms facing the ceiling. Take some deep breaths and relax.

Step Five

Imagine light, or colorless healing energies of high frequency and potency flowing from above into your head, down your face and throat from inside and filling up your heart.

Allow this energy to spread over your arms and flow into your hands. Let it concentrate in your palms.

Step Six

Place your left hand on your heart and your right hand on your tummy. Just sit and allow the energy to fill you up. It knows best where to go.

EXERCISE FOUR

Placing Someone in the Light

Step One

Sit comfortably and take a few deep breaths. Connect to your heart center.

Step Two

Imagine that your heart and chest expand, gathering all the light and love existing around you in the empty space of your room, beyond your home, over the town or city where you live, all the way up into the sky.

Step Three

Visualize a person you might feel worried about, someone who needs an energy boost or healing standing in front of you, and send them all that love and light from your heart to theirs.

Alternatively, you can visualize that love and light showers this special person from above.

Just use your imagination and intention. Trust the process.

Step Four

Lean back, place one hand on your heart and remember that love and light are infinite resources that you are inherently connected to.

Enjoy feeling this energy.

Bless the other person. Bring your full attention back to the space of the room surrounding you. Then become aware of your emotions. Hold those feelings as long as you can in your awareness.

EXERCISE FIVE

To Be, To Do, To Have

Step One

Sit down in a quiet moment where you can be undisturbed. Take a few deep breaths, make yourself comfortable and start writing down your answers to these questions:

- What would you like to be?
- What would you really like to do if time and money were no obstacles?
- What would you like to have?
- How would you need to be to do and have all the above?

Don't censor yourself. Allow yourself to get in touch with and express all your desires. That's where the juice is. Our desires nudge us to develop and expand.

Write down everything that comes to your mind, preferably on three different papers.

Step Two

Leave the exercise alone for a while and do something else, something completely different.

Step Three

Go back to the exercise and reread what you wrote. Check what the most important things are for you.

Write those priorities on a card. This is your roadmap.

Step Four

Look at it often. Stick it up on a mirror or carry it with you in your wallet.

This helps remember what you most want to draw in and cultivate.

EXERCISE SIX

Heartfocused Breathing

This is a deceptively simple technique that is at the core of the HeartMath system. It soothes the nervous system and feels deeply relaxing. This exercise creates more awareness of your heart, as well as your aliveness. It also leads to more harmony in your heart rhythm, and activates a sense of well-being while you recharge your level of vital energy.

Step 1

Sit comfortably on a chair, straighten your spine, plant both feet firmly on the ground. Take a few deep breaths, feel your diaphragm being moved by the breath.

Step 2

Close your eyes, place one hand on the center of your chest and focus on your heart. Feel the area behind your hand by bringing your awareness there. Breathe easily and gently.

Step 3

Try to feel your heart beat. Become aware of the heart pumping blood through your whole system. Energy is pulsating through you. Feel this sense of aliveness in your body while keeping your main focus on your heart.

After practicing this technique every day regularly for a while, you will reach a point where you can easily do it without placing one hand on your heart, or without closing your eyes. Just by remembering to do the exercise, the body, mind and emotions will willingly go along this new path through which you are setting a new baseline.

Simply slowing down your breath by watching it and focusing your awareness on your heart region activates the cascading of beneficial biochemical reactions throughout your various systems. Keep doing this exercise as often as you can. It's easy, super beneficial, and it feels good.

EXERCISE SEVEN

Send a Smile Into Your Body

Step One

Sit comfortably, relax and think of a beautiful situation or person you love. Allow a smile to appear on your face – a genuine warm smile.

Step Two

Notice the sensation of that smile on your face. Decide to allow your body to be nourished by it. Send the smile into different parts of your body.

Your brain is able to guide the flow of this energy in the form of enchantment and vitality.

You can send the smile into all your organs, or to those areas of your body that are tired or painful.

Step Three

Notice the feeling of pleasure expanding in your body. Just sit there and smile for at least five minutes.

This is a wonderful and easy way of cultivating appreciation, delight and love for yourself simply through smiling.

EXERCISE EIGHT

Bring On Laughter

Step One

Sit on the floor, take a few deep belly breaths and center yourself. Find a position that allows your spine to straighten and yet feels comfortable.

Step Two

Lean slightly backwards as you inhale, stretch out your arms in front of you in a circle form and then bring them towards your heart while breathing in, as if you would gather more air to enter your heart area.

Step Three

While breathing out, lean forward and push your arms forward, with stretched out hands, fingers pointing upwards, in front of you, as if helping to push out the stale air you have accumulated in your lungs. Make the sound *haaa* as you breathe out.

It's a soothing and relaxing sound. So repeat it a few times until your voice becomes louder.

Step Four

Make three of those loud *haaa* sounds. Enjoy hearing your voice and feeling the opening of your throat chakra.

Then make them five, and then make as many of those sounds as you possibly can in one exhale. Repeat several times.

Step Five

Do some simple stretches and giggle. Bring both hands together, with your palms touching each other in front of you with outstretched arms. While breathing in, open both arms wide to the side, and laugh.

Or raise your hands upwards to the ceiling and laugh. Let your body guide you. Enjoy the stretching and the different sounds of the laughter you let out. Allow yourself to goof around in this way for a few minutes. Then just sit still and laugh as long as you can.

Step Six

Make a promise to yourself to check out Laughter Yoga exercises on YouTube videos.

Commit to a time when you will take that step and write it in your agenda.

Step Seven

Find out about Online Laughter Yoga Clubs and try out laughing for free with others whom you don't see.

BIBLIOGRAPHY

Almaas, A.H. *Diamond Heart*. Book Four. Boston: Shambhala Press, 1987.

Beck, Martha. *Finding your Way in a Wild New World*. London: Piatkus, 2012.

Bennett-Goleman, Tara. *Mind Wispering*. New York: HarperCollings, 2013

Bloom, William. *Feeling Safe*. London: Judy Piatkus, 2002.

The Endorphin Effect, London: Judy Piatku, 2001.

Braden, Gregg. *The Turning Point*. Hay House, 2014.

Brown, Brenè. Daring Greatly. New York: Avery, 2012.

Childre, Doc and Rozman, Deborah.

    Transforming Anger. Oakland: New Harbringer Publications, 2003.

    Transforming Stress. Oakland: New Harbringer Publications, 2005.

    Transforming Depression. Oakland: New Harbringer Publications, 2007.

    Transforming Anxiety. Oakland: New Harbringer Publications, 2006

Chopra, Deepak. *The Ultimate Happiness Prescription*. Random House, 2009.

Co, Stephen; Robins, Eric (M.D.). *Your Hands Can Heal You*. New York: Atria, 2013.

Cohen, Lawrence (Ph.D.). *Playful Parenting*. Random House, 2001.

Downey, Miles. *Effective Coaching*. Cengage Learning, 2003.

Eden, Donna; Feinstein, David (Dr.). *Energy Medicine*. London: Piatkus, 2010.

Hedge, B. M. *You can be healthy*. New Delhi: Trinity Press, 2017.

Holford, Patrick and Lawsaon, Susannah Lawson. *The Stress Cure*, London: Piatkus, 2015.

Marx Hubbard, Barbara. *Conscious Evolution*. Novato: New World Library, 1998.

Flem-Ath, Rand and Rose. *Atlantis. Der Versunkene Kontinent unter dem Ewigen Eis*, Munich, 1977

Ford, Debbie. *Courage*. New York: HarperCollins Publishers, 2012.

Furst, Dan. *Surfing Aquarius*, San Francisco: Weiser Books, 2011.

Gallwey, Timothy. *The Inner Game of Tennis*. London: Pan Books, 1975.

George, Kim. *Coaching into Greatness*. Wilsey, 2006.

Golas, Thaddeus, *The Lazy Man's guide to Enlightenment*, New York: Bantam Books, 1972.

Goleman, David. *Emotional Intelligence.* London, Bloomsburry Publishing, 1996.

Goleman, Daniel and Davidson, Richard. *The Science of Meditation.* Penguin Life, 2018.

Kataria, Madan. *Laugh for no Reason*, Mumbai: Madhuri International, 2011.

The Inner Spirit of Laughter. Bangalore: Dr Kataria School of Laughter Yoga, 2016.

Kenney, Jim. *Thriving in the Crosscurrent.* Wheaton: Quest Books, 2010.

Khan, Hazrat Inayat. *The mysticism of sound and music.* Boston: Shambhala, 1996.

The Art of Being and Becoming. New York: Omega Publications, 1982.

Kinslow, Frank (Dr.). *When Nothing Works, Try Doing Nothing.* Lucid Sea, 2010

Kline, Nancy. *Time to Think.* London: Cassell Illustrated, 1999.

McTaggert, Lynne. *The Bond.* New York: Free Press, 2011

The Intention Experiment. London: HarperElement, 2008.

Nepo, Mark. *Finding Inner Courage.* London: Heron Books, 2013

Lyle, Lesley. *Laugh Your Way To Happiness.* Oxford: Watkins, 2014.

Lipton, Bruce. *The Biology of Belief*, Hay House, 2005

Osho. *Joy.* New York: St. Martin's Press, 2004.

Courage. New York: St. Martin's Press, 1999.

The Book of Secrets. New York: St. Martin's Press, 2010.

Emotional Wellness. Harmony Books, 2007.

Pearl, Eric (Dr.). *The Reconnection*, Hay House, 2001.

Raghunathan, Raj. *If You'Re So Smart Why Aren't You Happy?* New York: Portfolio/Penguin, 2016.

Rath, Tom. *Strengths Finder 2.0*. New York: Gallup Press, 2007.

Rice, Michael. *Search for Paradise Land*, Essex: 1985

Rinpoche, Sogyal. *The Tibetan Book of Living and Dying*. London: Penguin Random House, 2017.

Rubin, Harriet: *Soloing*: London: Random House, 2000.

Seligman, Martin (Ph.D.). *Authentic Happiness*. London: Nicholas Brealey, 2002.

Sharma, Krishnan; Sharma, Rashmi. *The Practical Book of Reiki*. New Delhi: Pustak Mahal, 2008.

Shimoff, Marcy. *Happy for No Reason*. New York: Free Press, 2008.

Shri Ram Chandra Mission. *Meditation*. Chennai, 1997.

Stutz, Phil, and Michels, Berry. *The Tools*. London: Vermillon, 2012.

Tolle, Eckhart. *A New Earth*. London: Penguin Michael Joseph, 2005.

Uhler, Jay. *How to Make Friends with your Feelings*. Andover: Ambassador Press International, 1993.

Whitmore, John. *Coaching for Performance*. Boston: Nicholas Brealey Publishing, 2009.

Whitworth, Laura; Kimsey-House, Karen; Kimsey-House, Henry; Sandahl, Phillip. *Co-Active Coaching*. Boston (u.a.): Davies Black, 2009.

Williamson, Marianne. *The Gift of Change*. New York: HarperCollins, 2004.

The Age of Miracles. Hay House, 2008.

Lightning Source UK Ltd.
Milton Keynes UK
UKHW011919150621
385566UK00003B/18